Rodeo Cowboys in the North American Imagination

ALSO BY MICHAEL ALLEN

Western Rivermen, 1763–1861: Ohio and Mississippi Boatmen and the Myth of the Alligator Horse (Baton Rouge, 1990), winner of the Phi Alpha Theta Book Prize

Frontiers of Western History, ed. with Mary L. Hanneman (Needham, Mass., forthcoming)

Michael Allen
Rodeo Cowboys
in the North American
Imagination

University of Nevada Press   Reno & Las Vegas

Wilbur S. Shepperson Series in History in Humanities

Editor: Jerome E. Edwards

University of Nevada Press, Reno, Nevada 89557 USA

Copyright © 1998 by University of Nevada Press

All rights reserved

Manufactured in the United States of America

Design by Carrie Nelson House

Library of Congress Cataloging-in-Publication Data

Allen, Michael, 1950–

Rodeo cowboys in the North American imagination / Michael Allen.

p. cm. — (Wilbur S. Shepperson series in history and humanities)

Includes bibliographical references and index.

ISBN 0-87417-315-9 (alk. paper)

1. Rodeos—West (U.S.)—History. 2. Cowboys—West (U.S.)—History.

3. Popular culture—United States. I. Title. II. Series: Wilbur S.

Shepperson series in history and humanities (Unnumbered)

GV1834.A55   1998   98–22963

791.8'4'0978—dc21   CIP

The paper used in this book meets the requirements of American
National Standard for Information Sciences—Permanence of Paper
for Printed Library Materials, ANSI z39.48-1984. Binding materials
were selected for strength and durability.

07 06 05 04 03 02 01 00 99 98   5 4 3 2

In Memory of Stewart Allen

(1915–1992)

Father, Westerner, Horseman, Businessman,

Public Servant, and Jeffersonian Republican

CONTENTS

ILLUSTRATIONS

(Following page 50)

(Following page 124)

ACKNOWLEDGMENTS

Over the past ten years, my journey down North America's rodeo road
has taken me to about as many towns as described in that old country-
western song "I've Been Everywhere (Man)": Ellensburg, Missoula,
Cookeville, Spokane, Deep Springs, Billings, Boulder, Tacoma, Oklahoma City, Austin, Colorado Springs, Pendleton, and many more. Along
the way, I've run up a lot of debts. If I forget to acknowledge some of
those debts here (which, despite my preparations, I fear may happen),
I deeply regret the omission.

First, I want to thank the taxpayers of Tennessee, Montana, and the
state of Washington for paying me to teach and do research in their uni-
versities. I hope I have returned their confidence in our democratic
educational system.

The editors of *Columbia, Magazine of Northwest History*; *Journal of the
West*; the *Ketch Pen* (Rodeo History Society); *Pacific Northwest Forum*; and
the *Pacific Northwest Quarterly* all generously granted permission to re-
publish in revised form material that originally appeared in their magazines.

At the various institutions where I have taught and conducted re-
search, colleagues provided valuable support and encouragement.
Thanks, Calvin Dickinson, the late B. F. Jones, George Webb, and Larry
Whiteaker (Tennessee Technological University); Buzz and Betty Ander-
son (Deep Springs College); Mumtaz Fargo (Montana State University,
Billings); Jim Brown, Jack Keating, Mike Kaltan, and Bill Richardson
(University of Washington, Tacoma); and Walter Grinder (Institute for
Humane Studies at George Mason University).

Librarians and archivists helped in mapping the trail of the history
of rodeo in North American popular culture. Thanks to the librarians
and archivists at Central Washington University, Ellensburg; Special
Collections, University of Colorado, Boulder; Library of Congress Division of Film and Sound Recordings, Washington, D.C.; Local History

Room, Ellensburg Public Library; National Cowboy Hall of Fame, Oklahoma City (Marilyn Pyle, Chuck Rand, Don Reeves, and Anne B. Wheeler); National Cowgirl Hall of Fame, Hereford, Texas; Professional Rodeo Cowboys Association, Colorado Springs; ProRodeo Hall of Fame, Colorado Springs (Patricia Hildebrand and Ruth Airlie); University of Washington, Tacoma, Library (Suzanne Klinger); and University of Washington, Seattle, Suzzalo Library.

Rick Gydeson, Paul Andrew Hutton, Dianne Kounalakis, Elizabeth Atwood Lawrence, Mary Lou LeCompte, William Savage, Murray Tinkelman, Charles Townsend, Jack Wells, and Laurel E. Wilson offered professional counsel. Betty Allen, Mike Birdwell, Keith Edgerton, James Hoy, Beth Kalikoff, Guy Logsdon, Bill Malone, Ron Tyler, and Larry Whiteaker read and criticized individual chapters in their fields of expertise. And the following folks read numerous chapters or the entire manuscript and offered criticism: Mary L. Hanneman, Mike Magie, Dave Morris, J. C. Mutchler, Walter Piehl, Bill Rorabaugh, Carol Zabilski, and Paul Zarzyski. Thank you for your advice, and please know that I hold you collectively responsible for any errors made in this book (ha!).

When I first began to write a chapter about country music, experts warned me off, saying the music industry moguls would never cooperate in the publication of copyrighted lyrics. Well, that may be true of dude musicians, but not cowboy and rodeo music folk. Many thanks to Chris LeDoux, Al LeDoux, Ian Tyson, Buffy Sainte-Marie, and Red Steagall for practicing the Cowboy Code tenet of generosity in sharing your words and music with me and my readers.

My longtime associate Margaret Dalrymple was kind enough to contract my incomplete manuscript when she first became executive editor of the University of Nevada Press; her excellent and friendly staff, copyeditor extraordinaire Gerry Anders, and anonymous referees have helped to sand the manuscript down and then polish it up considerably. I am very pleased to publish this book right in the heart of rodeo country, in the land of the Las Vegas National Finals Rodeo and the Elko Cowboy Poetry Gathering.

Finally, my wife, Mary, and our children, Jim, Davy, and Caroline, have made a lot of trips down the rodeo road while I was working on this book. They have spent many weeks residing at Howard Johnson's ("HoJo's" to Jim) and less luxuriant lodgings (three-year-old Davy spent a wild weekend camped out with me in a tent in downtown Pendleton). They have sat on many hard grandstand bleachers, eaten too many corndogs, and become top hands in the process. "We've Been Everywhere (Man)," and I am grateful and very happy that our family will travel many more roads together in the years to come.

Rodeo Cowboys in the North American Imagination

Frontier, Civilization, and the Meaning of Rodeo

By golly . . . a man would think Elvis was up here on
this horse. —William Crawford, *The Bronc Rider* (1965)

Before I researched and wrote my first book, *Western Rivermen* (1990),
I learned about riverboating by working for three years as a deckhand,
oil tankerman, and cook aboard Mississippi River diesel towboats. So,
naturally, ever since I began to research and write this book about rodeo
cowboys, people have asked me if I ride or ever rode in the rodeo. I answer that question with an emphatic no—as a young man I never longed
to ride a bucking bronc or wrestle a steer. And now, at forty-eight and
with a bad back and a young family, such an endeavor is certainly out of
the question. However, I do know something about horses and rodeo.
That knowledge grows out of my past.

When I was a kid growing up in Ellensburg, in eastern Washington
State, rodeo loomed large in my family's and neighbors' lives and
imaginations. My town hosted the Ellensburg Rodeo, a respected, professionally sanctioned annual Labor Day Weekend rodeo. In a rodeo
town, the show is present in one way or another all year round, and in
our house on the edge of town this was especially so. My dad, Stewart
Allen, was an Idaho boy—a fallen Mormon who in the 1930s left the farm
for town but never forgot his rural roots. During the few hours he could

squeeze from running an ice cream shop and serving as Ellensburg's mayor, Dad was a horseman and rodeo aficionado.

Every Friday night was "posse night." Dad came home from work early, hung up his restaurant clothes, and donned the cowboy garb of his southern Idaho youth. He ate a quick dinner, saddled up his horse, and since we lived only a few blocks from the rodeo grounds, rode over the tracks and into the rodeo arena, where the Ellensburg Rodeo Posse held its weekly drill. At about 8:30 P.M., my mom and I would walk over and join the other posse families around the arena or in the grandstands. The posse was just finishing the drill—a precision performance by twenty to twenty-five mounted posse members to the accompaniment of Eddie Arnold's "Cattle Call" wafting out of a tinny loudspeaker above the bucking chutes. After the drill, Dad and his fellow "cowboys" quickly gathered around several cases of Lucky Lager beer. After a couple of beers, the posse men ended their evening with horse races and a wild game of broomstick polo. I never much liked riding horseback myself, and I did not come to the rodeo grounds to watch the broomstick polo. But I did like to stand in the tall grass, watch the posse drill, and listen to Eddie Arnold.

As Labor Day approached, Dad and his posse buddies plunged into the time-consuming community effort that is so much a part of authentic rodeo folk festivals. They literally camped at the rodeo grounds, rode in the Saturday and Sunday downtown parades, rode in the daily rodeo grand entry processions, and raced the relay races. At night they conducted the posse-night shows, the junior rodeo, competition team-pulling, and cow-cutting exhibitions. They competed in drill, pole bending, and horse racing against their rodeo posse cohorts from around the Pacific Northwest. And they entertained the other posse men with breakfasts and drinking and country music parties. I helped my dad run the back gate at the night shows for years, and when I turned twenty-one I got to sell tickets and serve as a bouncer at the posse's dance.

On Labor Day, our whole family went to the Ellensburg Rodeo championship show. After riding in the grand entry, Dad always joined us in
the grandstand. We stayed until the champion cowboys got their prize
buckles, and then we ate barbecue for dinner and went home very tired.
The rodeo was over for another year, but for us and countless others in
our town it was a constant presence in our lives. I tell people today quite
candidly that the rodeo took on an importance to us secondary only to
the Christmas holidays. Though my dad is no longer alive, and though
I have long since moved from Ellensburg, I still attend the Labor Day
show every year and sit in the covered grandstand with my wife and kids,
just as our family did in the 1950s. For some of the folk, rodeo still possesses great meaning.

This redneck part of my past has combined, somehow, with an academic bent to lead to this book. Upon leaving Ellensburg, I continued to
follow rodeo during a stint in the Marine Corps, my brief career as a
towboatman, and studies at two institutions in rodeo country, Central
Washington State College and the University of Montana. My doctoral
training (at the University of Washington, Seattle) as a social historian
led me into the study of American folklore and popular culture. In my
first book it was the mythological riverman—the "Alligator Horse" boatman hero of nineteenth-century popular culture—whom I found particularly compelling. In searching for a twentieth-century counterpart
to the folkloric riverman, I returned quite naturally to my old rodeo
haunts. For it seemed to me that the rodeo cowboy—alongside perhaps
the logger, truck driver, soldier hero, railroadman, and astronaut—was
a minor but nevertheless fascinating twentieth-century occupational
folk hero. Moreover, he was a relatively unstudied twentieth-century
American occupational folk hero.

Much has been written about working cowboys—those men who
herded cattle during the height of the Great Plains "cattle kingdom."
Indeed, probably too much has been published on that subject.[1] And the
mythological working cowboy—the cowboy hero portrayed in dime nov-

els, silent and talking movies, television, comic books, country music, and pulp westerns—has also had more than his share of interpreters.[2] This is not so for the rodeo man of history or myth. During the long and complex history of rodeo, only a few historians and anthropologists have attempted to research and analyze this peculiar North American folk festival. And only a handful have investigated the mystique of rodeo or the role of the rodeo man in American popular culture. Their work thus constitutes a respectable, but by no means definitive, field of scholarship.

The first rodeo scholar was University of Colorado professor Clifford P. Westermeier. A transplanted New Yorker, Westermeier earned the respect of academics and rodeo men alike for his path-breaking 1947 book *Man, Beast, Dust: The Story of Rodeo.* It remains an important book to this day, for although it at times meanders into a chatty listing and praising of rodeo aficionados and the author's many cowboy friends, Westermeier writes evocative narrative prose, and readers can still savor his literary artistry.[3]

Man, Beast, Dust recounts the history of rodeo only until around the time of World War II. Kristine Fredriksson's *American Rodeo: From Buffalo Bill to Big Business* (1985) brought rodeo history up to date in a style that is highly competent, if less dramatic than Westermeier's (as this book goes to press, sociologist Wayne S. Wooden and journalist Gavin Ehringer have published *Rodeo in America: Wranglers, Roughstock, and Paydirt,* a portrait of contemporary rodeo). *American Rodeo* is a straightforward institutional or business history—an indispensable source of information about the twentieth-century development of modern professional rodeo. A recent historical monograph is Texan Mary Lou LeCompte's *Cowgirls of the Rodeo* (1993), which tells the important and previously neglected story of women in pro rodeo. Taken together, Westermeier, Fredriksson, and LeCompte have done a good job of relating the history of professional rodeo, but without any particular interest in analyzing just exactly what rodeo means and how it fits into the complex milieu of American folklore and popular culture. Fortunately, folklorists and anthropologists have stepped in where the historians left off.[4]

In the 1970s, Beverly June Stoeltje and Elizabeth Atwood Lawrence conducted independent field investigations of the world of North American small-town rodeo. Both worked among the common folk of the Great Plains, producing path-breaking works on the origins and meaning of rodeo. In her University of Texas Ph.D. dissertation, "Rodeo As Symbolic Performance" (on the Stamford, Texas, Cowboy Reunion and Rodeo), folklorist Stoeltje finds an almost religious significance in rodeo folk-festival "rituals."

On the northern Plains, anthropologist and veterinarian Lawrence reached many of the same conclusions. Her 1982 book, *Rodeo: An Anthropologist Looks at the Wild and the Tame,* places rodeo squarely into the Myth of the West matrix earlier explored and delineated by Henry Nash Smith, John William Ward, Roy Harvey Pearce, Leo Marx, and other American Studies scholars.[5]

The Myth of the West is a complex problem that Lawrence distills well. The defining American myth—the most important story of the American folk—is that of westward expansion. It is the epic story of the movement of early North American pioneers onto the frontier and their civilizing of the frontier by taming its savage forces—wild animals, raging rivers, and other hostile elements, such as outlaws and Indians. Rodeo, Lawrence argues, is no less than a folk ritual that reenacts and sanctifies the Myth of the West before an audience of modern North Americans who no longer have firsthand experience with the initial civilizing of the West. The terms *wild* and *tame* take on paramount importance in Lawrence's study (as *frontier* and *civilization* did for Smith, Ward, and Marx before her). The broncs, bulls, steers, and calves of the rodeo represent the wild forces of nature in the North American West. The cowboy represents the taming forces of North American civilization. In the arena, these great forces clash. The cowboy hero attempts to *tame the wild* quite literally (albeit temporarily), and in so doing he acts out the Myth of the West:

> The sport of rodeo, like the duties of working cowboys from which it was derived, deals with the relationships between man and animals ... and on a deeper level with the human relation to the land—the wilderness and the wild. Brought into focus by means of the various contests and displays of rodeo, these man-nature relationships are dramatically delineated, categorized, and manipulated. As an outgrowth of ranching, rodeo embodies the frontier spirit as manifested through the aggressive and exploitative conquest of the West, and deals with nature and the reordering of nature according to the dictates of this ethos. It supports the value of subjugating nature and reenacts the "taming" process whereby the wild is brought under control.

In acting out the civilizing of the frontier, Lawrence argues further, the rodeo man fully adopts the traits and values of historic working cowboys. These cowboy characteristics include individualism, courage, disregard for personal pain and injury, innovation, loyalty to the cowboy group, reticence, plain speech, humor, anti-intellectualism, and a strong belief in democracy and equality. Other scholars have labeled these same traits as the *Cowboy Code.* The Cowboy Code characteristics parallel those ascribed to frontier Americans by historian Frederick Jackson Turner in his famous essay "The Significance of the Frontier in American History."[6]

There is no small amount of irony in all of this, for the rodeo cowboy is himself wild, or at least aspires to that distinction. Thus, in civilizing the forces of the frontier he is in many ways taming that which he loves best—working himself out of a job, as it were. Lawrence attempts to unravel this tangled contradiction of *wild* and *tame,*[7] just as Henry Nash Smith and his colleagues did with *frontier* and *civilization.* It is the tension between the frontier and civilization embodied by the rodeo-cowboy hero that makes him such a potent force in our culture, placing him alongside other western folk heroes like the long hunter, scout, frontier soldier, riverman, lawman, and of course, the Plains cowboy. And it is this same tension that ultimately makes the rodeo cowboy, like the other western folk heroes, a tragic character. Having tamed the wild in the rodeo arena, there is nothing left for him to do. He must die or he must move on—not to the Rockies like Leatherstocking in *The Prairie* or down to Old Mexico like John Wayne in *Stagecoach,* but in good twenti-eth-century fashion, *down the road,* to the next rodeo show. There the rodeo-cowboy hero will find more broncs and bulls to tame.

I take exception to some of Lawrence's arguments. I do not subscribe completely to her direct equation of modern rodeo cowboys to frontier cowboys (and other nomadic pastoralists, for that matter); I disagree with some of her feminist theories and her Freudian talk of saddle horns and belt buckles as phalluses, and her overanalysis of the symbol-ism of cow excrement and other bodily excretions. Nevertheless, Law-rence has written a brilliant synthesis and analysis of rodeo. Some of the most promising facets of *Rodeo: An Anthropologist Looks at the Wild and the Tame* are short but tantalizing forays into the realm of popular cul-ture. In brief sections addressing country music, literature, film, and even bumper stickers, Lawrence exposes the tip of a mythological ice-berg. Indeed, looking at the small, sturdy field of rodeo studies as a unit, it is obvious that one of the last unexplored facets of rodeo is the role of the rodeo cowboy as hero in North American popular culture.[8]

The rodeo cowboy is only one of a number of modern occupational folk hero types, yet he is a fascinating one. He is, after all, a modern man—he lives in industrial America, rides to work in a car or truck (or airplane), and if he is lucky, sleeps at the Holiday Inn, not out under the stars with coyotes yelping in the background. Yet on the other hand he is a *cowboy*—representing facets of North America's past that evoke powerful rural and preindustrial images. This makes for a fascinating paradox. *Contemporary ancestor* is the term David D. Lee and others have used to describe modern-day folk heroes whose characteristics are simultaneously pre- and postindustrial (Hollywood has supplied the less weighty but equally potent term *urban cowboy*). Studies of Sergeant Alvin York and Charles Lindbergh are evidence that the subject of contemporary ancestors is a ripe one. The rodeo cowboy occupies an unexplored space within it.[9]

The rodeo cowboy is a *contemporary ancestor* idolized by a modern, industrial North American society. It is difficult to say exactly when this worship began, but sometime around World War II the status of the rodeo cowboy began to rise steadily, and he gradually acquired something of a mystique. The reasons for this are complex but no doubt have something to do with the triumph of a modern economy and centralized state as evidenced by American mobilization and victory in World War II. This pinnacle of modernization proved exhilarating and unnerving at the same time. It created a pronounced nostalgia for cowboys and the cattle-ranching frontier among a North American populace who had precious little personal acquaintance with those historical phenomena. Most Americans knew so little of cattle ranching by World War II that they could enthusiastically romanticize it and, in their confusion, somehow turn the rodeo man into a *real cowboy*. Earlier generations knew better, but by 1945 the path was open to idolization of the rodeo man as a hero in the growing Myth of the West.[10]

The rodeo cowboy had earlier been portrayed as a heroic figure in a small genre of rodeo folk music and poetry. Appropriately, more formal rodeo portrayals first took shape not in polished literature but in the movie houses, the primary venue for folk-based popular culture during the post–World War II years. Robert Mitchum's gripping 1952 performance as rodeo man Jeff McCloud in *The Lusty Men* marked the first effective portrayal of the rodeo hero in popular culture. It was followed by a number of rodeo films, most notably *The Misfits* (1961), *Junior Bonner* (1972), *J. W. Coop* (1972), *Urban Cowboy* (1980), and *8 Seconds* (1994). There were rodeo television shows as well, and country music produced a small, vital rodeo subgenre, written and sung by artists like Chris LeDoux and Red Steagall. During the Vietnam era, folk and counterculture musicians embraced the rural mystique of the rodeo, beginning with Ian and Sylvia's "Someday Soon" (1964), the Byrds' pivotal album *Sweetheart of the Rodeo* (1968), and Buffy Sainte-Marie's "He's an Indian Cowboy in the Rodeo" (1972). Meanwhile Hal Borland's *When the Legends Die* (1963) and William Crawford's *Bronc Rider* (1965) gave birth to a rodeo literary genre that eventually included works such as Larry McMurtry's *Moving On* (1970), Craig Lesley's *Winterkill* (1984), Cyra McFadden's *Rain or Shine* (1986), Michael Dorris' *A Yellow Raft in Blue Water* (1987), and Ken Kesey's *Last Go Round* (1994). And in the 1980s a new generation of "cowboy poets" incorporated rodeo themes into their work. In addition, there have been artistic and photographic representations of the rodeo man. Indeed, rodeo made the transformation from popular culture to "high" culture as early as 1942, when the Ballet Russe de Monte Carlo commissioned Aaron Copland and Agnes de Mille to create western-theme works, the much-acclaimed *Rodeo Suite* and the ballet *Rodeo*.

Yet it is in the realm of popular culture—not the fine arts—that the rodeo man takes his most evocative form in the American imagination. This is, I think, because popular culture lends itself much more readily to translation of what began as a folk tradition. Indeed, popular culture today arguably provides a generous supply of what we used to call "folk culture." I am not one of those who believe that movies, popular songs, and pulp literature are the products of elite capitalist groups, foisted off on gullible and mindless consumers. I believe that popular culture *means something* to those folks who choose, of their own free will, to embrace it. Folklorist Richard M. Dorson wrote in 1973 that the vital folklore of any period in American history reflects "the main concerns and values, tensions and anxieties, goals and drives of the period." More recently Lawrence Levine has been exploring "the degree to which popular culture functions in ways similar to folk culture," concluding that if one applies a judicious methodology, popular culture can serve as an "indispensable guide to the thought and attitudes of an asymmetrical and diverse people." With Dorson's and Levine's analyses and methodologies in hand, we can assume that popular culture will tell us some important things about the American folk. And in studying the rodeo cowboy in popular culture, we continue in a small way to pursue the complexities of North American civilization.[11]

This book, then, might best be termed a history of the rodeo-cowboy hero in popular culture. *Popular culture,* as used here, is an umbrella term under which we can find everything from folksy, independently published rodeo memoirs to "high art" such as Copland and de Mille's *Rodeo.* In between fall rodeo movies, paintings, novels, cowboy poems, and country-western songs that individually run the range from "high" to "low" art. At times I refer to specific examples of these greatly varied works as "folk art" or "folk-based art" or "art" or "representations" or "literature," etc., and this can get confusing. But again, I think "popular culture" serves as the best general description of the rodeo subgenre of movies, television shows, literature, art, and music.

Although this book deals in depth with movies and literature, it is not a work of literary criticism. I am a historian who also knows something about folklore and popular culture, but ultimately my historical methods prevail. Readers will not find much lit-crit jargon here, and no poststructuralist methodology. If we have learned anything in the last decade, it is that the literary left joins the "new" western historians in exhibiting surprisingly little knowledge about America, much less the American West. When I examine literature and movies here, I try to do so by first telling the story in narrative prose and then analyzing the story. I do not necessarily consider the latter endeavor more important than the first.[12]

In a somewhat related vein, I do not use this history as an opportunity to expound on the much-reviled "evils" of rodeo, e.g., "cruelty to animals." Indeed, I love rodeo. It is an integral part of my western folk culture. Folklore is rough and coarse ("salty," Dorson used to say), and rodeo most certainly fits this description. With that in mind, I should also explain my use in this book of the word *redneck*. Although born (along with *cracker*) in a southern milieu, *redneck* has, in recent decades, become very much a part of western folk culture and vernacular. In the West *redneck* signifies, most importantly, rural status and an individual's adherence to the norms of western folk culture (e.g., the Cowboy Code). Although *redneck* and *cowboy* are not synonymous, they are, in the West, linguistic and cultural cousins. Nor are they imbued with racist connotations. In the West some rednecks may very well be racists, but when all is said and done they have many more-important things on their minds, like four-wheel-drive rigs and deer hunting. Moreover, as we shall see, many nonwhite, nontraditional horsemen have in the past and present aspired to and attained cowboy status. They too follow the Cowboy Code. They too are cultural cousins of rednecks. So despite the fact that modern liberal sensibilities are disturbed by *redneck*, I use it here because it is an important, laudatory term in western folk vernacular.

Next, there is the problem of art and life—or more specifically, the problem of distinguishing between rodeo-cowboy art and rodeo-cowboy life. Readers of this book will note that my depictions of Plains working cowboys, historic rodeo cowboys, and popular-culture rodeo cowboys occasionally overlap. The most obvious example involves the Cowboy Code, a value system that permeates historic-cowboy and rodeo-cowboy behavior and popular-culture portrayals of both. The reason for this overlap is that I do not believe that Plains, rodeo, and pop-culture cowboys are mutually exclusive groups. Their blending is immediate because rodeo is in part a folk-based *performance.* It is a show—but a show based on historic ranch workways. And it is a show put on by rodeo cowboys who not only are highly skilled in nineteenth-century Plains cowboying techniques, but are also strict adherents to the Plains Cowboy Code. Thus when novelists, moviemakers, songwriters, etc. create popular-culture art about rodeo, they are making art about art that is based on life. And if we acknowledge that historic Plains cowboys and rodeo cowboys were and are themselves influenced by pop-culture representations of their mystique, then what we get is pop-culture artists making art about art based on lives that were and are influenced by art. I have charted the puzzle in this manner:

Plains (Working) Cowboys

↗   ↘

Pop-Culture Representations of Plains Cowboys ⟷ Rodeo Cowboys
(Folk-Based "Low" Art)   ("Performers")

↘   ↕

Pop-Culture Representations of Rodeo Cowboys
("Low" Art)

↓

"High" Art

In this very complex way, cowboy and rodeo-cowboy life and art have gotten all mixed up. Since there is no apparent solution to this puzzle, I have decided simply to acknowledge its importance and to describe it with as much precision as possible.[13]

Something similar occurs with my treatment of the long-standing debate over whether rodeo cowboys are *real cowboys*. I discuss this sore subject at some length. My conclusions may disappoint some cowboys— and some dudes. But when all is said and done, the distinction between *real cowboys* and rodeo cowboys is today inconsequential. The important thing is that rodeo cowboys *believe* they are *real cowboys*. And most other North Americans also believe rodeo cowboys are *real cowboys*. The rodeo man's role in the Myth of the West is thus based on actual folk belief. And since all such myths are in turn based on elements of truth, the rodeo myth is not "false," nor are its adherents "pretenders."

Let me mention one last conflation, involving the term *North American*, that might also spark some disagreement. I entitled this book *Rodeo Cowboys in the North American Imagination* because Mexico and Canada are so important in rodeo history and culture, and Canadian popular-culture artists (such as Ian Tyson and Buffy Sainte-Marie) have been particularly important in creating rodeo music, art, and literature. In making generalizations and drawing conclusions about the significance of rodeo popular culture, I often refer to all of North America. Some Canadians and Mexicans might disagree with generalizations that throw them together with the United States; many from the U.S.A. might disagree as well. And sometimes my generalizations *are* aimed specifically at the United States. Yet North American cowboy and rodeo culture thrives in an uninterrupted zone stretching from northern Mexico to the Canadian prairie provinces. Rodeo and cowboy culture together form a unifying force that knows no national or ethnic boundaries. Thus a history of the rodeo cowboy in popular culture must also disregard these boundaries. When you're a cowboy, you're a cowboy.

That much said, let me add that we probably do not really *need* a book-length monograph on the history of the rodeo cowboy in popular culture. I know that scholars are not supposed to preface their books with such remarks, but I cannot resist. I once hoisted a few beers with a wise professor who said that if all of his and his colleagues' scholarly monographs were placed on a ship going out to sea, and if that ship sank and all of the monographs were lost, Western civilization would somehow survive. I agree.

So why write a history of rodeo cowboys in popular culture? First, because I do believe that such a study does after all provide us with a small clue to the complex riddle of the American mind. I believe that the fundamental problem of North American civilization is that of an agricultural people enduring the agony and joy of industrialization and modernization. If a book about rodeo can somehow shed a little light on that paradox, then it is certainly worth the effort to write it.

But I also wrote this book in large part for personal, nonprofessional reasons. As I stated at the outset, my life has from childhood been surrounded by rodeo and rodeo cowboys. Two of my uncles competed professionally in the 1920s and 1930s. I grew up on the edge of town, around horses, cattle, tack, irrigation equipment, alfalfa, bolo ties, and country music. I stood out in the tall grass and listened to "Cattle Call" as the Ellensburg Rodeo Posse drilled. After all those posse practices and rodeo parades and all those Labor Day championships, rodeo is, quite simply, on my mind. And so I write about it. It is at the very least a constructive use of my time. And surely truth can result from historical method.

My dad was a great lover of rodeo, and I share that feeling, although as a scholar and teacher, not a competitor. This is in a way ironic, for Dad never spent even one minute intellectualizing rodeo, and he would have been a bit puzzled by anyone who did. In this he was typically American. But I think that rodeo evinced his Americanness in another way as well. In retrospect, I believe that participation in the rodeo somehow evoked the positive facets of his rural Idaho youth—a youth spent on his own father's dryland wheat farm near Pocatello. After a childhood around livestock, horses, and rodeos, he left the farm forever during the Great Depression. I am sure he never regretted his move to town; he felt no yearning for the agricultural West with its backbreaking labor and meager earnings. Yet he always kept a part of southern Idaho with him— he always wore western duds, grazed a horse or two and a steer out back, rode in the posse, volunteered in the rodeo, and pretended to be a cowboy every Friday night and Labor Day weekend. In this too, I think, he was very American—a modern businessman who lived in town but was still tied, somehow, to his agricultural roots and the Myth of the West. The North American ambivalence over the loss of a real or imagined agrarian Eden is no small part of our consciousness, even in "postmodern" times. My dad represents one small example of the ubiquitous agrarian vision.

On Labor Day, September 7, 1992, at approximately 4:00 P.M., rodeo cowboys received their championship buckles in the Ellensburg Rodeo arena. In doing this they carried on a local folk tradition of more than seventy-five years' duration. At a nursing home a few blocks away, my dad died after a long illness. This book is dedicated to his memory.

CHAPTER ONE

"Real Cowboys"
A Brief History of Rodeo

There's a hundred years of history and a hundred before that
All gathered in the thinkin' goin' on beneath his hat.
And back behind his eyeballs and pumpin' through his veins
Is the ghost of every cowboy that ever held the reins.
—Baxter Black, "Legacy of the Rodeo Man" (1986)

"A plain where a round-up is taking place offers a picturesque sight,"
wrote North Dakota cattleman Theodore Roosevelt in 1888. "I well remember one such. It was on a level bottom in the bend of the river . . .
in shape a long oval, hemmed in by an unbroken line of steep bluffs so
that it looked like an amphitheater." Cowboys camped among the cot-
tonwoods, their *remuda* of horses grazing at the outskirts. "In the great
circular corral, towards one end, the men were already branding
calves," and "shouting, galloping cowboys" continually herded more
cattle toward the corral. The scene seemed one of "dust, noise, and confusion; but in reality the work was proceeding all the while with the utmost rapidity and certainty."[1]

"On cow ranches, or wherever there is breeding stock, the spring
round-up is the great event of the season," Roosevelt observed. Montanan Teddy Blue Abbott, who cowboyed a couple hundred miles west of
Roosevelt's spread, agreed that roundup was "something everybody
looked forward to on the range." It was a time for cowboys to count the
results of the spring calving, brand the young calves, cut their ears for
identification, and "doctor" the sick ones. Yet these jobs were probably

not exactly what cowboys "looked forward to" the most. "Cowpunchers was alone so much," Abbott remembered, they relished the roundup as a chance to "see a lot of people and hear all the news." It was also a time for gambling, drinking, footraces, and wrestling. And it was a time for "cowboy fun"—horse racing, roping, and bronc-riding contests among the working cowboys and vaqueros of the nineteenth-century North American cattle frontier.[2]

That the "cowboy fun" described by Roosevelt, Abbott, and many others bears a resemblance to what we now call rodeo is, of course, no accident. Rodeo is derived from the Spanish verb *rodear,* meaning "to encircle" or "to round up," and American rodeo is a direct descendant of the work festivals of early North American cowboys and vaqueros. Aside from this obvious fact, however, there is little agreement among rodeo participants, observers, scholars, and Americans in general as to just exactly what rodeo *is.* Today's Professional Rodeo Cowboys Association (PRCA) competitors call rodeo a "sport" and sometimes refer to themselves as "professional athletes." Yet they also cling tenaciously to the title of "cowboy." Most rodeo fans now also see rodeo as a spectator sport, albeit a unique one—with animals and aspects of pageantry and theater unlike, say, a professional basketball game. Dudes (non-westerners who watch rodeo only on ESPN or the Nashville Network) see rodeo as a quaint yet exciting remnant of the "Wild West." And animal-rights activists (an unfriendly set of dudes) see rodeo as a cruel, Roman-circus type of spectacle, a sort of Americanized bullfight where the bull gets to live (most of the time).

The few scholars who have seriously studied rodeo shy away from the sports categorization. Most, though not all, view rodeo as a folkway—a western folk festival. Folklore is made up of the verbal and nonverbal traditions of the common folk. Given rodeo's origins in the workways of the western cattle roundup, it seems to fit this definition handily. But we ought to be very careful here. Richard M. Dorson defines *fakelore* as ersatz folklore—commercialized, marketed, and diluted for the sake of popular entertainment. As it has progressed in this century, rodeo (especially big-money PRCA rodeo) certainly has moved away from folklore toward fakelore, although the extent of that evolution is highly debatable. Thus it seems that the proper definition of *rodeo* is floating around in a never-never land somewhere between folklore on the one hand and popular entertainment, or popular culture, on the other. Since rodeo is undoubtedly rooted in folk traditions, I define it as a *folk-based* popular entertainment.[3]

By this definition, rodeo left the pure folk idiom as soon as paying customers arrived. And that happened relatively early. Townspeople soon heard there was a good show to watch way out in the country, and they began to travel to cattle ranches to see the action. No one charged admission to these "Sunday rodeos," and spectators packed their own food and watched from rough seats on corral rails and bales of straw. But someone soon got the idea that a more organized and orchestrated rodeo, staged in an area of population concentration, could be a real crowd-pleaser and perhaps generate some revenue for local merchants. Rodeo was on its way to town.[4]

Several North American communities boast the distinction of having hosted the "first rodeo," and it is futile to try and sort out their claims here. As with all folklore and folk-based phenomena, point of origin is difficult, if not impossible, to pinpoint. Certainly the steer-roping, bronc- and bull-riding, and bull-wrestling contests observed by chroniclers of 1820s and 1830s Mexican Texas and California fiestas contained elements of what we now recognize as rodeo. There are descriptions of rodeolike contests in San Antonio, Texas, in 1844, and Santa Fe, New Mexico, in 1847. San Antonio reportedly hosted a rodeo event featuring Indian, Mexican, and Anglo- and Celtic American horsemen shortly following the Civil War, but details are sketchy. Rival ranch crews competed on bucking broncs in Deer Trail, Colorado, in 1869, and ranchmen came to Pecos, Texas, to compete at roping steers in 1883. Albuquerque, New Mexico, and Denver, Colorado, hosted rodeos in 1886 and 1887, and in 1888, citizens in Prescott, Arizona, staged a very important rodeo event. Because the Prescott rodeo's organizers charged admission and awarded trophies for the first time on record, Prescott now claims to have hosted the first professional rodeo. Miles City, Montana, followed in 1891, and Cheyenne, Wyoming, held its initial "Frontier Days" celebration in 1897. In 1911 and 1912, respectively, the Pendleton (Oregon) Roundup and Calgary (Alberta) Stampede joined Cheyenne as enduring rodeo spectacles. By the 1920s, North American rodeo was off and running.[5]

The Ellensburg Rodeo, a respected central Washington State show founded in 1923, provides an excellent case study of how the rodeo folk festival evolved into folk-based popular entertainment in the early-twentieth-century North American West. First settled following the Civil War, Ellensburg lay in the heart of a thriving cattle region. Thousands of cattle and horses grazed the rich meadows and semiarid plains of the Kittitas Valley, and the roundups that characterized cattle country were commonplace among the Kittitas cowboys. So, too, were the impromptu competitions and "cowboy fun" that had emerged elsewhere. By the early 1920s, cowboys on at least two Kittitas Valley ranches were staging regular contests or, as the locals called them, "Sunday rodeos."

Ben Ferguson, a local cowhand and rodeo competitor, described his family's promotion of one such rodeo: "We had all them horses and my brother and a couple of friends put on a rodeo. . . . My brother, he just wanted to have some fun. Just got a neighbor boy or two here, went out and rounded them [cattle and horses] up. They got a wagon load of poles and made the corral and made the arena [and] chutes." During the early 1920s the Fergusons staged rodeos "every other Sunday," and it was not unusual for 100 to 300 spectators to attend. The economic potential of all this activity did not go unnoticed. Ferguson remembered that several townspeople saw "that we was having a big time" and began to discuss the possibility of staging a rodeo in the Ellensburg city limits. Sometime around 1922, a group of townspeople came to ask the Ferguson brothers to assist in staging the first Ellensburg Rodeo: "They come out and got us to go in there and furnish the horses and then they took it over."[6]

Three distinguishable socioeconomic groups combined to found the Ellensburg Rodeo. Ranchers and cowboys like the Fergusons, the Kittitas County Fair Board (which included townspeople and area farmers alike), and local businessmen and professionals formed the nucleus. But these diverse citizens faced large obstacles. Although community leaders allocated an excellent parcel of land in a natural amphitheater on Ellensburg's east end, there was not enough money available to pay for the lumber, tools, horse teams, and huge labor force necessary to construct a rodeo grounds. In an important move, the Kittitas County Fair Board called upon valley residents to donate materials and labor for the construction of the rodeo grounds, and they set aside Thursday, June 14, 1923, as a "field day" for building the new arena.

Communal work projects like the Ellensburg Rodeo Grounds field day show the other side of the coin of historic Western individualism: a Code-like loyalty toward and willingness to assist fellow westerners. Barn raisings, corn-husking parties, quilting bees, and cattle roundups all exemplified this communal side of western American values. During Ellensburg's field day, scores of men came to work on the grounds. Local cowboy and rodeo contestant Howard Thomas remembered: "I was riding for Cooke's [ranch]. . . . 'Can you spare me a few days to work on the Rodeo?' [I asked Mr. Cooke. He said,] 'I can give you a week.' So I brought four horses, plows, and a spring tooth harrow, and a scraper. I drove them in town. . . . When it was light enough to see I was going to the grounds and when it was too dark to see I was coming home."[7] The work reached a crescendo on June 14, when more than 500 valley men and women turned out to work on the rodeo grounds. They graded a road, a racetrack, and the arena, rerouted Wilson Creek around the site, built corrals, fences, three bridges, and a grandstand, plumbed new water mains, dug ditches, and pruned trees. Their accomplishments were amazing, as the *Ellensburg Evening Record*'s headlines shouted: "COMMUNITY EFFORT IS SUCCESSFUL. Business Men, Farmers Work on Fair Grounds. Sight of Toilers Working in Common Cause Inspiring." The rodeo arena was ready to go.[8]

Kittitas County Fair Board members, businessmen, and rodeo enthusiasts spent the remainder of the summer planning the first Ellensburg Rodeo for September 13–15, 1923. The rodeo's "superintendent," Dr. H. E. Pfenning, and his steering committee invited the Yakima Indians to participate, scheduled eighteen major events, and advertised the rodeo as the "greatest Wildwest Roundup in the State." September 13, 1923, arrived and so did large crowds of rodeo participants and fans. Howard Thomas remembered this first rodeo as "a good one," and a local woman, Lillian Pope, noted, "You knew pretty near everybody that was riding in it. . . . It really made a difference [because] it was really more of a local show." Another Kittitas Valley old-timer described the competitors as local ranch hands—"real cowboys" competing in "wild horse races, stagecoach races, chariot races."[9] In addition to these events, there were grand entry parades, bucking broncos and bulls, calf roping, relay races, bulldogging, and special races for Indian contestants. The *Record* noted that "Hundreds Are In Overflow Crowd; Grandstand Filled," and most in attendance reportedly "yelled and cheered and thoroughly enjoyed Ellensburg's first real rodeo."[10]

It is interesting to speculate on the motives of the Ellensburg Rodeo's founders and, in so doing, to assess the motives of founders of other early North American rodeos, from Texas to Alberta. Although it is no doubt true to say that Ellensburgers staged a folk festival—a celebration of their frontier lifestyle—there is more to the story. The Ellensburg Rodeo was more commercial than a truly folkloric roundup, ranch rodeo, or even "Sunday rodeo." It certainly was not a direct offshoot of the pioneer, cattle-frontier lifestyle, for by 1923 there was very little of that lifestyle left; the Kittitas Valley frontier had vanished two generations earlier. With these facts in mind, I suggest that the desire to stage a rodeo was partially due to pronounced nostalgia—a nostalgia felt by townspeople and valley residents for a pioneer, cattle-ranching life that was becoming foreign to their world of automobiles, airplanes, moving-picture shows, and radio broadcasts.

At the same time, a modern, Chamber-of-Commerce-type boosterism and promotion are also characteristic of Ellensburg's and other western towns' first rodeos. Town business and professional men and women, most of whom had themselves spent little or no time hauling hay or riding horseback, were in the forefront of the rodeo movement. They were joined by local cattlemen and farmers, but nearly all looked upon the rodeo as a good way to foster business and promote their community around the Pacific Northwest. Of course, memories and folk traditions of the frontier still lingered, and the people of the Kittitas Valley certainly relied upon their frontier folk heritage to create their rodeo. Volunteerism—the community spirit of the pioneer days—provided part of the base upon which the Ellensburg Rodeo was built.[11]

The birth of American rodeo in the late nineteenth and early twentieth centuries was paralleled by the rise and decline of the "Wild West shows." Rodeos and Wild West shows have some important common traits, including commercialism and nostalgia, yet there are very important differences between the two. Wild West shows were not folk festivals; they were pure popular-entertainment spectacles. Their ties to authentic folk traditions were much weaker than those of rodeo, and their commercialism much more pronounced. When all is said and done, the Wild West shows are a sidelight—a fascinating footnote in the history of North American rodeo.

On July 4, 1882—six years before Prescott, Arizona, held its first rodeo—Wild West shows emerged when Buffalo Bill Cody, the most famous of the Wild West entrepreneurs, staged the "Old Glory Blowout" at North Platte, Nebraska. For the next sixty years, Wild West troupes traversed the United States and the world, entertaining huge audiences that included common working folk and the crowned heads of Europe. Buffalo Bill's "Wild West" (Cody never used the word *show* to describe his theaterlike entertainment—he advertised and referred to it as, quite literally, "The Wild West") gave rise to at least 116 other Wild West shows. From approximately 1882 to 1942, audiences thrilled to the performances of Cody's troupe, as well as the famed Pawnee Bill's Historic Wild West, Miller Brothers 101 Ranch Real Wild West, Colonel Tim McCoy's Real Wild West and Rough Riders of the World, the Tom Mix Circus and Wild West, Gene Autry's Flying A Ranch Stampede, and many others.[12]

Millions of Wild West show fans, most of them in cities in the eastern United States and Europe, flocked to witness what one Wild West program touted as "the most completely-appointed delegation of frontiersmen and Indians that ever visited the East." In 1893, for instance, Cody grossed over $1,000,000 and claimed to have entertained more than 6,000,000 paying customers. On a typical afternoon, a Wild West show audience witnessed a program that included a "Grand Processional Parade" (a motif borrowed from circus tradition), rifle-shooting exhibitions by male and female performers alike, a stagecoach race, Indian dancing and horsemanship, a "buffalo hunt," and a dramatic reenactment of Plains Indian warfare—usually Colonel George Armstrong Custer's "Last Stand" at the Little Bighorn. In addition, there was horse racing and "Cow-Boy's Fun," including "Cow-Boys and Mexicans" riding "Bucking Ponies" and "Roping and Riding Wild Texas Steers."[13]

It is the "Cow-Boy's Fun" section of the Wild West program, of course, that has led many to link the Wild West shows to rodeo. Certainly both entertainments share event motifs and the larger symbolism and nostalgia of cowboys taming wild animals in an open-air performance. Yet Wild West shows originated in the commercial form, and their performers were contracted, salaried professionals, not entry-fee-paying competitors. Wild West shows tended to cater to city audiences, whereas rodeos, in the early days, were confined to western towns and villages.

Women played a relatively minor role in early rodeo, but Wild West show women like Annie Oakley and Lillian Smith achieved international star stature. In sum, the early rodeos enjoyed a closer tie to the folkloric, cattle frontier "cowboy fun" than the Wild West shows; the early rodeos' commercialism was, during this period of time, much less pronounced. This may be why North American audiences preferred rodeos to Wild West shows and why Wild West shows began a gradual decline around the time of the World War I. By the late 1930s, the Wild West shows had nearly vanished, while the rodeos were thriving.[14]

During the two decades before World War II, new rodeos appeared and crowds grew. Cheyenne, Pendleton, and Calgary were joined by hundreds of smaller but durable rodeo entertainments like the Ellensburg Rodeo. And Wild West performances in eastern cities were superseded by huge annual rodeos in Madison Square Garden and the Boston Garden. Top cowboys such as Washington State's Yakima Canutt, Oklahoman Ike Rude, and Pete Knight of Alberta, Canada, gained national fame for their rodeo prowess. In 1936, in the middle of the Great Depression, more than 250,000 paying customers viewed the nineteen-day Madison Square Garden show, and Cheyenne, Denver, and Pendleton each drew 100,000.

In 1929 the management and entrepreneurial elements of rodeo—the local rodeo boards, sponsors, and stock contractors—had banded together to form the Rodeo Association of America, later renamed the International Rodeo Association. The organization aimed to systematize and professionalize the rodeo "sport" by forbidding false advertising (of high prize purses) and by policing a number of self-proclaimed "championship" rodeos. Member rodeos adhered to a new points system to determine championships and adopted specific RAA judging criteria. These changes definitely marked progress, but many rodeo cowboys complained that the RAA represented only management and failed to address their needs. Their complaints were genuine, but it took a crisis to organize this dispersed and individualistic group of rodeo hands into a coherent labor organization: in 1935, complaining of inadequate prize money and bad judging, cowboys struck the Boston Garden Rodeo, and soon afterward they formed a permanent alliance of their own.[15]

It took the rodeo cowboys so long to organize professionally that they dubbed their first coalition, founded on November 6, 1936, the Cowboy Turtles Association. One remembered naming it that because they had "been slow as turtles doin' somethin' like this." Later renamed the Rodeo Cowboys Association (RCA), and today the Professional Rodeo Cowboys Association (PRCA), the Cowboy Turtles used strikes and the threat of strikes to battle the RAA for higher prize money and better judges. After excesses and mistakes by both groups, the situation stabilized. With 105 RAA-sanctioned shows and hundreds of amateur events, North American rodeo approached World War II as a maturing and prospering popular entertainment spectacle.[16]

The war temporarily sidetracked rodeo. As early as 1941, 28 percent of scheduled rodeos, amateur and professional, were canceled. From 1942 to 1945, fuel shortages, rationing, conscription, and other war-related phenomena forced scores of shows to close. Hardest hit by the war were the rodeo cowgirls. Although the Wild West shows had been their prime venue, cowgirls had enjoyed a visible minor role in professional rodeo throughout the 1920s and 1930s. Champion cowgirls such as Mabel Strickland, Fannie Steele, and Montana's famous Greenough sisters, Alice and Marge, competed against one another and staged exhibitions in relay racing, trick riding, bronc riding, and calf roping. With gas rationing and other constrictions, rodeo boards had to cut costs; they often chose to eliminate all of the ranch-related cowgirl events and replace them with low-cost barrel racing and beauty contests. Although men's rodeo emerged from the war alive and well, the restrictions on women's events persisted, probably reflecting the men's (debatable) belief that roughstock events and—except for barrel racing— even timed events were too dangerous for women. In response, dedicated cowgirl competitors in 1948 founded the Girls Rodeo Association, now the Women's Professional Rodeo Association, and have held their own gender-segregated rodeos ever since. Cowgirls have only recently returned to non-barrel-racing competition at PRCA-sanctioned events, riding bulls at the Cheyenne Frontier Days rodeo.[17]

The emerging professional rodeos should be distinguished from the strictly amateur shows, or "punkin' rollers," as some cowboys call them even today. A punkin' (pumpkin) roller was and is a small, amateur rodeo not sanctioned by the RAA and Turtles, RCA, or PRCA. Punkin' rollers were akin to authentic folk festivals; less commercialized than the pro events, they were therefore more true to the folk idiom. Like the Ellensburg Rodeo, they were usually held in conjunction with a county fair (another type of folk festival), and many of their founders were ranchmen and farmers with ties to the vanishing agricultural society. Cowboy competitors were local and regional hands, not dues-paying Turtles or RCA professionals. True, punkin' rollers had a commercial component in local business sponsorship, gate admission charge, small cash prizes for winners, and the hawking of food and drink at the rodeo grounds. But they were down-home, down-to-earth events compared with, say, a 1930s Madison Square Garden Rodeo or today's PRCA National Finals Rodeo in Las Vegas.[18]

If the punkin' rollers remained true folk festivals, the emerging professional rodeos were gradually becoming less so. Nevertheless, pro rodeo did remain partly true to its folk origins throughout the World War II years, the 1950s, and the 1960s. Nearly all professional shows had begun as punkin' rollers and inevitably carried earlier traditions with them as they evolved and professionalized. Pro rodeos almost always took place in an outdoor arena in or near rural environs, and in conjunction with a county fair. Contestants were often local or regional RCA or PRCA cowboys, cheered on by the hometown crowd. Moreover, the program in professional rodeos and punkin' rollers alike took on an identical, folk-based form. A "grand entry" parade initiated a carefully orchestrated sequence of events, all narrated by a rodeo announcer.

Bareback bronc riding came next, followed by calf roping, saddle bronc riding, barrel racing, and steer wrestling (bulldogging). Brahma bull riding provided the spectacular finale. Interspersed variants included steer roping, wild-horse races, wild-cow milking, relay ("pony express") races, team roping, cow cutting, and contracted clown and novelty acts. This carefully prescribed, folk-based form exists in all authentic rodeo shows, amateur or professional, to this day.[19]

Rodeo aficionados call the 1950s the "golden age" of rodeo, a time when, according to one observer, rodeo "did very well and just kind of exploded." New shows and contestants revitalized the game, and national magazines such as *Newsweek, Saturday Evening Post,* and *Sports Illustrated* joined the trade publications *Hoof and Horns* and *Rodeo Sports News* to bring new fans into the fold.[20] Perhaps one reason for the charm of this era is that, despite pronounced growth, the commercialization of rodeo had not overwhelmed the folk idiom. Modern rodeo fans could have it both ways—viewing first-class rodeo contests that nevertheless exuded real western flavor. The punkin' rollers and professional shows still shared not only identical programs but also authentic, outdoor, western settings. Even the rodeo "superstars"—cowboys like Casey Tibbs, Jim Shoulders (who raked in an unheard-of $39,000 winnings in 1959), Everett Shaw, and Freckles Brown—boasted authentic rural roots on the ranches of the North American West. They were, some said, the last of an old breed, and like their predecessors, these rodeo hands claimed to be *real cowboys.*

Of course, some would debate that claim. There have always been detractors who discount the authenticity of rodeo cowboys' claims to be *real cowboys.* This question of exactly what a cowboy is and how one qualifies to be a cowboy is a very important one within cowboy culture. I define cowboys by using a strict historical criterion: a *real cowboy* was a man who worked cattle on horseback during the days of the Great Plains "cattle kingdom"—the late-nineteenth-century cattle-drive period. By this definition, cowboys disappeared with the long drives and the advent of ranching—especially the introduction of technologies and business cycles that turned the rancher into an "agribusinessman" and his hired help into ranch hands. Thus I believe that, with a small number of notable exceptions, *real cowboys* disappeared sometime in the early twentieth century.

There are today perhaps a few hundred *real cowboys* left: western men (and some women) who make their living on horseback, working hundreds of cattle on large spreads in a manner akin to the Great Plains drives of the late nineteenth century. This tiny group of cowboys spends days at a time out on the range, isolated from the technological innovations and comforts that have revolutionized cattle ranching during the twentieth century. These *real cowboys* continue to work, dress, talk, and live according to the Code of traditional cowboy culture. Yet they are so few today that we can scarcely even call them an endangered species; they are too fast approaching extinction. Throughout the twentieth century, the number of *real cowboys* has declined drastically, while the number of *pretenders* has grown out of all measure. Today there are only a handful of *real cowboys*, but countless dudes, drugstore cowboys, rednecks, agribusinessmen, and ranch hands who sincerely *wish* they were *real cowboys*.[21]

Yet without exception, rodeo cowboys have always referred to themselves simply as "cowboys," with no modifier (as I noted, the pros today use the word *cowboy* while also calling themselves "professional athletes"). Since the late-nineteenth-century birth of rodeo (and, for all practical purposes, the demise of a viable working-cowboy profession), rodeo hands have staked a tenacious claim to the title of *cowboy* proper. The vast majority of North Americans today do not seem to understand or care about the marked historical difference between a rodeo cowboy and a working cowboy. And so the myth of the rodeo man as cowboy has today become institutionalized and acculturated. But this has not always been the case.

In the late nineteenth and early twentieth centuries, there were still actual cowboys around, and there were rural Americans who had known and who remembered historic Plains cowboys. For these old-timers, the rodeo hand did not possess the mystique he possesses for North Americans today. Indeed, there was a clear dichotomy between working cowboys and professional rodeo hands—a dichotomy upon which any working cowboy or his defender was glad to expound. One Pacific Northwest old-timer, remembering an early punkin' roller rodeo, noted that most of the contestants were "regular cowboys. They wasn't these drugstore cowboys or these fellas that don't do nothing only follow rodeos. They was real cowboys." Texas folklorist A. C. Greene remembers as a young boy hearing old cowboys disparage a local rodeo, complaining that there "were just rodeo cowboys doing the riding, anyway, not working cowboys." These statements, and many others like them, document a pronounced prejudice against professional rodeo hands that prevailed throughout the late nineteenth and early twentieth centuries but ended, for the most part, sometime after World War II. From the early ranch cowboy's point of view, a rodeo man was undependable—he drank too much, caroused with women, and had bad work habits. He was constantly quitting ranch work to follow the rodeo, leaving ranch cowboys to pick up the slack. Ranch cowboys prided themselves on dependability and loyalty to the ranch, and they accused rodeo men, sometimes enviously and unfairly, of breaking this Code of behavior.[22]

At the same time, some ranch folk derided the rodeo cowboys' skills and insinuated that rodeo men were second-rate hands or, worse yet, dudes and city slickers. One defender of ranch cowboys wrote in the 1930s: "A man can learn to be a bronk rider or a calf roper without getting out of the city limits of Chicago, or New York," and although some of "those contest riders are cowboys and good ones, there's just one helluva lot of them that *ain't.*" Moreover, "if these modern boys used the old timers' horses and equipment, they would slow up considerably and nobody but a fool would argue otherwise."[23]

So, are rodeo men *real cowboys* or not? This difficult question can lead to violent disputes (literally). A rodeo man's claim to cowboy status is a mighty touchy subject, and rodeo men argue, quite rightly, that their cowboy credentials are strong. For starters, and disparagers notwithstanding, rodeo men possess many of the skills of range cowboys in spades. They are excellent ropers and riders; the best of them are probably more sharply focused on and skilled at their events than the multifaceted working cowboys could possibly be. On the other hand, no working cowboy would have ever bulldogged a steer or ridden a bareback horse or a Brahma bull as part of his job; those events are purely for "show." Yet rodeo men can counter truthfully that they adhere closely to other features of Plains cowboy culture. They certainly dress like cowboys, and they speak in the slow, laconic drawl that characterizes cowboy vernacular. They lead a nomadic life, traveling from rodeo to rodeo in a manner somewhat akin to that of nineteenth-century cowboy drifters. Of course, they travel in trucks, vans, and four-wheel-drive rigs, not on horseback. There were no Dodge pickups on the trail to Dodge City.[24]

The rodeo cowboys' strongest claim to being *real cowboys* is their strict adherence to the Cowboy Code, a set of unwritten rules of behavior that evolved among late-nineteenth-century Great Plains cowboys and was subscribed to almost universally by cowboy occupational folk groups. The Code contained many features that resemble the unique characteristics ascribed to American frontiersmen by historian Frederick Jackson Turner in "The Significance of the Frontier in American History." Cowboys were democratic, practical, innovative, and courageous. They disliked intellectuals. Cowboys were individualistic, yet closely bound by the Code mores of their peers. These included an aversion to city life and "civilization," fancy talk, and boasting. Many cowboys spoke only when necessary. They said what they wanted to say in slow, deliberate vernacular, with perhaps a dash of dry humor to enliven their "lingo." A variant to this slow drawl was the quick-witted retort, also served up with healthy portions of irony and vernacular. A cowboy admired a good horse and took good care of it; he stood by fellow hands and his outfit at all costs. He showed hospitality to cowboys from other outfits and shared important trail information with them. He was deferential to women, showing an exaggerated courtesy toward "good women"—although by and large he shunned the company of "good women" in favor of the prostitutes and bar girls he knew would not "tie him down" and end his wandering lifestyle.[25]

Allowing for the passage of decades, the intrusion of modern technological society, and the virtual demise of authentic Plains cowboy culture, there nevertheless remain recognizable variants of Cowboy Code traits in the culture of twentieth-century rodeo cowboys. As noted, they dress, talk, and wander like Plains cowboys. A look at rodeo behind the chutes reveals other variants of the Cowboy Code at work. Rodeo men are democratic, resourceful, and most certainly courageous. They are individualistic when compared with society at large, yet loyally conformist in following cowboy norms. They show hospitality, sharing cash, beer, motel rooms, and their gear and riggin'. More important, they share precious information about competition roughstock with their rodeo opponents, just because they respect them as fellow cowboys. They love their roping and bulldogging horses, and they show a profound respect for the wild animals they seek to ride. And although many rodeo men today are married, many are not; their treatment of women continues to hold at least the form of authentic cowboy culture.[26]

Are rodeo men *real cowboys?* One final way to sort out the question is to ask it about the 1950s "golden age" of rodeo and its cowboy superstars. Were they *real cowboys?* If we define a cowboy as someone who made his living working cattle on the late-nineteenth-century Great Plains trail drives, then of course Casey Tibbs, Jim Shoulders, Everett Shaw, Freckles Brown, and their 1950s cohorts were not cowboys. But clearly these top rodeo hands were not dudes or city slickers. Perhaps we can compromise a bit. To achieve a synthesis, an assessment of the rural connection and mystique is essential.

Most of the rodeo hands of the post–World War II era were, like their late-nineteenth- and early-twentieth-century predecessors, *ranch-trained*—a term rodeo folks use to describe a rodeo man who learned his trade on a working cattle ranch. There was a solid core of rodeo competitors who lived and worked on cattle ranches, migrating to and from the rodeo arena as their finances and lifestyles dictated; some aspired to save enough prize money to buy land and become full-time cattle ranchers. Casey Tibbs, Everett Shaw, and Jim Shoulders each had a personal connection with cattle ranching, though in varying degrees. Tibbs, one of the all-time-great bronc riders, grew up on his parents' homestead near Pierre, South Dakota. Shaw, a steer roper, was born in 1903 on a Hogshooter Creek spread, between Nowata and Bartlesville, Oklahoma. Four-time all-around champion Shoulders was a city boy, born and raised in Tulsa, where he graduated from East Central High School in 1946, but he always spoke of his childhood visits to his grandparents' farm and the expertise he gained there working cattle. So all of these rodeo men claimed to be cowboys in that they were ranch-trained. And if their cowboy credentials might pale a little in comparison with those of the men who worked the long cattle drives of the late-nineteenth-century Great Plains, these 1950s rodeo hands nevertheless came closer to being bona fide cowboys than the vast majority of other folks in North America at that time. And if any man doubted their claims to the title of *real cowboy*, he kept his mouth shut.[27]

With more growth and commercialization of rodeo in the 1960s and 1970s, even the tenuous ranch-training connection was fast disappearing. A self-styled "new breed" of cowboy—including Larry Mahan, Don Gay, Gary Leffew, Tom Ferguson, and many others—emerged on the rodeo circuit in the late 1960s. The new breed were highly skilled athletes who eschewed some—although certainly not all—of the traditions of North American rodeo men. Most of these cowboys were *arena-trained*, not ranch-trained. In other words, they had learned their initial rodeo skills by actually rodeoing, bypassing the workways of the ranch cowboy. Increasingly, post-1965 rodeo cowboys were western town boys who had learned and honed their skills in high-school rodeo clubs, calf-roping teams, and 4-H groups, and even as college athletes in the National Intercollegiate Rodeo Association (NIRA). Some attended the "rodeo schools" and courses that began to pop up in the North American West. Rodeo historian Kristine Fredriksson could write in 1985 that one-third of the members of the PRCA, a group that had always maintained a rural and decidedly anti-intellectual posture, had attended college. And, amazingly, one-half of the mid-1980s PRCA cowboys admitted that they had never worked on a cattle ranch. Only one-half of PRCA cowboys, then, claimed any sort of a connection, however slim, to actual ranch work.[28]

Big-money PRCA rodeos underwent marked change. Rodeo announcers found themselves introducing a few cowboys who actually hailed from New Jersey and New York. An airline credit card became as important to the rodeo man as a good bronc saddle. Some of the new age cowboys even flirted with pop psychology and the mental mastery techniques of "psycho-cybernetics." If they proved to be winners—and many of these superb athletes did—then another transformation occurred: The new-breed cowboy with big winnings often behaved like an astute businessman, not an old-time rodeo rake out on an all-night drunk. Business acumen led to advertising, recording, and television contracts, diversification, stock portfolios, and planned retirements for the most successful of the new breed.[29]

The career of Larry Mahan—"the cowboy in the gray flannel suit," as *Time* once called him—provides a microcosm of the rise of the new breed and the final evolution of big-money PRCA rodeo from folk festival to professional athletic contest. Born in 1943 near Salem, Oregon, Mahan earned his spurs in youth calf-roping clubs and junior rodeos, not the rigors of ranch life. In a sixteen-year PRCA career that grossed him $506,441, Mahan used scientific method—writing, filing, and restudying copious notes on the hundreds of broncs and bulls that he rode so well. He called rodeo a "sport" and referred to himself as a "professional athlete." He flew to competitions in his own Cessna 310 and, much to the dismay of Jim Shoulders and other old-timers, grew sideburns and let his hair hang down over his ears (he had the audacity to wear *sweater vests* while riding roughstock). Moreover, Mahan revolutionized the rodeo profession by diversifying into promotions and advertising, a western clothing line, publications, and his own highly lucrative rodeo schools and seminars. Indeed, one rodeo colleague remembered Mahan as "the only cowboy I know who hands out his business card when you say hello."[30]

Today, one can argue that big-time PRCA rodeo is no longer a folk festival—it is a folk-based popular-entertainment spectacle. Big-money rodeos have essentially become commercial athletic contests. Fans watching televised PRCA rodeo find much to recommend it, for the pro rodeo contest—like other professional athletic events—has taken on an engaging and glitzy aesthetic in its own right.

The 1990s heirs of the new breed now often perform in the indoor, climate-controlled sports stadiums of major North American cities. Televised rodeo shows on ESPN and TNN have removed many rodeo fans from the arena altogether. The recent move of the National Finals Rodeo from its traditional home in Oklahoma City to the bright lights of Las Vegas has even further accelerated the stampede toward commercialization. There the rodeo announcers sound more and more like AM radio disc jockeys, and they even play rock-music clips to accompany bronc-riding performances (Queen's "We Are the Champions" is a favorite). Big-money rodeo sponsors today greatly alter the nature of the game. R. J. Reynolds, Copenhagen, Skoal, Levi Strauss and Wrangler, Dodge trucks, Black Velvet Whiskey, Coors, Schlitz, and Budweiser, Frontier Airlines, and Justin boots make prize money soar while underwriting state-of-the-art arena scoreboards, promotions, concerts, beauty pageants, and even roughstock breeding (one old-timer complained recently of the proliferation of broncs and bulls with "Copenhagen" or "Skoal" surnames). As prize purses escalate, a cadre of "cowboy plutocrats," as one historian has dubbed them, move even farther from rural ranchways into the world of professional athletes and media stars, perfecting the philosophy and methods of Larry Mahan and the new breed. No matter how tenaciously he claims to be an authentic cowboy, the big-time PRCA rodeo man has in some ways become very much an *urban cowboy*. One might argue (at risk of personal injury) that today's big-money rodeo cowboy is, in a very special way, a professional actor. He is a highly skilled athlete who *portrays* a working cowboy in front of thousands of admiring fans.[31]

However, I must stress that even if the rodeo man is not a *real cowboy*, but in fact a professional athlete who *portrays* a *real cowboy*, he is nevertheless a unique professional athlete. For unlike professional football and basketball players, the rodeo man is tied irrevocably to the Myth of the West—the central myth in North American history and culture. The rodeo man works, dresses, behaves, talks, and adheres almost religiously to the Code of *real cowboys*. If he is an actor, then he is a damn convincing one. Indeed, he is convincing as only an actor who has fully embraced his persona can be. Listening and watching a sports announcer interviewing six-time PRCA all-round champion Ty Murray, for example, one is struck by the similarity of Murray's dress, stance, demeanor, accent, and language to that of Teddy Blue Abbott. When asked to what goals a six-time all-round champion roughstock rider can still aspire, Murray intones in classic Cowboy Code understatement: "When I'm done rodeoing . . . and people look back and my name's brought up, I hope that I'm remembered as a great cowboy. Not as a great bull rider or a great bronc rider. I hope when they think back they'll just say I was a great cowboy."[32]

Only a few cowboy competitors can claim the winnings, fame, and material comforts of the new breed of rodeo men like Larry Mahan and Ty Murray. At least for the time being, small-town, folk-based rodeos and rodeo cowboys continue to thrive, paralleling and complementing the slick, commercial big-money shows. Big-time PRCA rodeo makes up only a portion—albeit the most visible portion—of North American rodeo performances. Many medium-sized and small PRCA rodeos—shows like the Bishop (California) Pioneer Days and Montana's Dillon Jaycee Rodeo and Red Lodge Home of Champions Rodeo—still clearly evince folk-based traditions. And there are always the punkin' rollers. Just as some baseball purists have retreated from major league Astrodomes to the green grass of AAA farm-team ballparks, rodeo fans tired of Las Vegas glitz seek out the punkin' rollers of the North American West. Shows like the Omak (Washington) Stampede, Ennis (Montana) Fourth of July Rodeo, Miles City (Montana) Bucking Horse Sale, Grover (Colorado) Rodeo, Vernal (Utah) Rodeo, Stamford (Texas) Cowboy Reunion, some of the small International Professional Rodeo Association (IPRA) shows of the Midwest, and many others still provide rodeo hands and their fans a taste of the real rodeo folk festival.[33]

Thus North American rodeo continues to grow, prosper, and evolve. It will no doubt keep on doing so. Until the Great Plains are depopulated or animal-rights activists gain sway in western state legislatures (sobering but not altogether impossible scenarios!), authentic folk-based PRCA shows and punkin' roller rodeos will carry on the North American rodeo tradition. Meanwhile, big-money PRCA rodeo will also continue to sustain some rodeo traditions, even in its highly commercialized venues. Hundreds of thousands of North Americans will keep looking to rodeo and rodeo cowboys as symbols of our frontier heritage. And the rodeo cowboy will, for the time being at least, continue to ride in these popular shows, shouting "Let 'er buck!" as he explodes from the chutes.

CHAPTER TWO

"Goin' Down That Road"
The Rodeo Cowboy in Movies and Television

Boy, I'm beginning to smell wages all over you.
—Gay to Perce, in *The Misfits* (1961)

In John Huston's 1961 movie *The Misfits,* rodeo cowboys repeatedly disparage "wages." Introduced as a "good for nothin' cowboy," rodeo roper Gay (Clark Gable) quickly retorts, "That may be, but it's better than wages." His rodeo compatriot Perce (Montgomery Clift) shares the same view, agreeing to join Gay in a wild-horse hunt of dubious financial reward simply because "anything's better than wages." When Gay's lover Roslyn (Marilyn Monroe) implores the men to leave the wild horses alone—"you know it's wrong"—Gay counters, "All I know is everything else is wages." Later he chastises the vacillating Perce with the remark given in the epigraph above. The choice for Gay seems clear: to remain free and independent he must stay a cowboy, avoiding regular jobs and the "wages" they bring. It seems easy, but as the wild-horse chase reaches its grisly climax, Gay begins to change his mind. Ultimately, he sets the horses free, declaring, "I'm finished with it. . . . I've just gotta find another way to be alive now. If there is one."[1]

But is there "another way" for the twentieth-century cowboy? Can the rodeo cowboy find a middle road between freedom and "wages," between the ways of the frontier and civilization? While *The Misfits* does not answer this central question, it addresses it in a dramatic way, and in so doing it carries on the tradition of classic westerns. This tradition is also evident in other post–World War II rodeo movies (and one television series): *The Lusty Men* (1952), *Stoney Burke* (1962–1963), *Junior Bonner* (1972), *J. W. Coop* (1972), *Electric Horseman* (1979), *Urban Cowboy* (1980), *8 Seconds* (1994), and *The Cowboy Way* (1994). Although they vary in their approaches, all of these rodeo movies explore the tension between the ideals of the frontier and civilization.

To understand and appreciate the rodeo movies requires a brief review of the origins and motifs of the classic western. The first westerns date back more than 150 years to the *Leatherstocking Tales* (1823–1841) of James Fenimore Cooper. The tales (the most famous of which is *The Last of the Mohicans*) are set in the northeastern wilderness and feature a frontiersman hero who appears under five monikers in five novels but whom scholars have dubbed Leatherstocking (after his deerskin leggings). The five novels are remarkably similar. As each work begins, the reader finds Leatherstocking in the wild, living in complete harmony with nature, a man alone—with the notable exception of a male Indian companion. Together they are the Eve-less Adams in the Garden of Eden, adhering to an unwritten frontier code. But the silence of the forest is soon broken by the exertions of civilized folk—pioneer families, soldiers, government officials, and the forces of business, society, law, and order. These civilizers waste no time in getting themselves in terrible predicaments at the hands of the forces of the frontier—ferocious animals, raging rivers, outlaws, and most often, bloodthirsty Indians. Without hesitation Leatherstocking befriends and intervenes on behalf of these civilized folks and aids them in subduing the forces of the wilderness. But the victorious result is ironic and tragic. In aiding the civilizers, Leatherstocking has facilitated his own demise, for he cannot possibly settle in the villages (or marry the women) he has helped to survive and prosper. He must move on. In *The Prairie* (1827), Leatherstocking assists one final group of pioneers and then dies an old man; he is buried on the Great Plains, among the Indians and within sight of the Rocky Mountains. Civilization follows close behind.[2]

For the next hundred years, the American western evolved around this taletype first painted by Cooper. Of course, variations appeared regularly (in Owen Wister's 1902 novel *The Virginian*, for example, the hero actually settles down to married life at the end of the story). But even with variations the westerns still addressed the fundamental motif: the clash between the frontier and civilization—the wild and the tame—in the nineteenth-century American West. Always the forces of the frontier (wild animals, blizzards and thunderstorms, bad men and Indians) await and threaten to destroy civilized folks (farmer settlers, soldiers, townspeople, and government officials) as they head west to make their new homes. Between the two forces stands the western hero—a scout, hunter, cowboy, mountain man, or "good" gunfighter. He follows a variant of Leatherstocking's frontier code of behavior—the Cowboy Code. He knows well the ways of the wild but has accepted the rightness (and inevitability) of "progress." He enters the fray and helps the civilized folks prevail. Tragically, he simultaneously works himself out of a job; there is no place for this hero in a West of farms, towns, churches, and families, and he has to "move on." Thus the Ringo Kid (John Wayne) saves the domesticated passengers in *Stagecoach* (1939) and heads for his ranch in Old Mexico. Similarly, Shane (Alan Ladd), the hero of *Shane* (1953), helps upright farmers to make a community and a civil way of life for families and "decent folks." He helps them fight off the wily cattlemen and their hired gun (Jack Palance), then rides off into the Grand Tetons as the little boy (Brandon de Wilde) cries after him futilely and hauntingly, "Shane! Come back, Shane! Come back!"[3]

Rodeo movies all address this taletype, but in unusual and innovative ways. The difference is due largely to their twentieth-century settings. All of the classic films discussed so far are set on the eighteenth- or nineteenth-century American frontier. The rodeo movie belongs to a new genre, the urban, or contemporary, western. The contemporary western continues the classic juxtaposition of the frontier and civilization, but in a far different, modern context. Interestingly, the subgenre began with Roy Rogers and Gene Autry, whose grade-B cowboy movies and serials were often set in modern America, complete with automobiles, telephones, and gangster bad guys. John Wayne's early *Three Mesquiteer* serials also superimposed the twentieth century on the nineteenth. Later, 1950s television gave us Sky King, who added an airplane to the cowboy accoutrements, and the *Roy Rogers Show* featured Roy's sidekick Pat Brady in his beloved Jeep "Nelly Belle." All of this technology appeared, incongruously, right alongside the horseback chase scenes and six-gun shoot-outs of the classic western.⁴

Later, in the 1960s and 1970s, more artistically ambitious moviemakers produced *Lonely Are the Brave* (1962), *Hud* (1963), *Coogan's Bluff* (1969), *Monte Walsh* (1970), *The Last Picture Show* (1971), *Billy Jack* (1971), *Kid Blue* (1973), and many other contemporary westerns. These movies are all set in the post-frontier West, with all of its trappings of industrialization, urban centers, and material progress. Obviously, the western hero's environment has changed drastically. Horses are sometimes supplemented or supplanted by pickups, four-wheel-drive vehicles, automobiles, and airplanes. Shootists have abandoned their revolvers for automatic weapons with immense firepower. Most important, many of the old evil forces of the wild are gone. Rivers are dammed, and the buffalo and grizzly bear are nearly extinct. The Indians have been killed or shoved onto reservations; they appear now only in a new, cross-acculturated context. Although outlaws abound, they have given up their horses, neckerchiefs, and six-guns for Cadillacs, pin-striped suits, and semi-automatic firepower. The hero is still a courageous and plain-spoken fellow, but his new dramatic station is even more ironic than the old. He is a cowboy in a land of cities, alone now as never before. The hero of the contemporary western movie is a *contemporary ancestor,* exiled forever from his beloved nineteenth-century wilderness.[5]

Rodeo, a late-nineteenth- and twentieth-century historical phenomenon, provides an excellent subject for the contemporary western. Its form fits the classic taletype because real rodeo cowboys are actually in the business of subduing the wild—roping calves, bulldogging steers, and riding wild broncs and bulls in the rodeo arena. Rodeo cowboys literally act out the taming of the West. But this direct relationship with the classic western motif raises problems as well as opportunities for the filmmaker. Compared with movies about, say, cowboys and rustlers, rodeo movies are more complex and less predictable in their treatment of the poles of frontier and civilization. The twentieth-century context rules out the usual bad guys, and so, with the exception of the obligatory barroom brawl, the forces of the wild are almost always the wild animals in the rodeo arena. The forces of civilization loom more ominously, in the form of commercialization and "progress" in a vanished West. The rodeo-movie cowboy is truly the last of his breed, but he has precious little wilderness to which he can escape. Indeed, some of these heroes have grown so disillusioned as to actually consider marriage and settling down. Yet most often the rodeo cowboy of film stays true to his literary and cinematic predecessors, riding off alone into the sunset (if he has not been killed in the arena, that is). When the rodeo is over and the wild animals conquered, the rodeo man jumps into his pickup or car and, as they say in the trade, keeps "movin' on down that road." There is another rodeo ahead, and more calves to rope and broncs to ride. After all, it's better than wages.[6]

Interestingly, the first rodeo movies appeared long before the first commercial western novels with rodeo themes, such as William Crawford's *Bronc Rider* (1965). Rodeo movies were themselves relatively rare before 1952, although a few early examples of the genre exist. A. D. Kean, a turn-of-the-century Canadian bronc rider turned filmmaker, shot and marketed *The Calgary Stampede* in the nineteen-teens (chapter 4), and movie cowboy superstar Hoot Gibson appeared in his own *Calgary Stampede* feature in 1925. Meanwhile, Yakima Canutt, a Washington State rodeo star turned movie actor/stuntman/producer, starred in his own production, *The King of the Rodeo,* and other silent and grade-B western potboilers. Bill Pickett, also a rodeo competitor turned actor, starred in *The Bull-dogger,* a 1920s movie notable for the fact that its hero, Pickett himself, was an African American (chapter 7). The Roy Rogers and Gene Autry serials and features also used rodeo sporadically, but like Rex Allen's grade-B *Rodeo King and the Señorita* (1951), these early movies failed to utilize the rodeo milieu as an important dramatic component of the plot. Rather, they employed rodeo events only to supply action or to supplement an otherwise unrelated story, usually about love.[7]

In the early 1950s, Hollywood at last discovered the potential of the rodeo cowboy as a powerful, albeit tragic, modern western hero. Within one year, no less than three feature-length rodeo movies appeared. Budd Boetticher filmed the action shots for *Bronco Buster* (1952) in rodeo arenas stretching from Cheyenne to Calgary and added veracity with cameo appearances by top rodeo hands Casey Tibbs, Pete Crump, Jerry Spangler, and Manuel Enos. *Bronco Buster*'s plot centers on a romantic rodeo triangle. In Richard Fleischer's *Arena* (1953) the story centers on a "washed-up rodeo rider" (Gig Young) who attempts a comeback, only to meet a disastrous end. Yet while both of these movies are good entertainment, they are notable here mainly for their attempts to emulate Nicholas Ray's 1952 rodeo classic, *The Lusty Men.*[8]

The Lusty Men was the first of a string of solid westerns directed by Ray. Shot in black-and-white on location at several western rodeos (including the venerable Tucson Rodeo and Oregon's Pendleton Roundup), *The Lusty Men* is the first and, to this day, one of the most successful movie portrayals of the life of a North American rodeo cowboy. The foremost reason for this success is the effective use of the frontier/

civilization dialectic in the rodeo context, but with a compelling romantic twist. For rodeo man Jeff McCloud (Robert Mitchum) encounters much more fighting spirit from home-loving Louise Merritt (Susan Hayward), the wife of his traveling partner, than he does from any of the wild broncs and bulls he has ever ridden.'

The Lusty Men opens with a melancholy Texas homecoming for the permanently injured McCloud. After eighteen years of competition, a bull has "sat on him" and he has little to show for his life except the prestige of being a former rodeo champ. He hires on at a local ranch, thanks to the efforts of a starstruck rodeo amateur, ranch hand Wes Merritt (Arthur Kennedy). The two agree to hit the rodeo road, with Jeff acting as Wes's coach—but only over the strenuous objections of Wes's wife, Louise. Like the women of all of the classic westerns, Louise symbolizes civilization. A child of itinerant fruit pickers (one of several Great Depression references in the film), she despises rodeo and its roving "saddle tramps"; she fears Wes will lose the money they have carefully saved for a down payment on a ranch. She reluctantly agrees to accompany the men but implores Wes to remember their goal: a "decent, steady life."

Jeff utters what amounts to a rodeo-cowboy soliloquy when he and Louise first clash. Countering her skepticism about the remunerative aspects of rodeo, he explains that "some things you don't do for the cash. Some things you do for the *buzz* you get outta them." She remains unconvinced and hostile, and Jeff waxes eloquent: "I've come out of those chutes a lot of times. Heard the crowd hollerin'. The force of a bull jumpin' and twistin' underneath. I always felt the same thing. For a little bit there you're a lot more than you are just walkin' down the street or eatin' and sleepin'. Maybe it's somethin' you can't explain to a woman . . . it's a different kind of buzz." Interestingly, after this first clash, Louise remains resistant but somewhat intrigued by Jeff and his wild ways. Indeed, much of the power of *The Lusty Men* comes from its characters' inability to finalize their choices between the wild and the tame.

We glimpse this dilemma in Louise's eyes at the end of her and Jeff's first confrontation, but even more in Jeff's behavior soon afterward, when he bids the Merritts good night. As the obviously happy, loving couple retire to their ranch bungalow, the former rodeo champ casts a longing glance at them and a life he has never known. Perhaps Jeff would like to settle down after all.

The rodeo road of *The Lusty Men* is not an attractive or romantic one. The camps of the rodeo performers closely resemble the fruit camps of Louise Merritt's Depression youth. Although several of the cowboys and cowgirls are clever, upright folks, many evince the tragedy and pathos of their wandering lives. Arthur Hunnicutt's Booker, a former roughstock rider turned rodeo hanger-on, is a likable but pathetic character whose grotesque leg has been broken so many times that he charges a quarter for greenhorns to view it (the widowed Booker embodies the wild/tame conflict in that he is trying to raise a teenage daughter while on the rodeo circuit). Curly, a rodeo hand whose face has been gashed horribly by a Brahma bull, drives his wife to despair with his drinking and gambling before, finally, he is fatally gored by a bull in the arena.

Louise is revolted by what she sees, but Jeff and Wes seem to thrive in this violent, exciting milieu. Wes, a talented roper, bulldogger, and roughstock rider, experiences an unusually successful rookie season; he fully embraces the rodeo lifestyle, including heavy drinking, gambling, and flirting with women. When Louise announces that they have saved enough money to buy their dream ranch, her worst fears are realized: Wes does not want to quit the rodeo road. She rebels, and Jeff McCloud makes his move, announcing his love for her as best he knows how: "I've made a thousand bartenders rich in my time. I've thrown away the down payment for a dozen spreads of my own over a crap table. . . . If I'd had somebody like you it mighta been a different story." Louise is moved but ultimately cannot betray her man. Jeff, spurned, takes an honorable way out. Although aging and out of shape, he mounts a bucking bronc in the Pendleton Roundup; his foot catches in the stirrup, and he is dragged around the arena. Finally rescued, he dies in back of the chutes in Louise Merritt's arms. Then she and Wes, thrown together by this tragedy, leave the rodeo world together and forever, reborn and bound for their Texas ranch.

The Lusty Men is a powerful and entertaining movie. Its black-and-white images provide the first actual rodeo footage ever viewed by a mass movie audience. This realism combines with an outstanding supporting cast and a very strong performance by Susan Hayward as the steadfast defender of home and stability. Most important is an excellent script (by Horace McCoy and David Dortort) that drapes the wild/tame conflict around the shoulders of Robert Mitchum's magnificent Jeff McCloud. McCloud provides the image to which, with exceptions, rodeo-movie cowboys from *The Misfits* to *8 Seconds* aspire. He is independent, skilled, courageous, and knows how to turn a clever phrase. Yet Jeff is ultimately a tragic character. Too old to follow the rodeo road and too set in his ways to win Louise Merritt, he opts for what amounts to a ritual suicide. Dying, he still can drolly say, "Never was a bronc that's never been rode. Never was a cowboy that's never been throwed. Guys like me last forever." In fact, the movie shows that guys like Jeff—and the West they represent—are nearly gone.[10]

Nine years later, in 1961, another movie explored not only rodeo but also larger themes of the plight of the cowboy on the vanished frontier, and his relationship to wild animals. Playwright Arthur Miller first envisioned *The Misfits* while residing near Reno, Nevada, to secure a divorce. He became acquainted with a group of local cowboys who had resorted to capturing wild mustangs in the surrounding desert mountains and selling them for dog food in order to maintain a vestigial cowboy lifestyle. The pathos and irony of their endeavor was spellbinding to Miller, who roughed out a screenplay about these "misfit" men and horses, including a key role for his actress wife, Marilyn Monroe. John Huston, "deeply impressed" with Miller's script, agreed to direct *The Misfits*, and the movie has become a cult classic, partly because each of its three stars—Monroe, Clark Gable, and Montgomery Clift—died soon after its completion.[11]

Rodeo and the taming of wild animals are the glue that holds Miller's sometimes overwritten script together. Cowboy Gay (Gable) and his car mechanic buddy Guido (Eli Wallach) are drifters who find Reno and its wilderness environs much to their liking. Roslyn (Monroe) comes to town for a divorce and falls in love with Gay, and the two spend a brief, idyllic time together in Guido's unfinished, abandoned home in the desert mountains. But soon Roslyn is introduced to the world of rodeo by Gay and his friend Perce (Clift), an archetypal drifting rodeo cowboy whom the men enlist to help them in a wild-horse hunt. After Perce first competes unsuccessfully in the local Dayton Rodeo, the four go on a drinking binge, and then for two days they hunt the wild horses, using an airplane and a flatbed truck as their mounts. The engine noise in an otherwise silent desert, combined with the black-and-white spectacle of these cowboys chasing down mustangs with a flatbed truck and securing them with ropes attached to truck tires, is incredibly ugly. Roslyn condemns the men for hounding the animals, and Gay fires back that they are "misfit horses." Ultimately all but Guido accept Roslyn's view, and they set the horses free. Indeed, they are all of them misfits.

Gay and Roslyn first fight over animals when he tries to shoot a rabbit that has invaded their garden; later, after viewing her first rodeo, she is so repulsed that she begs Perce to withdraw. Perce himself evinces an intriguing love-hate relationship with the broncs and bulls that thrash him about in the Dayton Rodeo. He speaks glowingly of the bronc: "That ol' horse. He sure was rank, wasn't he?" Gay replies, "Oh, he was a real killer." Bandaged, bleeding, and drunk, Perce takes on a Brahma bull, only to be thrown and further injured. "He was somethin', though, wasn't he?" exclaims Perce, blood running down his face. "Oh, I want no part of that bull," Gay declares, "except on a plate, medium rare." Yet Gay obviously respects these rodeo animals, just like the mustangs he captures and sells for dog food. The hypocrisy of this latter pursuit finally hits him, but not before he has shown his mastery over the animals and staked them to the desert floor. Thus, in setting them free, he is still the master.[12]

Huston's movie is perhaps the most ambitious of the rodeo movies. It is weakened at times by Miller's tendency to make his cowboys overly philosophical, articulate, and talkative ("We're all blind bombardiers, killing people we never saw," Guido reflects at one juncture). But ultimately the movie is a riveting portrayal of cowboy life in the twentieth-century West. Rodeo and the taming of the wild frontier provide the vehicles for this drama, and *The Misfits* travels down the streets, into the barrooms, and then into the arena of a real, small-town Nevada rodeo. Clift's Perce, like Mitchum's Jeff McCloud before him, embodies the classic rodeo cowboy, stoic in his individualism, movin' down the road to escape wages and civilized ways, but realizing finally that the road leads nowhere for a twentieth-century man. Perce and Gay do the only thing they know how to do, but in the end there is no place for them.[13]

The Misfits is the most bittersweet of the rodeo portrayals because its cowboys at last have to admit that they have more in common with the mustangs they capture than with the dog-food manufacturers they sell them to. This sort of irony proves most confusing to a cowboy like Gay: "Somehow or other it all got changed around," he confesses to Roslyn at movie's end. "See, I'm doing the same thing I always did. It's just that they changed it around." Who, exactly, "they" are remains a mystery to this cowboy, who has finally acknowledged, a century too late, the end of the frontier: "Damn 'em all. They changed it. Changed it all around. Smeared it all over with blood. I'm finished with it."[14]

Rodeo-cowboy television shows stand in marked contrast to the high drama and irony of *The Lusty Men* and *The Misfits*. With the notable exception of post-1970s sports television venues (see chapter 7), television producers have never successfully produced and marketed the rodeo subgenre. In fact, only three television shows have ever focused on a rodeo theme, and all three fall far short of the artistic scope of *The Lusty*

Men, The Misfits, and later rodeo movies. The first rodeo television show actually bridged three electronic media—radio, film, and television—producing the pilot for the classic 1950s television series *The Adventures of Ozzie and Harriet.* In the movie *Here Come the Nelsons* (1952), Ozzie, Harriet, David, and Ricky Nelson add visuals to their weekly 1940s radio program fare, setting the stage for their long-running television series. *Here Come the Nelsons* features Rock Hudson, Ann Doran, Jim Backus, and others in an amusing, forgettable tale about a visiting rodeo trick rider (Doran) and a big misunderstanding. The misunderstanding results in Ozzie's riding a rodeo bronc named Dynamite and assisting an undergarments salesman (Hudson) in capturing some bad guys (with a girdle roadblock). *Here Come the Nelsons* is definitely not Academy Award or Emmy material. Yet some viewers might understandably prefer Ozzie's good humor and rodeo antics to Guido and Perce's rodeo existentialism.[15]

One year after the release of *The Misfits,* two major television networks premiered their first (and last) weekly rodeo dramatic series. NBC's *Wide Country* (1962–1963) is notable mainly for its attempt to emulate its more memorable rival, ABC's *Stoney Burke* (1962–1963). Rodeo aficionados are still puzzling over the unrealized potential of *Stoney Burke,* which had all the makings of a durable television series. Debuting on October 1, 1962, in the 9:00–10:00 P.M. Monday-night time slot, *Stoney Burke* was based on the life story of South Dakota's Casey Tibbs, an all-round champion roughstock rider who served as the series' technical adviser. A young Jack Lord (later of *Hawaii Five-O* fame) played Stoney, working hard to master Great Plains rodeo-cowboy lingo and learn the fine points of the rodeo sport. Lord was supported by an outstanding cast that included regulars Warren Oates and Bruce Dern playing Stoney's traveling buddies E. J. Stocker and Ves Painter. Set on the southwestern rodeo circuit and filmed in black-and-white, each episode featured actual rodeo roughstock and timed-event footage. This live action was woven into a plot centering on guest stars playing the varied folks Stoney encountered on the rodeo road. It seemed like a natural—a veritable rodeo *Route 66*—yet *Stoney Burke* somehow never gelled.[16]

In "Tigress by the Tail," an episode that aired on April 22, 1963, we get a little sample of the ups and downs of *Stoney Burke*. As in Buck Owens and the Buckaroos' "Tiger by the Tail," a then-current country-music hit, Stoney Burke's tiger is a young woman, although not a love interest (at least not from Stoney's perspective). Donna Wesson (Elizabeth Ashley) is the only daughter of Stoney's recently deceased cowboy compatriot Del Wesson. Freshly expelled from prep school when she meets up with Stoney—after a high-speed automobile chase—Donna is broke (with creditors in hot pursuit), driving a stolen car, and definitely looking for a little romance and a lot of trouble. Since Del Wesson once saved Stoney's life (carrying the critically injured young cowboy out of the Montana mountains just before he "ended up dinner for timber wolves"), Stoney feels a solemn duty to help Donna. But as Ves Painter (Warren Oates) remarks in one of numerous wry asides, Stoney is taking on "all the responsibilities of fatherhood and none of the rewards." Donna is "too old to adopt and too young to turn loose."

Donna goes right to work. Dodging a tenacious credit agent (Ed Asner) and immediately vanishing from the job Stoney arranges for her, she seduces a married rodeo roper, sets him up for a fistfight with another suitor, and then heads for Mexico for a quickie marriage to the roper. In a rare moment of respite from writing checks to cover Donna's bills, Stoney intervenes and tries to talk some sense into her. She in turn tries to seduce him ("I could love you—please love me back"), but Stoney is not about to court his deceased friend's young daughter. Donna then promises her "Sir Galahad in spurs . . . not to act wild and crazy as long as I'm in your hands." But by story's end Stoney has to conclude that Donna, at this stage in her life at least, is hopelessly irresponsible. "I feel sorry for you, Donna," he states gravely after a final confrontation at the episode's conclusion. "I've never felt so sorry for anyone in all my life."

Then, as the closing credits appear, Stoney executes his signature departure, walking slowly away, bronc saddle thrown over his shoulder,
headin' on down that road to the next rodeo.

Woven into this story line are three scenes of live arena action (bulldogging, trick riding, and bronc riding) and some pretty good one-
liners from Oates's Ves Painter. If Donna's story, even with this accompaniment, lacks the muscle to make a tight one-hour television show,
Stoney Burke's writers nevertheless do one thing very well. *Stoney
Burke*'s forte is its portrayal of frontier and cowboy values as they relate,
in this case, to Donna and Stoney's situation. Viewers learn that although a rodeo man may at times live as wildly as Stoney's girl tiger, a
rodeo man also has a set of values—a code of behavior—to which he must
adhere. *Stoney Burke* introduces and delineates the Cowboy Code in
this, and all, of its episodes. Stoney does not hesitate to help and keep
on helping "Del Wesson's little girl" because "I owe Del my life." It is as
simple as that. He tries his best to teach Donna to honor her word and
meet her obligations in the same way he has met and honored his. When
she tries to elope, he warns: "Before you belong to somebody, you've got
to belong to yourself." But Donna persists in her dishonesty, selfish-
ness, disloyalty, and cowardice; she continues to break the code of behavior. When she shrieks at Stoney, "This is the way you repay my father
for saving your life!" he chastises her one last time and then turns her
loose: "Yeah! That's the best way [to repay him] I know how. To give his
little girl a way to straighten out her life by takin' her punishment. A life
for a life, Donna—mine for yours—that makes us even. If Del were alive
he'd mark the bill paid . . . maybe someday you'll thank me, and that's
the day you'll finally grow up." Ves Painter, ready himself to hit the road
again, puts it more succinctly: "Good riddance to that tiger."[17]

Perhaps *Stoney Burke* appeared a decade too early. In movie theaters,
the iconoclastic 1960s and especially the early 1970s proved fertile
ground for the enigmatic rodeo-cowboy hero. Nearly a dozen rodeo
films appeared in succession, among them *When the Legends Die* (1972),

The Honkers (1972), *Black Rodeo* (1972), the Academy Award–winning documentary *The Great American Cowboy* (1974), and *Goldenrod* (1977). *The Honkers* and *Goldenrod* are important for their workmanlike assemblage of a standard rodeo subgenre motif—aging and (in *Goldenrod*) crippled cowboys gritting their teeth and trying, but not quite succeeding, in living new lives without rodeo. In *The Honkers* (cowboy vernacular for mean horses), James Coburn's rodeo-cowboy hero Lou Lathrop is actually no hero at all. Life on the rodeo road has made him unfit for any civilized company; he is an outlaw who breaks the Cowboy Code by disrespecting good women and cheating his best friend and fellow rodeo cowboys. *The Honkers* ends with Coburn walking into the sunset, but unlike in *Shane* (or *Stoney Burke*), no one is calling him back. The movie's strongest suits are authentic portrayals of rodeo competition and a memorable supporting role by Slim Pickens (himself a former 1950s rodeo competitor and clown) in his only rodeo movie. In the 1977 Canadian television movie *Goldenrod*, Tony LoBianco's rodeo hero is much more sympathetic than Lou Lathrop; he is trying to change his life and raise two young boys as a single parent. Permanently injured and no longer a rodeo competitor, he is an exile, lost and striving to learn about the tame nonrodeo universe.[18]

Cliff Robertson directly addresses the 1960s counterculture in *J. W. Coop* (1972), for which he served as producer, director, and star. Robertson's J. W. Coop hits the rodeo road after a ten-year stint in a Texas state prison, only to find that times have changed greatly since he last rodeoed. Commercialism, greed, and racism have entered a world where rodeo cowboys now commute in Lear jets and boast lucrative television and advertising contracts. J. W. is puzzled and somewhat bemused by all of this, but his hippie lover (Christina Ferrare) is appalled. Together they travel the circuit in an old army ambulance as J. W. advances in the standings and is simultaneously drawn into the materialism of his glitzy new rodeo world. Ferrare gets fed up and leaves. As the movie ends (at the National Finals Rodeo), Coop, with one leg broken, secures his

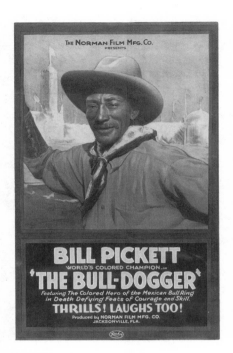

1. One of the earliest rodeo movies, *The Bull-Dogger* (ca. 1925) featured Texas rodeo hand and Wild West show star Bill Pickett. Courtesy, Buffalo Bill Historical Center, Cody, Wyoming.

2. The first great rodeo movie was *The Lusty Men* (RKO Radio, 1952). In this scene, rodeo roughstock veteran Jeff McCloud (Robert Mitchum) and his protégé Wes Merritt (Arthur Kennedy) eye a rank bronc Wes is about to ride. From the author's collection.

3. One of television's only weekly rodeo dramas was *Stoney Burke* (United Artists Television, Inc., 1962–63), starring Jack Lord (of *Hawaii Five-O* fame). The short-lived television series also produced a Dell comic book series, one number of which is pictured here. From the collection of Paul Hutton.

4. Cliff Robertson produced, directed, and starred in *J. W. Coop* (1972), a rodeo movie that combined cowboy culture and counterculture with interesting results. In this scene, J.W. (Robertson) stands along Myrtis Dightman, one of several contemporary rodeo stars who played themselves in the movie. From the author's collection.

5. Steve McQueen delivered one of his greatest performances in *Junior Bonner* (ABC Pictures Corp., 1972), the story of an archetypal courageous, individualistic wandering rodeo man. Here, Junior (McQueen) takes a short break from demolishing a Flagstaff, Arizona, barroom in order to exchange some words with his mom Elvira, brother Curly, and dad Ace Bonner (Ida Lupino, Joe Don Baker, and Robert Preston, with back to camera). From the author's collection.

6. John Travolta took the cowboy mystique from the country to the city in his authentic portrayal of Bud Davis in *Urban Cowboy* (Paramount Pictures, 1980). Bud is an earnest Texas country boy who moves to Houston and ends up, in country singer Johnny Lee's famous refrain, "Looking for Love (in All the Wrong Places)." In this pose, Bud (Travolta) courts Pam (Madolyn Smith) while temporarily estranged from his one true love, Sissy (Debra Winger). From the author's collection.

7. *(left)* Rodeo poet and former roughstock rider Paul Zarzyski prepares to give a lively reading of his *Roughstock Sonnets* at the 1996 Elko Cowboy Poetry Gathering. Courtesy, Sue Rosoff.

8. *(below)* Western Swing revivalist and Texas Poet Laureate Red Steagall is pictured here with his 1970s band, the Coleman County Cowboys. Steagall helped pioneer the rodeo country-music subgenre with his album *For All Our Cowboy Friends* (1977). Courtesy, Red Steagall.

9. The rodeo genre found one of its few high-culture venues in Agnes de Mille's ballet *Rodeo*, danced to Aaron Copland's *Rodeo Suite* (1942). Here, David Justin dances the role of The Roper in a San Francisco Ballet production (ca. 1985). Photo by Marty Sohl. Courtesy, San Francisco Ballet.

hand in a suicide knot and rides a Brahma bull for the last time into the arena. *J. W. Coop* owes its success largely to its 1960s countercultural motifs, multiethnic backdrop, a stellar, understated performance by Robertson, and an excellent supporting cast.[19]

More traditional and more successful is Steve McQueen's inspired portrayal of a rodeo man in *Junior Bonner* (1972). Junior is definitely old-school, and there is no pot smoking or alternative transportation (Junior drives a beat-up Cadillac) in this Sam Peckinpah movie. Yet Junior is appalled by the same materialism and moral indifference that confronts J. W. Coop. A former bull-riding champ down on his luck, Junior returns to his hometown of Prescott, Arizona, to compete in the annual rodeo. He finds trouble brewing. His daddy, Ace Bonner (Robert Preston), a former rodeo champ himself, has been swindled out of the family ranch by Curly (Joe Don Baker), his other son, who is bulldozing the old place and converting it to a double-wide trailer subdivision he has dubbed "Curly's Reatta Rancheros." Thus we have our frontier/civilization dialectic: Junior and Ace represent the individualism and virtue of the vanished frontier, while Curly, a twentieth-century materialist, sees the Old West only as a marketing tool. "I just want you to get a grip on your future," says Curly, offering Junior wages to sell off plots of the family ranch. Junior refuses, adding, "I've gotta go down my own road." To which Curly snaps, "What road? Hey, I'm working on my first million and you're still workin' on eight seconds."

With this philosophical backdrop, Peckinpah goes on to devote much of *Junior Bonner* to rodeo itself, and to Junior's obsessive adversarial relationship with the bull Sunshine. Riveting split-second, split-screen images by cinematographer Lucien Ballard draw us into Prescott's famed Frontier Days rodeo. Alternately, smoky flashbacks trace the long-running rivalry between Junior and Sunshine. Junior is obsessed with taming the beast and, after much family squabbling, an obligatory bar fight, and an appropriately short romance with a gorgeous Phoenix bank teller named Charmagne, he does just that. The wild ride on Sunshine nets a $950 purse that seemingly can jump-start Junior's lagging career, yet he will have none of it. He gives the money to his dad. Ace, it seems, has his heart set on an Australian mining adventure ("big money in rare metals," the luckless old-timer informs Junior early on). And so, at movie's end, Junior buys Ace and his dog one-way, first-class tickets to Sydney—"The Last Frontier"—telling the travel agent to inform Ace that "Junior sent ya." Broke once again, Junior heads off in his Cadillac with horse trailer in tow, bound for the Salinas, California, Rodeo.

With the possible exception of Jeff McCloud, Junior Bonner is the most convincing and memorable rodeo-movie cowboy. Simplicity is the key to his success; Junior is a totally uncomplicated man who lives only for rodeo. While Jeff entertains dreams of settling down with Louise Merritt, and Gay ultimately sees the futility of his attempts to live in the past, Junior suffers absolutely no doubts whatsoever about his wandering ways. McQueen, in one of his finest performances, plays the stoic, brave rodeo cowboy to the hilt, with an engaging western accent and just the right amount of humor. In his quick fling with Charmagne (whom he woos away from a fat-cat Phoenix banker), we learn a great deal about Junior's ways. He is gentle and kind to her but has no interest whatsoever in settling down or otherwise pursuing the relationship. He is a rodeo man and, like Leatherstocking, Shane, and the Ringo Kid before him, cannot be tamed. "Rodeo time," he informs the smitten Charmagne, putting her on a plane for Phoenix. "I gotta get on down the road. So long."[20]

After the burst of 1972 rodeo movies, the rodeo subgenre faded considerably until 1994 and the recent western revival. Moreover, of the three intermediary movies, two—*Electric Horseman* (1979) and *My Heroes Have Always Been Cowboys* (1990)—pale in comparison with the more solid and entertaining rodeo movies discussed above and below. Only *Urban Cowboy* (1980), with its solid cast, script, and production team can rightly join the 1952–1994 rodeo subgenre stalwarts.

One of the best things about Sydney Pollack's *Electric Horseman* is its paradoxical title, which succinctly juxtaposes the tame and the wild— modernity and the frontier—(the title *Urban Cowboy*, of course, accomplishes the same thing). However, the movie goes quickly downhill, borrowing bits from prior rodeo movies, mixing them up with David Miller's classic *Lonely Are the Brave* (1962), and serving it all up in a mildly entertaining but overdrawn offering. Robert Redford plays a former world rodeo champion who, unlike Jeff, Gay, and Junior, is drawing wages in his middle age: he represents a breakfast cereal company. But the job is degrading—the former roughstock rider finds himself promoting "Ranch Cereal" in Las Vegas glitter, dressed in a cowboy costume lined with Christmas-tree lights, astride a $12-million thoroughbred as much a captive as he. Driven to drink and despair, the cowboy salvages lost honor (and individualism) in heroic style. After learning that the cereal company is drugging the thoroughbred to facilitate his promotional usage, Redford kidnaps him. With horse in tow, he heads into the Nevada desert wilderness, pursued by corporate and governmental bad guys and a newswoman (Jane Fonda) who becomes his accomplice and lover. Together the two turn *The Misfits* on its head, taking us from civilization quickly back to the frontier and its inherent virtues. It is a great idea, but the movie is overly long, the script lacks subtlety, and Kirk Douglas had already done it better (though without the rodeo motif) in *Lonely Are the Brave*.[21]

James Bridges' *Urban Cowboy*, by contrast, has enough muscle and creative energy to hold up well two decades after its release. Moreover, it is important in the historical as well as the artistic milieu. Adapted from an Aaron Latham article in *Esquire*, the movie spearheaded a popular-culture movement that can only be described as a phenomenon, as millions of Americans became fascinated by the greater Houston, Texas, urban-cowboy scene. The "rural urban" (read wild/tame) lifestyle, country music, clothing, hats and boots, dance steps, pickup trucks, redneck workways, and outlandish leisure pursuits of these Gulf Coast "cowboys" were documented and aped throughout America and beyond during the 1980s and still impact the world of rural nostalgia. The important (and unique) portrayal of rodeo in this film ranks it in the rodeo subgenre right alongside *The Lusty Men* and *Junior Bonner*.

With the Charlie Daniels Band blasting a background score, moviegoers meet Bud Davis (John Travolta), a snuff-dipping Texas farmboy bound in his pickup truck for Pasadena, Texas, a suburb of Houston. Bud is seeking his fortune in this redneck gas-and-oil boomtown, and his uncle Bob (Barry Corbin), a former rodeo bull rider retired due to injury, is there to show him the way. But Bob also shows Bud the way to Gilley's, a three-and-a-half-acre Pasadena honky-tonk ("Holy shit. This place is bigger'n my hometown," Bud exclaims upon entering the establishment for the first time). Gilley's boasts a country-music-star proprietor, headliner bands, a dance floor where literally hundreds can Texas two-step the night away, and a "rodeo arena" equipped with a mechanical bull for those urban cowboys who aspire to a new, high-tech kind of "rural" amusement. At Gilley's Bud meets Sissy (Debra Winger), a south Texas pistol who drinks and dances all night and works days driving her daddy's tow truck. They quickly fall in love, marry, suffer the adversities of newlyweds, break up, seek consolation in the arms of others, and fall in love again at movie's end. Central to all of this is the sinister Wes Hightower (Scott Glenn), an ex-con and rodeo champ who woos Sissy, teaches her to ride the mechanical bull, and ultimately loses out to Bud in a spectacular, mechanized "indoor rodeo" finale. With the villain licked and the bulls ridden, the reunited couple drive off in their pickup to the accompaniment of Johnny Lee's "Looking for Love (In All the Wrong Places)."

One of the intriguing facets of this movie is a new portrayal of women in the wild/tame dialectic, probably ascribable to 1970s feminism. Sissy emerges as a cowgirl hero the likes of which we have never seen. Unlike Louise Merritt or Monroe's Roslyn, Sissy does not represent the tame; indeed, she tries to emulate Bud's redneck ways of drinking, promiscuity, and rodeoing. "There's certain things a girl can't do," the tradition-bound Bud implores, but Sissy shuns housework and insists, "I wanna ride that bull." She does just that, angering Bud and furnishing viewers with the most sensual scene in rodeo-movie history. Finally Sissy settles down—but so does Bud. The two evolve as equals in the urban western landscape.

Rodeo and cowboy images are inextricably and uniquely woven into the fabric of *Urban Cowboy.* Barry Corbin's Uncle Bob is a pivotal character whose past rodeo glories are central to Bud's development. Bob sports a championship buckle that he "won for bull ridin' in '64," and Bud thinks Bob "would have been better than Larry Mahan if it hadn't been for that accident." Bud himself is farm-raised and brags that he "rode some pretty rank horses" growing up. On one of Bud and Sissy's first outings, they attend a prison rodeo where convicts in full prison attire don cowboy hats and boots and play a haunting version of the rodeo game. "Damn, these outlaws make good cowboys," Bud observes after Wes Hightower rides a swirling, raging beast. Soon afterward, Wes and the entire rodeo milieu are quickly, and somewhat incongruously, transferred to Gilley's "wide open indoor spaces," where a mechanical bull supersedes the flesh-and-blood version. "Do you think you can help me ride that bull? . . . I mean good enough that I can enter [Gilley's] rodeo and kick ass?" Bud implores Uncle Bob, who answers simply, "Why, hell, yeah."

Throughout all of this, the mythical image of working cowboys is quickly and radically altered to equate it with, first, that of rodeo cowboys, and ultimately, that of the pickup-driving rednecks who frequent Gilley's. Bud's transformation to urban cowboy is apparent immediately as we view a slow, powerful camera tilt from black boots to black hat as he leans against the bar at Gilley's, sipping on a long-neck Lone Star beer. "Are you a real cowboy?" Sissy asks upon meeting him, the first of a half dozen such inquiries in the movie. Bud answers coolly: "That depends on what you think a real cowboy is." Later, when Sissy leaves Bud for Wes (who she thinks is a "real cowboy"), Bud finds solace in the arms of Pam (Madolyn Smith), a sophisticated Houston society girl whose hobby, it seems, is searching for her own "cowboy" hero. "Got myself a cowboy," Pam tells her friends at Gilley's when Bud asks to take her home.

Writer/director Bridges serves up fast-paced sequences that move quickly from Gilley's to rodeo arenas to "Tudor-style" prefabricated homes and double-wide trailers to gas refineries and back to Gilley's again. The movie is too lengthy but nevertheless strong, owing its success largely to the crazy blending of frontier and civilization—wild and tame—that is expressed in the film's title. Country boys become citified but somehow remain country; a barroom entrepreneur invites "shit-kickers" to his "all-indoor rodeo back there on the south forty," guaranteeing it to be "just like any rodeo across the country"; and bulls become mechanized "buckin' machines" that still command the cowboys' respect and their need to tame the wild. At no point is this paradox (and the confusion it creates) better expressed than in Bud's first romantic night with Pam. In her fashionable high-rise penthouse, the two gaze at the glittering lights of Houston below. It is apparent that Pam loves city life, but she wants the country too. Her thoughts are intriguing: "I have a thing about cowboys. It just drives my daddy crazy. I told him, 'Daddy, most men today are just too complicated . . . I like a man with simple values. I like them independent, self-reliant, brave, strong, direct, and open.' 'You mean dumb,' he said. Daddy's a real scream."

Pam tries to sort all of this out by proposing a toast, "To cowboys and all that implies," but the viewer remains mystified. Fortunately, Bridges straightens it out for us in a rather simple way that nevertheless provides a strong conclusion for the film. The land and a love for it run as themes throughout *Urban Cowboy*. The movie begins with Bud leaving the country for the city but, as we learn, holding strong hopes of going home. "You come to Houston to make money," he explains to Pam, "then go back home and get yourself a piece of land." "I never met a cowboy who *didn't* talk about goin' back to the country," Pam observes. Bud, however, has not "been able to save a dime." Gilley's rodeo and its generous prize money provide a possible solution. "If I win that rodeo," Bud speculates, the dream of land in the country "could all come true." When Bud and Sissy depart Gilley's at the end of *Urban Cowboy*, we can assume they are bound for the country and the rural values of hearth and home. Bud, like the hero of *The Virginian* before him, aims to settle down on the land. "Come on, Bud, I'll buy you a beer," a friend offers after the cowboy hero has ridden the bull and vanquished the bad guy. "No way," Bud fires back, Sissy at his side. "We're goin' home."[22]

In the 1990s, after a hiatus of nearly a decade, the North American movie western made a triumphant return. Soon after Clint Eastwood accepted the best picture Academy Award for *The Unforgiven* (1992), traditional westerns such as *Tombstone* (1993), *Wyatt Earp* (1994), and *Maverick* (1994) joined contemporary westerns *City Slickers I and II* (1991 and 1994), *Even Cowgirls Get the Blues* (1994), and a dozen other western movies in a 1990s western renaissance. The western movie revival was paralleled by a television resurgence boasting a 1993–1994 season with thirteen prime-time westerns, including *Young Guns; Dr. Quinn, Medicine Woman; Walker, Texas Ranger;* and *Harts of the West*. The western was back in a big way, and the revival included four new rodeo movies and the promise of more to come.

The first of the 1990s rodeo subgenre movies, *My Heroes Have Always Been Cowboys* (1990), ultimately trivializes the rodeo motif so carefully crafted by Nicholas Ray, John Huston, Cliff Robertson, Sam Peckinpah, and James Bridges. It stars Scott Glenn, reprising his *Urban Cowboy* bull-rider role, but this time as the good guy H.D. Dalton, a former world rodeo champ who, severely injured by a bull, has fallen on hard times. Returning to his Oklahoma hometown, H.D. finds that "a lot of things have changed" since he left. His rancher daddy (played by western star and former all-round champion roper Ben Johnson) is in a nursing home, put there by evil in-laws (Tess Harper and Gary Busey) who want to sell off the family ranch to feed their materialism and greed. Anyone who has seen *Junior Bonner* can finish the script: H.D. breaks his dad out of the nursing home, enters the bull-riding contest to end all bull-riding contests, and despite his former injuries, walks away with the $100,000 purse that will solve all of his family's problems.[23]

In 1994 and 1995, audiences saw three new rodeo movies that proved the vitality of the contemporary western subgenre and the ability of modern filmmakers to emulate and build upon the motifs of earlier rodeo-movie makers. I will return to two of these movies later in this book: *Convict Cowboy* (1995), which starred Jon Voigt and built upon the prison-rodeo themes of *J. W. Coop* and *Urban Cowboy*, and the most commercially successful of the 1990s rodeo movies, *8 Seconds* (1994), in which actor Luke Perry made the leap from television (*Beverly Hills 90210*) to a stellar performance as Lane Frost, the late-1980s all-round champion bull rider who met a violent arena death in the Cheyenne Frontier Days Rodeo—*8 Seconds* exploits live-action scenes in the mold of *Junior Bonner* and a tragic cowboy hero in the mold of *The Lusty Men* and *J. W. Coop*.

The remaining movie of the 1994–1995 trio, *The Cowboy Way* (1994), superimposes the traditional frontier/civilization and Cowboy Code motifs of the 1951–1994 rodeo movies onto a stark urban landscape in ways that are, during the film's best moments, humorous, dramatic, and visually appealing. Writer Bill Witliff introduces the frontier/civilization paradox immediately: The opening credits appear over a scene in which team ropers Sonny Gilstrap (Kiefer Sutherland) and Pepper Lewis (Woody Harrelson) win the "New Mexico State Championship Rodeo"—a scene that gives way to the dark visage of an ocean vessel loaded with illegal immigrant laborers sailing into the port of New York City. Flashing back to the rodeo, we learn that despite their team-roping victory, Sonny and Pepper are feuding over Pepper's irresponsibility in "pull[ing] a no-show at the National Finals Rodeo" the previous year. But they quickly relegate this argument to the back burner when they learn that their friend Nacho Salazar (Joaquin Martinez) has "run into some kinda trouble" on a trip to New York City. Nacho went east to retrieve his daughter Teresa (Cara Buono), for whose illegal entrance into this country he paid $5,000 to the thuggish sweatshop entrepreneur John Stark (Dylan McDermott). Sonny and Pepper hit the road to rescue Nacho and Teresa. In so doing, they follow the same path from frontier to city worn by country boys like Yankee Jonathan (the antebellum folk hero), Arizona's Deputy Coogan (and his televised cover version, Deputy McCloud), Crocodile Dundee, and even Tarzan. Sonny and Pepper learn from Sam Shaw (Ernie Hudson), a black policeman (and Bill Pickett aficionado), that Nacho has been murdered. The two rodeo ropers spring into action, trailing the evil city boys and giving them a taste of western justice and the "cowboy way." The movie ends with Sonny and Pepper, friends once again, moving on down the road, leaving New York City, driving Teresa to a new life and home in New Mexico.²⁴

Sonny and Pepper exhibit pronounced western traits that add up to an archetypal rodeo-cowboy portrait. Sutherland's Sonny Gilstrap strikes a classic pose, adorned in hat, boots, and sheepskin jacket, a cigarette planted in the side of his mouth (or behind his ear). He is chivalrous toward women but keeps his distance. Sonny will put his life on the line for a friend, and he despises liars and cheats. He seldom speaks, but when he does his remarks go right to the heart of things. When the attractive female desk clerk at the Waldorf-Astoria asks, "You're a real cowboy, aren't you?" Sonny replies simply, "Been accused of it a time or two." On the other hand, Harrelson takes the cowboy persona dangerously close the realm of the southern good ol' boy with his Pepper Lewis, overplaying the role but ultimately complementing Sutherland and winning the audience over with his wild ways. Pepper dresses in cowboy duds, chews tobacco, tosses back mescal, and administers red-pepper cowboy folk remedies. He talks incessantly in a nasal twang, cursing and tossing out witty asides. Unforgivably, he breaks Cowboy Code with displays of vanity (taking a showy bow in the arena) and, much worse, lying to his best friend. Yet despite his failings, Pepper sort of grows on you. Who else would appear naked on his front porch, a cowboy hat hanging over his erect penis? Who else would take a New York modeling job (for Calvin Klein underwear) to earn enough money to rescue his best friend's rodeo trophy buckle from a pawnshop? And who else, when asked by a pretentious waiter how he wants his steak prepared, could make an old, old joke ring: "Well, just knock its horns off, wipe its nasty old ass, and chunk it right down here on the plate. . . . We're kinda particular about our meat." Even when Sonny is angry at Pepper, he has to admit, "Ol' Pepper sure can cowboy when he wants to."

Director Gregg Champion portrays the frontier/civilization paradox in numerous and innovative ways. The opening New Mexico State Rodeo scene is scored with the Gibson Miller Band's cover of "Mamas, Don't Let Your Babies Grow Up to Be Cowboys," and Sonny and Pepper's arrival in New York City in their old pickup truck is accompanied by a raunchy Jeff Beck/Paul Rodgers version of "On Broadway." The obligatory western barroom fight is staged in Havanita, a cosmopolitan Cuban *salsa* club, which also becomes the setting for a radicalized version of the classic western motif of the cowboy riding his horse into a bar when Pepper drives his pickup through the front entrance, "the cowboy way." The humorous and ironic potential of the two cowpokes moseying around the Waldorf-Astoria is realized: Pepper tries to impress the desk clerk with his intention to "go to a museum" and "take in a opera or two." And Pepper steals the show at a swanky fashion-industry cocktail party (and lands himself the underwear-modeling job).

The twenty-minute chase scene that concludes *The Cowboy Way* provides five innovative (albeit outlandish) wild/tame juxtapositions. First, Sonny incapacitates a pawnshop thug calf-roper-style, literally throwing him and hog-tying him with a "piggin' string." Then, trailing John Stark to his sweatshop, Sonny and Pepper engage him and his gang in a shoot-out, complete with the western-style six-guns Sonny has liberated from the pawnshop. When Stark flees, holding Teresa hostage, a high-speed motor chase ensues along New York City's streets, Pepper in the pickup bed, one hand gripping the roll-bar, one in the air, bronc-buster style, shouting "Yahoo!" at each bone-jarring landing. Stark next drags Teresa aboard a Lexington Avenue subway train. Sonny and Pepper borrow two horses from the New York police and launch a train chase to "head 'em off" before they reach Brooklyn. With radicalized motifs borrowed from *The Great Train Robbery* (1903) and countless other westerns, the rodeo riders chase down the subway train, their horses' hooves pounding the concrete (a little boy inside the train yells, "Look mom, cowboys!") until they can climb atop the train and bring it to a halt at the 62nd Street Station. Stark flees, holding a gun to Teresa's head and taunting Sonny and Pepper, now on the opposite side of the track, "You cowboys. You're a dyin' breed, man." But director Champion delivers an outrageous rodeo-inspired surprise. A train momentarily blocks Stark's view of the two rodeo ropers. Grabbing a long strand of electrical cord, Sonny tosses one end to his partner and commands, "Pepper, heel it!" As the train's last car rumbles by, Pepper tosses his loop around its coupling. Simultaneously twirling the other end of the electrical cord like a lariat over his head, Sonny ropes Stark, who is dragged to a horrendous death behind the speeding train. "Nice throw," Sonny notes. Pepper replies, "Not bad yourself."

This finale leaves only one loose end in *The Cowboy Way*: the issue of Sonny and Pepper's friendship—and Pepper's betrayal, which has driven them apart. "A friend don't pull a no-show at the National Finals Rodeo," Sonny states early on. "Pepper, I've had it with you . . . you lyin' son of a bitch." It seems Sonny had big plans for his National Finals prize money. In the tradition of rodeo movie cowboys from Wes Merritt to Bud Davis (with J. W. Coop in between), Sonny wanted to buy his own land and some cattle and settle down. The prize money was to be a down payment. But near movie's end, Pepper, in a moment of uncharacteristic humility, owns up to why he skipped the National Finals. "Sonny . . . I didn't want you to buy that ranch," he confesses. "Guess I just always figured we were better together than we were apart. I didn't want to split up the team." Thus Pepper proves himself an adherent to the Cowboy Code after all. A man might well be a cowboy on his own ranch, but this is not the destiny of a true rodeo man. The rodeo cowboy's place is moving on down that road. It's better than wages. That's the cowboy way.[25]

More than a hundred years ago, Frederick Jackson Turner argued that the frontier was the formative influence in American history. Frontier conditions, Turner declared, fostered an American populace characterized by individualism, self-reliance, courage, pragmatism, coarseness, anti-intellectualism, nationalism, egalitarianism, and a belief in democracy. Although Turner's thesis was, and is still being, debated, students of cowboy and rodeo culture are struck by how closely the traits Turner described match the Cowboy Code attributes ascribed to and embraced by working cowboys and their rodeo-cowboy descendants. And if the extent to which Cowboy Code traits are based on historical fact is debatable, what is irrefutable is the impact of Turnerian ideas and the Cowboy Code on the Myth of the West—a powerful set of beliefs through which many North Americans view and define their history and culture. Henry Nash Smith, Leo Marx, John William Ward, Harold P. Simonson, and many others have demonstrated the importance of the myth of frontier individualism in American folklore, literature, art, theater, film, and popular culture. The western—be it literature or film—is the culmination of Turner's thesis as applied to art.[26]

Yet as easy as it is to find Turnerian themes throughout the western genre, it is considerably more difficult to explain that genre's great persistence and importance. Why did North Americans become so enamored of the western in the first place? And why has the genre proved especially popular and durable from World War II to the present day? What was it about the cold war that fostered westerns? The answer to these questions is no doubt related to the profound psychological impact of industrialization and the rise to world power upon a formerly simple, agricultural people. The western emerged and flourished exactly as the industrial revolution changed the face of North America. As Americans embraced machines and material progress in their economic lives, they simultaneously embraced westerns in their cultural expression. The result was, and still is, rural nostalgia. Through the western, Americans can have the frontier *and* civilization; they can modernize while clinging to and romanticizing their rural, preindustrial past.[27]

Rodeo movies from *The Lusty Men* through *The Cowboy Way* manifest this rural nostalgia in extremely interesting ways. Indeed, Pam in *Urban Cowboy* unwittingly paraphrases Frederick Jackson Turner when she describes her cowboy heroes as "independent, self-reliant, brave, strong, direct, and open." The rodeo cowboys of Pam's vision, like most of the rodeo-movie cowboys, tend toward the wild side of the frontier/ civilization paradox, but it is important to stress that they never completely embrace the wild. For one of the most intriguing aspects of the rodeo-movie cowboy is that he is caught between the two poles of the dialectic. He leans toward the wild in his personal characteristics and rambling ways, yet his entire raison d'être is to tame and "civilize," momentarily at least, wild beasts. Thus the rodeo-cowboy hero is a *contemporary ancestor,* a folk hero with nineteenth-century values and characteristics who, ironically, lives and works in modern, postfrontier North America.[28]

The rodeo cowboy's ambiguous relationships with wild animals and with women epitomize this tension. Jeff McCloud, Perce, Junior Bonner, and J. W. Coop are all obsessed with taming broncs and bulls, and yet they admire and respect those animals they cannot break. Gay feels this respect but cannot bring himself to set the wild mustangs free until he has staked them to the ground. Similarly ambiguous is the way these cowboys are drawn to, but strongly resist, the civilizing influences of the women in their lives. Jeff McCloud entertains notions of settling down with Louise Merritt but ultimately must go it alone. Gay is drawn to Roslyn, but as *The Misfits* ends, both are heading their separate ways. Neither J. W. Coop nor Sonny Gilstrap (nor Stoney Burke) finds permanent solace in the arms of a woman, and Junior Bonner (like his daddy) does not even try. Only Bud settles down, but with a woman who has proved herself just as wild as he.

The rodeo-movie cowboy thus never resolves the paradox of the frontier and civilization—the wild and the tame. He vacillates between the two, just as his fellow Americans looked back longingly even while they embraced the industrial revolution and all of its material benefits. Since the rodeo-movie cowboy is a fictitious character, he can usually have his frontier and tame it too, but only after his creator has figured out a way to end the movie. There is no place for a wild man in a civilized world, and so rodeo-movie writers have had to be creative, to say the least. The endings to the best rodeo movies manage to avoid the inevitable civilizing of a preindustrial man. Thus Jeff McCloud, like Leatherstocking in *The Prairie* 150 years earlier, must die. Gay vows to find "another way" to live, and so *The Misfits* must end just as his futile search begins. In *8 Seconds* (as in real life), Lane Frost dies in the rodeo arena. J. W. Coop rides a Brahma bull to his demise. Only Bud settles down. The rest all die or, like Stoney Burke, Junior Bonner, Sonny Gilstrap, and Pepper Lewis, keep moving on, away from civilization, movin' on down that rodeo road.

CHAPTER THREE

"Wild Side of Life"
The Rodeo Cowboy in Folklore and Literature

Riding a bull was the kind of thing you did to prove you didn't give a shit.
—Lonnie Bannon, in *Horseman, Pass By* (1961)

Rodeo and rodeo cowboys seem heroic to Lonnie Bannon, a young man coming of age in the 1950s West Texas of Larry McMurtry's *Horseman, Pass By*. Although Lonnie enjoys living and working on his grandfather's ranch, the teenager is often lonely and bored; the closest town, Thalia, is twenty miles away. Meanwhile, the ranch-cowboy life that Lonnie's family has known since the mid-nineteenth century is gasping for breath. Lonnie's grandfather Homer Bannon, an old-time Texas cattleman, loses his entire herd to hoof-and-mouth disease; government health inspectors shoot all of his cattle and cover them in huge bulldozed trenches. Meanwhile, Lonnie's alcoholic uncle Hud is a misanthrope—he beats the hands and rapes Halmea, the ranch cook, and tries to steal Homer's ranch. Eventually he shoots Homer (although quite literally to put the old man out of his misery). As Lonnie watches his world disintegrate, he does so in the company of rodeo cowboys, who seem to offer at least a faint hope of satisfying his many questions and yearnings. The backdrop to *Horseman, Pass By* is the Thalia Rodeo, a small, annual rodeo festival that somehow excites Lonnie's imagination: "During all that time there was nothing but beer drinking and rodeo talk, courting and dancing. . . . Rodeo was the one big get-together of the year. Since it came like Christmas, only once a year, I was careful not to let any of it pass by me."[1]

Lonnie regularly makes the trek to the Thalia Rodeo to try to put the pieces of his life together again. At first, rodeo seems to offer great promise. Lonnie admires the cowboys "drinking cans of cold beer" behind the chutes, "squatting on the ground checking their rigging," their girlfriends close at hand. He even admires the cowboy skills of his Uncle Hud, who once "rodeoed a good deal." Lonnie's friends Hermy and Buddy enter the bull-riding competition, and Jesse, the Bannons' hired hand, borrows one of Homer's horses for the cow-cutting event. It is Jesse, the drifting ranch hand, who really opens Lonnie's eyes to the glories and pitfalls of the rodeo road. "How is it rodeoin'?" Lonnie asks him at the beginning of the story. "Isn't it pretty excitin'?" Jesse responds with understatement (in good cowboy fashion). "Oh, it gets in your blood like anything else you do," he drawls. "For a while it's right excitin'." Later, Jesse advises Lonnie that "it might not hurt you to see the world some," and Lonnie's wanderlust is excited by the myth of the rodeo road:

> He got to talking about places he'd been on the rodeo circuit, and just hearing the names was enough to make me restless. He'd been to practically every town in Texas, big or little, Lubbock and Amarillo and Houston, Fort Worth and Dallas and San Antone, Alpine and El Paso, Snyder and Olney, Vernon and Dumas and Newcastle and a hundred more, and then on into New Mexico and Colorado, to Tucumcari and Clovis and Gallup and Cimarron, Raton and Walsenburg and Denver, on up to Cheyenne and Pendleton and Pierre and Calgary, over to St. Louis and Sioux City, Chicago and Kansas City and New York, and a hundred more I couldn't even remember. I could tell by the way he rolled the names around in his mouth that he must have

liked rodeo, or at least have liked seeing places. But he wouldn't admit it.[2]

"I run that road for ten years and never caught up with nothin'," Jesse
concludes, but Lonnie remains very interested. Indeed, by the end of the
story, Lonnie has no choice but to search for happiness on the road. With
his grandfather dead, the cattle gone, and Uncle Hud in charge of what
little is left, the cowboy ranch life has ceased to be a viable alternative
for Lonnie Bannon. The road might also prove a dead end, but it provides at least a chance for freedom and happiness. Lonnie ponders his
prospects with a melancholy prompted by "one of those songs of Hank
Williams, the one about the wild side of life." Hearing Williams' bittersweet ode to the hard-drinking, drifting, honky-tonk rednecks of twentieth-century rural America, he reflects that "city folks probably
wouldn't believe there were folks simple enough to live out their lives
on sentiments like those—but they didn't know." The song reminds
him of "Hermy and Buddy and the other boys I knew," he states sadly.
"All of them wanted more and seemed to end up with less; they wanted
excitement and ended up stomped by a bull or smashed against a highway. . . . Whatever it was they wanted, that was what they ended up doing without."[3]

By the end of *Horseman, Pass By*, Lonnie has chosen to leave the ranch
and Thalia: "I got my suitcase and decided to make a start." Hitching a
ride on a westbound cattle truck, he heads for Wichita Falls to visit his
buddy Hermy, hospitalized after being crushed by a Brahma bull. "I used
to ride them bulls when I was a young fucker," the truck driver informs
Lonnie. "But I got two boys now. Mama don't let me rodeo no more.
Sometimes I miss it, you know." Lonnie meanwhile is "tempted to do
like Jesse once said: to lean back and let the truck take me as far as it was
going." In keeping with the understatement of all of *Horseman, Pass By*,
the reader is left to ponder Lonnie's fate. But it seems that Lonnie is

bound to roam, at least for a while. Like Gay, Perce, Jeff McCloud, J. W. Coop, and Junior Bonner, he has no place left in the dying Great Plains cattle country. He ponders his dilemma as the "truck roll[s] on across the darkened range."[4]

Horseman, Pass By is an important work in the rodeo subgenre of western literature. This subgenre includes published rodeo reminiscences, novels, and poetry. In studying rodeo literature, however, one must begin with folklore, for the rodeo reminiscences, novels, and poetry all grow from roots in the complex, lively oral traditions of cowboy culture. The nineteenth-century Plains cowboys' world was one without books and learning, a lonely world of herding cattle in a semiarid wilderness. In such a world, the cowboys' primary means of expression and entertainment were quite naturally oral—talking to one another, telling stories, and sometimes singing or reciting coarse songs and poetry. Along the way, cowboy speech developed distinct and identifiable characteristics, the most important of which are a pronounced midland accent, a slow drawl (punctuated with an occasional quick-witted retort), and a vernacular peppered with Indian and Spanish words and a heavy dose of profanity. Stylistically, cowboy speech is known for irony, understatement, and dry humor. Doing a difficult job in a harsh land, Plains cowboys developed a rich and fascinating folk speech.[5]

It has always been difficult for "green hands" to "savvy" cowboy "lingo." A cowboy had a talent for "sayin' a whole lot in mighty few words"; he never "used up all his kindlin' to get his fire started." On a night on the town, he "raised hell *and put a chunk under it,*" so drunk "he couldn't hit the ground with his hat *in three throws.*" A man for whom he felt contempt wasn't "worth eight eggs" and "had a license to be pretty sorry." "I'd like to buy him for what he's worth and sell him for what he thinks he's worth," the cowboy would remark dryly, possibly not long before promising the subject of this comment to "fight y'u till hell freezes over, *then skate with y'u on the ice.*" Yet someone he respected might have "a heart in his brisket as big as a saddle blanket," and the cowboy could wax poetic about a gal "pretty as a red heifer in a flower bed," her hair as "soft as a young calf's ears." Asked by a neighbor how a wild young bronc was "coming along," one cowboy replied in typical fashion: "Well, he keeps us up in the air most of the time, but he's a-comin' along nice." "How deep do you reckon this snow is?" one cowboy asked another, who replied, "What the hell difference does it make? You can't see nothin' but the top of it nohow." In the summer following a particularly hard winter, a lone cowhand reportedly looked up at the blazing sun, paused, and asked, "Where the hell was you last winter?"[6]

Because early rodeo cowboys were directly connected to ranch-cowboy culture, they talked like ranch cowboys and passed this vernacular down to the younger rodeo hands. While it is debatable to what extent rodeo cowboys are today like *real cowboys*, their use of authentic cowboy vernacular is pronounced. Rodeo-cowboy speech is cowboy speech, with all of the drawling, Indian, Spanish, profanity, and ironic humor of the original folk idiom.

Rodeo cowboys also adopted cowboy folk beliefs and superstitions, expressing them in their own nonverbal and partly verbal folkways. A rodeo man's lucky talisman might be a brightly colored hat feather or a hatband made from the mane of an unusually rank bronc. Eating peanuts before or during a rodeo was taboo, as were yellow shirts and brand-new ropes. A rodeo cowboy might wear a lucky hat, but a brand-new hat was strictly taboo, and a hat thrown on a bed was the worst hex of all. Elizabeth Atwood Lawrence collected one story of a rodeo clown who unthinkingly put his hat on his bed one morning—that very afternoon, he reported, a bull hit and injured him. Clifford P. Westermeier shared a similar tale. Visiting an injured calf roper in his bedroom, Westermeier mistakenly threw his hat on the cowboy's bed, alongside the man's broken leg: "a few seconds later, upon seeing the hat, in a bated breath he suggested that it be removed to a nearby window sill—'just in case.'"[7]

Rodeo-cowboy folktales such as these constitute a large body of oral tradition. Like all folktales, they may be based on historical incidents, but their historical accuracy is not as important to folklorists as their recurrence, or the recurrence of their motifs. Rodeo-cowboy folktales provide many themes that also appear in more formal rodeo literature and poetry. Although it is difficult to generalize about such a large number of tales, several themes are obvious. Trickster tales, for instance, abound—stories in which a mischievous rodeo man outwits his fellow cowboys, rodeo animals, and "dudes" with comical results. In a 1975 oral history interview, rodeo man Howard Thomas told a long tale in which he outwits a mean Brahma bull and wins the awe of the local dudes. The bull, a clever beast, escapes the rodeo arena in Toronto, Canada, in 1927, with Thomas and friends in hot pursuit on horseback. The bull leads them on a three-week chase through the rodeo grounds, a cemetery, a railroad switchyard, downtown Toronto, and the local police headquarters (which the bull supposedly enters and tears "all to pieces"). Finally, Thomas uses his wit and rodeo skills to outfox and subdue the animal. Locals then insist on shooting the beast because "he's dangerous," to which Thomas replies, "Well, they're all dangerous, what do you think we want, a bunch of bucket calves to ride?" Finally, the cowboys hogtie the bull, take him back to the rodeo grounds, and set him loose in the bull pen. In the meantime, Thomas has become a local hero: "You couldn't get within three blocks of that hotel what with people wanting to see the cowboy that roped that bull," he reminisced. "I think there was seven major newspapers in Toronto and they all carried big stories about this thing. It was quite a write-up."[8]

A more modern trickster story tells how famed bronc rider Casey Tibbs would hitchhike around the rodeo circuit, hustling his lifts by lying down in the middle of the highway to attract passing motorists' attention. In 1971, world-champion saddle bronc rider Chris LeDoux fooled his fellow hands by dressing up like a hippie (complete with wig and love beads), entering a rodeo bar at the Calgary Stampede, and offering a bogus marijuana cigarette to world-champion bull rider Ronnie Rossen. When Rossen yanked LeDoux up by the hair, the wig came off and the joke was on the bull rider. And then there is the tale of a fast-talking rodeo rider who supposedly cajoled a charter airplane pilot into landing him on a small rodeo arena during the show so that he would not miss his event. The small plane overshot the arena and landed in a nearby potato field, "plowing up fifty yards of ground in the process." The cowboy nonchalantly stepped out over the side of the plane, proceeded to the rodeo, and won his event.[9]

Another recurring rodeo taletype is the injury story. Lawrence has interpreted the rodeo cowboys' legendary indifference to pain and injury as an important psychological means of achieving "mastery" over themselves and nature. They "flaunt their injuries," she writes, as badges of honor. The injury folktale serves up this important motif in narrative form, with the major character of each story behaving cavalierly in the face of danger, injury, and pain. Thus 1920s Pacific Northwest rodeo cowboy Clovis Chartrand could speak of another contestant's brush with injury in almost indifferent terms, tempered with a little humor: "He banged his head . . . and it knocked him out. His dad was there . . . it was kind of pitiful too, he just cried and run out there and picked him up . . . 'He's dead, he's dead, he's killed.' Pretty soon he came to and all that was the matter with him was that he had swallowed his chew of snoose." Chartrand summed it up laconically: "Nobody really got hurt bad out there. There was a few broken legs and such things, but personally I never got hurt very bad. I got banged up a few times, but no bones broke."[10]

There are many adulatory stories of rodeo riders entering and winning their events despite one or two broken limbs. Cowboys tell of Gene Ross riding in Cheyenne with his broken leg in a cast, and of cowgirl Fox Hastings escaping a New York hospital (the "hospital escape" is a recurrent motif) to win her event at Madison Square Garden. Bob Henry once won the steer wrestling at San Francisco's Cow Palace Rodeo with casts on both arms. Rodeo-clown and rodeo-announcer jokes, important subgenres of rodeo folklore in their own right, are replete with injury motifs. The announcer might warn the clown that a particular bull "could make a shish-ke-bob out of you," or report that "this bull got a clown down a few weeks ago" and "the clown is still in the hospital. . . . He's in rooms twenty, twenty-one, and twenty-two!" When the clown states he is quitting work because he's "got a leg botherin' me," the announcer innocently queries, "Well, what's the matter?" The clown replies, "It's up there in the fourth row."[11]

One of the most incredible tales combines the trickster and injury motifs with a heavy dose of cowboy folk medicine. During his famous rodeo career, "Wild Horse Bob" Crosby of Roswell, New Mexico, reportedly broke every bone in his body, except his spine and left leg, at least once. In 1930, Crosby broke his right leg five times and, because of a medical complication, developed gangrene. When "Mayo Clinic" doctors advised amputation, Crosby refused, reportedly walking right out of the operating room. He returned immediately to New Mexico, where he utilized an old cowboy remedy to arrest the gangrene: he wrapped his leg in an inner tube packed with cow manure for two days. It did the trick, according to Crosby: "the red sentipedes plumb disappeared." Although this experience evidently motivated his retirement from steer wrestling and bronc riding, Crosby continued to rodeo. He returned to the circuit a few months later and achieved even greater fame as a steer roper.[12]

Injuries resulting in death form a more sobering taletype, combining the dramatic injury theme with a gripping death scene that results in true folk-hero status. The Cheyenne Frontier Days arena death of bull rider Lane Frost (subject of the movie *8 Seconds*) is a recent example of this taletype. It descends from Plains cowboy bronc-busting tales and from stories about early rodeo riders Bonnie McCarrol and Pete Knight. When McCarrol's bronc threw her at Pendleton in 1929, cowgirl Ollie Osborn remembered, "everybody just stood there speechless . . . cause we all knowed she was hurt bad." Stories of the fatal incident spread rapidly, playing a major role in the banning of women's roughstock events from professional rodeo. Eight years later, Pete Knight's equally dramatic death ensured his status as a rodeo icon. Knight was a four-time world-champion bronc rider when he drew the bronc Duster at the Hayward (California) Rodeo on May 23, 1937. "Pete rode Duster until almost the last second before the signal," related Clifford Westermeier. But then Knight "fell in such a position that the horse could not avoid trampling him." A friend reached his side and asked, "Are you hurt?" Pete responded, "You're goddamned right I'm hurt!" They rushed him away in an ambulance, his wife, Babe, following close behind. But when Babe arrived at the hospital, she learned that Pete had died en route.[13]

The classic story of Freckles Brown has a much happier ending—one that has made Brown one of the most celebrated of all rodeo roughstock riders. This gripping tale is about the aging but fearless cowboy who subdues a Brahma bull believed by all to be "untameable." Oklahoman Freckles Brown was already a respected bull rider long before his 1967 National Finals Rodeo ride on Tornado. A competitor since 1937, he won the world title in 1962 despite advancing age and a broken neck in October of that year. "I've been hurt a lot," he once commented, "but I never think of gettin' hurt. . . . It never crosses my mind that I might get hurt." In Oklahoma City in 1967, at age forty-six (long past a roughstock rider's prime), Freckles found himself once again in the National Finals Rodeo. He drew Tornado, a notorious Brahma with a perfect record—in two hundred competitions Tornado had thrown every cowboy who tried to ride him. Freckles mounted the bull, burst out of the chute, and for eight unforgettable seconds rode the awesome, swirling, lunging Tornado. The ride earned him a hefty paycheck, a five-minute standing ovation (from a crowd not given to overdisplay of emotion), and a permanent place in rodeo folklore and history. Rodeo cowboys still tell the story, and Texan Red Steagall has celebrated it in poetry and song (chapter 5). Indeed, Freckles Brown's ride on Tornado is comparable to the legends about Babe Ruth.[14]

Although rodeo folktales evince a vast and complex oral tradition, one can nevertheless make some generalizations about them. Spoken in western accent and vernacular, these stories always feature a cowboy hero engaged in dramatic action. As in the rodeo movies, the folkloric rodeo cowboy is a freedom-loving individualist, a drifter, and of course a "top hand"—a real "buckaroo" highly skilled in his line of work. The dramas around which his stories unfold may involve superstitions and trickster motifs. But almost always they are tales of riding, roping, or 'dogging wild broncs, steers, and bulls—the rodeo man's raison d'être—a taming pursuit in which the cowboy hero is always courageous and oblivious to pain and injury. The hero who emerges from these tales is a *real cowboy*, not a dude or drugstore cowboy or some other pretender. He withstands the test, and he can call himself a cowboy. Indeed, this concern with *real cowboys* is the focus of much rodeo oral tradition, and there is a constant judgment of criteria by storytellers to determine just who really stacks up. One old rodeo hand addressed this issue when asked to recall the greats of his day. He replied as eloquently as cowboy vernacular allows: "We had a lot of good boys in the old days . . . the Bowman boys . . . Bob Crosby, Ike Rude, [Hugh Bennett]. . . . They were good hands, they were top hands"; Bob Crosby "was a real cowboy, I'll tell you that, he was a real buckaroo," and "Pete Knight was the best bronc rider I ever knew." But times have changed: "Nowadays you don't have buckaroos at rodeos, you have athletes. . . . Look at these twenty-three-year-old kids that's a world champion won over eighty thousand dollars last year. He's not a cowboy, he is just a good athlete, that's all they are." But the new rodeo men "make a nice show, they fill the bill," the old-timer conceded, giving the modern generation a little credit. "There is no use carrying on a grudge saying there's no buckaroos because buckaroos are just a thing of the past . . . there aren't any, that's all there is to it."[15]

Upon these oral traditions and rodeo folktales is built a small, fascinating body of rodeo literature—prose and poetry. I use the terms *literature* and *prose* and *poetry* with some hesitation here, because rodeo prose and poetry are so closely tied to the folk idiom that, at times, they might be more aptly called "folk literature." We can certainly call them a *folk-based* prose and poetry in deference to their intermediary status somewhere between folklore and high culture. This is certainly the case with rodeo reminiscences, a genre that forms a bridge between the folktales and novels of rodeo.

Rodeo reminiscences first appeared in the 1950s, when the first generation of rodeo cowboys and aficionados put pen to paper and recorded the stories of the early years of professional rodeo. Although a handful of these books are autobiographies, not many rodeo folk possessed the ability or desire to engage in such sustained literary endeavor. Vera McGinnis' *Rodeo Road* (1974) is an engagingly written autobiographical rodeo narrative, but it is one of the few. Most rodeo reminiscences are less-polished biographies or loosely constructed "histories" written by relatives, friends, rodeo announcers, journalists, and other insiders in the rodeo world. These works include Foghorn Clancy's *My Fifty Years in Rodeo* (1952), Gene Lamb's *Rodeo Back of the Chutes* (1956), Thelma Crosby's *Bob Crosby, World Champion Cowboy* (1966), David G. Brown's *Gold Buckle Dreams* (1986), and several more. Published privately or by obscure presses in affordable paperback editions, they are available today only in the homes of rodeo cowboys or the libraries of the National Cowboy Hall of Fame and the ProRodeo Hall of Fame.[16]

Written in an informal style with a heavy reliance on cowboy vernacular and oral anecdote, the rodeo reminiscences utilize a freewheeling methodology that defies categorization as history, fiction, journalism, or recorded folk narrative. At times they bear an interesting resemblance to the nineteenth-century folk-based southwestern newspaper stories of Davy Crockett and Big Mike Fink. Gene Lamb's introduction to *Rodeo Back of the Chutes* exemplifies their style. Lamb, a rodeo insider and founding editor of *Rodeo Sports News*, writes: "This book makes no pretense at being a history of rodeo . . . nor is it a novel. Every incident is true or based on truth, although some of them go a long way back and may have picked up a little color, and I have taken the liberty of some embellishment." Together, the rodeo reminiscences expand and formalize somewhat the traditional motifs of rodeo-cowboy folktales.[17]

The trickster of rodeo folktales is also a mainstay of the rodeo reminiscences. And like the Alligator Horse boatman of nineteenth-century folk literature, the rodeo trickster sometimes spikes his wily ways with a little violence and a lot of alcohol. Gene Lamb taps all of these themes in an outrageous story, supposedly true, entitled "Throwing Your Goddam Hotel Out That Window." Set in New York City during the annual Madison Square Garden Rodeo, it effectively contrasts the uncultured rodeo contestants and the cosmopolitan environs. The cowboys in one large hotel get "cabin fever" and throw a big party where "the grog" is "flowing in large quantities." When the desk clerk arrives to shut the party down, the cowboys throw him out the door, complaining, "Hell uva *hotel*. Can't even have a few quiet drinks. . . . Whole town's full of fairies." The rodeo men become more and more disgruntled until one of them finally forms a plan. "Let's throw the sunuvabitch out the window," he declares, and when a partner asks, "Throw what out the window?" he replies, "The whole goddam *hotel*."

The cowboys proceed to do just that, tossing lamps, carpets, chairs, and other furniture and furnishings out the window. "We'll form a line and work tha far side of tha room. Heavy stuff we'll have a double line," commands a rodeo man; "by gawd she's gonna git done right." Not surprisingly, the hotel manager soon appears, storming into the room and upbraiding the cowboys as a "bunch of ignorant savages." "They should never let you within city limits," he screams. "They should keep you in cages." He soon regrets his words. "Savijs, huh?" snarls one cowboy. "The little old idiot don't even know cowboys from injuns." In seconds the manager finds himself hanging upside down from a tenth-story window, held "firmly but with nonchalance around the ankles by a grinning cowboy." The rest of the crew returns to mixing drinks and making merry. A little later they pull the petrified manager back inside and shove a glass of "rye and coke" into his hand. He does not tarry, however, vanishing out the door at high speed while the cowboys explode in laughter. The police arrive, but "somehow it was all explained to the law." The cowboys "settled for damages done . . . [and] checked out without protest. And at least one small group of New York's Rodeo contestants had relieved the monotony."[18]

In vivid descriptions of arena action and the riding, roping, and 'dogging of wild animals, rodeo reminiscences, like folktales, stress cowboys' physical prowess, courage, indifference to pain and injury, and willingness to risk death in the arena. All of the writers relate variants of the classic stories of Bonnie McCarrol and Pete Knight, and the story of Freckles Brown's ride on Tornado is ubiquitous. In between lies a range of tales about cowboy heroes who casually endure serious injury while taming the rodeo beasts. Typical is Ken Adams' grisly yet somehow humorous story of a cowboy named Chet riding a bull named Pretty. "Pretty gave him a love tap with a horn, right at the hair line," but none of the other cowboy contestants showed much concern. "Sympathy evaporated" when they "saw he didn't have any damage that four or five stitches wouldn't cure."[19]

Gene Lamb devotes an entire chapter to injury stories that might unsettle readers unaccustomed to rodeo folk culture. He tells the standard tales of Bill Linderman's thrice-broken arm, Bob Henry's prize-winning Cow Palace bulldogging run "with both arms fractured between elbow and wrist," and Casey Tibbs's 1956 postretirement bronc-riding spree with "broken ribs and torn muscles." The story of Oklahoman Buck Rutherford includes the standard hospital escape after "specialists" supposedly recommended a spinal tap and "as a last resort drilling a hole for something or other." Lamb attempts to explain the injured cowboys' irrational disregard for pain in an unnerving story about a roughstock rider who fractures his pelvis and thereafter competes in a "harness" to keep him from "falling apart." "Well, why for gawd's sake doesn't he do something else [to make a living]?" Lamb asks the cowboy's partner, who answers simply: "He likes to rodeo, he's a good bullrider so what else could he do that would give him as a good a living?" Sometimes a cowboy just has to ride—even if his pelvis happens to be "falling apart."[20]

In a different but equally important vein is the famous tale of the formation of the Cowboy Turtles Association in 1936. Based on a historical incident, the story is told in some detail in nearly every rodeo reminiscence and constitutes nothing less than a rodeo-cowboy creation myth. Gene Lamb recounts the story. So does Foghorn Clancy, in *My Fifty Years in Rodeo*. And in *Mr. Rodeo Himself*, Cecil Cornish writes proudly of "the year the cowboys went out on strike and formed the Turtles Association," to which Cornish himself belonged.[21]

Much of the strength of the Turtles story springs from its Depression-era setting, which contrasts with its Old West cowboy-hero motifs. As I have already related, the Cowboy Turtles, ancestor to today's Professional Rodeo Cowboys Association, was born out of a Boston Garden Rodeo labor dispute in November of 1936. Angry over their powerlessness in management's decisions about prize money and judging, rodeo cowboys walked out on the eve of the rodeo and signed a declaration that, in rodeo-cowboy circles, ranks second only to the one signed by American patriots on July 4, 1776. Led by Everett Bowman, Hugh Bennett, Everett Shaw, and others, the cowboys fought attempts by the promoter, Colonel William T. Johnson, to stage the rodeo with "scab" labor. At the last moment Johnson backed down and agreed to bargain. Thus the Cowboy Turtles and the modern rodeo profession were born.[22]

This story possesses a number of interesting features, one being the name "Turtle" itself, and why the cowboys chose it. Numerous explanations circulate. Some say the rodeo men called themselves Turtles because they wore turtleneck sweaters while competing. Others say that the name comes from the cowboys' agreement in the beginning not to "give this outfit no highfalutin name." The most common explanation is self-mocking, as cowboys poke fun at themselves for being "slow as turtles doin' somethin' like this."[23]

More important is the story's 1930s setting and the incongruous casting of rodeo cowboys as modern labor agitators. The emergence of the cowboy hero as a "union man" who (temporarily) forsakes his beloved individualism for cooperation turns the myth of un-American, left-wing labor agitators upside down. The drama is intensified by the strong personalities of Everett Bowman and his fellow hands—common, plain-spoken men who rise to the occasion and do their duty for their fellow cowboys. Then there are the heroic details of the walkout and the confrontation with Colonel Johnson, who plays Sheriff of Nottingham to Bowman's Robin Hood. "These young fellows in Rodeo now, or starting out, will never realize how much they owe to Everett Bowman," Turtle Everett Shaw reminisced; "if he thought he was right, he stayed with it. And he stood for helping the rodeo."[24]

The result is a story that is good because it is exciting *and* true—a story that features a modern, urban cowboy hero. Significantly, this 1930s Turtle hero relies on frontier *and* modern traits to survive in a changing America. Frontier individualism has to be temporarily set aside. And this is no easy task, for as one chronicler of the Turtles noted, the rodeo cowboy "is the most independent creature on earth," and "when somebody suggested they form a group to set up rules and regulations . . . the cowboy objected. He wanted no interference in his personal freedom." Yet the Turtles did act as a group, and they triumphed. Even so, the contemporary urban labor-agitation theme is never allowed to override the rodeo cowboy's romantic, individualistic frontier mystique for long. If the mythologizers had their druthers, after all, the rodeo cowboy would most certainly be roping steers and riding broncs, not confronting management and scabs, much less engaging in collective bargaining discussions.[25]

Like the moviemakers and storytellers who preceded them, the reminiscence writers present a rodeo-cowboy hero who belongs more to the nineteenth century than to his own time. This rodeo man is a frontier individualist, a trickster and a drinker, and he is brave and impervious to danger. His nomadic life brings hardship, "countless hours driving all night, choking down rank black coffee . . . hoping you can win a couple of hundred bucks so you can . . . take more punishment." But bronc rider Chris LeDoux, who wrote those words in his biography, *Gold Buckle Dreams,* also describes the upside to this lifestyle: "Then, on that special day, you may be at Cheyenne or the Podunk County Fair, and it may be pouring down rain or 110 degrees in the shade, but everything clicks. . . . The horse blows in the air, you get tapped. You feel the power under you and in your own body. You are right on the ragged edge, taking it to the limit, making that wild ride."[26]

The rodeo-cowboy hero of the reminiscences is thus a twentieth-century frontiersman. He is a Plains cowboy drifter moving on down the interstate highway. He is, in sum, a *contemporary ancestor.* Relying upon the values and traits of an earlier, preindustrial society, the rodeo man of folktales and reminiscences continues the American pioneer lifestyle in the urban, industrial age. He is our ancestor, yet he rides before us right now, in today's rodeo arena. He is a wish fulfillment, representing the rural fantasies of an industrialized people, a people divorced from their land. In this sense, the hero of rodeo folktales and reminiscences is at once a historical and mythological creation. The rodeo cowboy's story tells us as much about his romanticizers' fantasies as it does about himself.[27]

During the decades following the publication of the first rodeo reminiscences, a more formal literature of rodeo novels appeared, authored by Larry McMurtry, William Crawford, Cyra McFadden, Hal Borland, Craig Lesley, Michael Dorris, Ken Kesey, and others. But writing a rodeo novel proved much more difficult than spinning tales or writing reminiscences. Translating oral tradition into formal prose is no easy feat. Like nineteenth-century southwestern folk humor, oral rodeo tales do not lend themselves to sustained development—usually they are effective only in a short, anecdotal form akin to that of their oral roots. For an artistic literary treatment, rodeo needed an author like Mark Twain, who translated southwestern folk humor into *The Adventures of Huckleberry Finn*. Rodeo never got a Mark Twain, but several authors succeeded at various levels in writing rodeo fiction. Their successes usually hinged on moving away (literally and figuratively) from the rodeo arena and making rodeo only one of several important elements in a modern urban western. In other words, the rodeo novelists used rodeo as a backdrop to stories that contained other essential elements of modern fiction. The most important of these elements, of course, are human relationships, including romance—subjects hard to find in a strikingly male-specific cowboy and rodeo oral tradition.

In this sense the rodeo novelists emulated the rodeo-movie makers who adapted James Fenimore Cooper's classic formula to the emerging urban western genre, with the rodeo cowboy substituting for the nineteenth-century Plains cowboy. Yet in portraying the rodeo mystique, moviemakers possess several advantages over novelists. The short (approximately two-hour) length of a feature film means that moviemakers can sustain the thinner facets of the rodeo genre. And in a visual medium, of course, they can bypass and downplay oral traditions somewhat (although movies do enable viewers to *hear* the cowboy's voice). Filmmakers also introduce family and interpersonal relationships into rodeo stories; in particular, they introduce women and story lines revolving around them, and thus present the rodeo cowboy in a more modern, romantic format. The performances of Robert Mitchum in *The Lusty Men* and Steve McQueen in *Junior Bonner* have never been equaled in rodeo literature.

Rodeo novels, lacking the powerful visual element, combine rodeo oral tradition with the motifs of the classic western and urban western rodeo movies, aiming to make the folk-based rodeo story into polished literary art. Larry McMurtry, William Crawford, and Cyra McFadden have accomplished this difficult task, and there are other notable authors of rodeo novels as well. However, we will postpone for another chapter a discussion of the works of Michael Dorris, Hal Borland, Craig Lesley, and Ken Kesey (all of whom experiment with the traditional racial and gender motifs of the classic western) and address at this time McMurtry's *Horseman, Pass By* (1961) and *Moving On* (1970), William Crawford's *Bronc Rider* (1965), and McFadden's *Rain or Shine* (1986).

One can count on one hand the number of rodeo novelists before Larry McMurtry, and then let them rest in peace. Curiously, exemplary western writers such as Zane Grey and Louis L'Amour ignored the rodeo mystique altogether, leaving the field to amateurs and buffs. B. M. Bower's *Rodeo* (1928), Gene Lamb's *Rodeo Cowboy* (1959), and Stanley Noyes's *Rodeo Clown* (1961) are important not because of their literary merit, but rather because they started a small subgenre of rodeo fiction—and because they helped to spark the work of William Crawford, who is probably one of the only novelists to have read them all and kept them in his library. If there are any other good rodeo novelists before Crawford and McMurtry, I have been unable to discover them.[28]

Horseman, Pass By, McMurtry's first novel, is not exclusively a rodeo tale, but the familiar themes of rodeo-cowboy individualism and wanderlust are ubiquitous in it. The Thalia Rodeo is integral to the story; Lonnie Bannon's friends Hermy and Buddy, the hired man Jesse, and Lonnie's uncle Hud are all rodeo men. Lonnie himself is drawn to rodeo cowboys because of the major dramatic event in the story, the loss of the family ranch and death of his grandfather, Texas ranchman Homer Bannon. Homer's death and, shortly before it, his symbolic shooting of the last remaining Texas Longhorns mark the end of the frontier. Homer is the last true cowboy in Lonnie's world, and his death leaves the boy reflecting on "the horseman that had passed." Lonnie sees no way to remain a *real cowboy* in 1950s America. His only hope lies in the rodeo arena.[29]

Most Americans know Lonnie, Homer, and Hud Bannon not from *Horseman, Pass By* but from the 1963 movie adaptation, *Hud.* Starring Paul Newman as Hud, Brandon de Wilde as Lonnie, and Melvyn Douglas as Homer, this evocative black-and-white movie stands as one of the great urban westerns, a classic depiction of the Great Plains horsemen passed by. Yet in adapting the novel for the screen, the moviemakers struck out much of its earthy rodeo milieu. Jesse's rodeo memories and reflections are gone, as is Lonnie's pivotal truck ride to visit the injured Hermy at story's end. The Thalia Rodeo still serves as the backdrop, and we see the milling crowds, the crowded cafes, and the drunken carousing of the rodeo cowboys and their fans. But the rodeo competition itself has nearly vanished. It is reduced to Hud's and Lonnie's ludicrous participation in a greased-pig chase, a children's event that no *real cowboy* would deign to enter.[30]

Even with the rodeo scenes pared back, *Hud* accomplishes its aims as an urban western. Cinematographer James Wong Howe's stark portrayal of 1950s Texas cattle country; raincoated government men shooting hundreds of Homer's cattle in a huge bulldozed trench; Hud's attempted rape of the Bannons' cook (Patricia Neal); Homer's funeral, with its beleaguered ranch men in black suits, cowboy hats and boots, and string-tied, pearl-buttoned, white western shirts; Lonnie's final departure, leaving a bitter and hateful Uncle Hud behind the slammed screen door of a ranch house Hud has purged of his kin—all of these images are gripping and unforgettable.[31]

A few years later, McMurtry used the rodeo cowboy's *contemporary ancestor* status and the Cowboy Code themes of individualism, courage, and nomadism to much greater extent in *Moving On.* Like *Horseman, Pass By,* this hefty novel is today a sleeper in the large body of work of the Pulitzer Prize—winning novelist. A descendant of Texan ranch folk, McMurtry is perhaps the most accomplished writer of urban westerns, a genre he was instrumental in creating. The most fascinating aspect of *Moving On* is probably also the main reason for its relative obscurity. In this tale of modern Texas, McMurtry somehow blends a rodeo story with one of academia, all the while exploring the adventures and tumultuous marriage of Patsy and Jim Carpenter. "Few novels, then or ever, have attempted to merge the radically incongruent worlds of graduate school and rodeo," McMurtry wrote in 1986, adding dryly, "I am now completely at a loss to explain why I wished to attempt this." Yet as a Texas artist (a combination some might also label "incongruent") who grew up in the land of rodeo and was drawn simultaneously to the life of the mind, McMurtry quite naturally hit upon this paradox as a basis for a novel. The result was much more entertaining and important than either McMurtry would admit or his critics have ever noted.[32]

Moving On opens in the early 1960s with Patsy and Jim Carpenter, newlyweds and pampered children of wealthy Texans, hitting the rodeo road. Jim, a would-be photographer and author, aims to "do a book of pictures" about rodeo cowboys. Like his many other quixotic schemes, Jim's rodeo book never quite pans out. In the meantime, however, he and Patsy meet real rodeo men and women in a world that profoundly influences their lives. Traversing the western United States in their beat-up Ford, sleeping in cheap motels, eating and drinking with the rodeo folk, Patsy and Jim become close friends with Pete the rodeo clown, his cowgirl wife, Boots, bronc rider Pee Wee Raskin, and most important, the vain, hard-living "world-champion cowboy" Sonny Shanks. Before the season ends, Patsy tires of the rodeo life, and Jim decides to return to Rice University to pursue a Ph.D. in English literature. But their rodeo memories and friends follow them back to Houston. Amid the lush green environs and bohemian trappings of Rice's university district, the story's final drama, the unraveling of Patsy and Jim's marriage, plays itself out.[33]

Sonny Shanks and Patsy Carpenter quickly emerge as the key figures in this classic urban western because they represent the opposing forces of frontier and civilization. Sonny, rodeo's "king of the sport," appears

early on atop a dangerous Brahma bull that he rides confidently to a winning score. Later, Sonny tries to score with Patsy as well, inviting her
into his rodeo rig, a white hearse littered with bronc saddles, first-aid
gear, "a case of whiskey," and a narrow mattress from which Patsy, to her
great shock, detects the unmistakable smell of a recent sex act. Undaunted by her departure and enmity, Sonny tries again, meets rejec-
tion, and retaliates by hog-tying Patsy and leaving her overnight in a deserted rodeo arena. "He's crazy . . . he has absolutely no respect for
civilization," Patsy cries angrily to Jim, who remains strangely drawn to
Sonny's wild ways. And Jim is not alone. Until his untimely demise (in
an amphetamine-fueled automobile crash), Sonny attracts a legion of
idol-worshipers, male and female alike. One of them, a young hand
riding the rodeo circuit, summarizes Sonny's mystique in cogent cowboy style: "I guess he's living proof that no amount of pussy can hurt a
man."[34]

Patsy Carpenter stands somewhere between Susan Hayward's Louise
(*The Lusty Men*) and Debra Winger's Sissy (*Urban Cowboy*) in the eternal
battle between women and rodeo men. Like Louise, Patsy will not abide
the uncouth and violent ways of the rodeo folk. "I hate cowboys . . . and
the whole business of cowboyism," she informs Jim early on, adding that
Sonny Shanks is "awful" and "cowboyism personified." As the story
develops, Patsy refines and finalizes her opinion of "cowboyism" and the
"insane violence this life seems to breed." "I hate it," she declares
finally. "I won't stay around it any longer. We're going back to Houston."
Yet Patsy has her wild ways too. Her hot temper and spunky independence, her flirtations and love affair, and her own unique brand of rambling fever all form a frontier individualism with a touch of feminism
thrown in. (Oddly, it was knee-jerk feminist literary criticism of Patsy
and her crying fits that compelled McMurtry, with tongue in cheek, to
defend her so strongly in the preface to the 1986 reprint of *Moving On*,
where he sings her praises and confesses that the book should have been

entitled *Patsy Carpenter.*) Patsy is one of McMurtry's finest heroines. Although she would never mount a mechanical bull at Gilley's Bar like Sissy, she is no debutante or Houston belle either (not by a long shot). And pity the poor cowboy or dude who provokes her.[35]

Sonny Shanks and Patsy Carpenter combine with several other elements to make *Moving On* a memorable work. The varied rodeo characters, along with Patsy's and Jim's families and Houston friends (including Emma and Flap Horton of *Terms of Endearment* fame), certainly add to the mix, as does the story of the marital woes and parenthood of the volatile newlyweds. Yet the key to the book's power, I think, is in the paradox of the "radically incongruent" worlds of rodeo and university to which McMurtry alludes in the preface and which he plays with throughout the novel. Complaining about the mundane, pedantic concerns of Rice graduate students, Patsy comments dryly, "The one nice thing about rodeo is that it doesn't operate on the semester system." After resisting an amorous advance from Jim's adviser, the lecherous academic "super-star" William Duffin, she informs Jim, "I just met the Sonny Shanks of the scholarly world." And even after leaving rodeo to return to a life of books and ideas, Jim, under the influence of a couple of beers, readily admits, "Rodeo isn't bad. I think it compares favorably with graduate school."[36]

Of course, Jim is much like McMurtry himself in being drawn irresistibly (and impossibly) toward two opposing worlds. One must be awfully careful in intellectualizing McMurtry (or any of America's country *philosophes,* for that matter), but it is certainly worthwhile to hazard a conjecture or two. Most western writers (and singers and painters and moviemakers) take pride in their purported anti-intellectualism and freewheeling literary style. But in fact they gravitate toward an established artistic framework, the dialectic of the frontier and civilization first patterned by Cooper. Larry McMurtry is no exception.[37]

In *Moving On* the rodeo represents the old America, and Houston and the Rice University milieu the new. Jim quite naturally finds himself torn as Patsy and Sonny pull him in separate directions. And because this is an urban western, the choices prove even trickier for all concerned. Patsy may be "tame," but Jim and Sonny soon learn that she is strong-willed and a powerful force. And while Sonny shows his "wild" ways atop broncs and bulls, he is nevertheless a *contemporary ancestor*, residing in four-star hotels, riding from town to town in a white hearse, popping amphetamines, and pondering a career as a "cowboy hippie . . . the Joe Namath of rodeo" right up until the moment of his death on Hollywood Boulevard. What to make of all of these contradictions is simultaneously the reader's problem and pleasure, and McMurtry revels in presenting the paradox and providing some possible clues to its unraveling. Throughout *Moving On*, the themes of individualism, freedom, and nomadism appear and reappear in modern garb. Perhaps the automobile and the two-lane highway form the point where wild and tame meet in this twentieth-century western. "This is like *On the Road*," Patsy says during an all-night starlit auto sojourn to a Denver, Colorado, rodeo. "All we've done is circle around. We are all a beat generation."[38]

Like *Moving On*, William Crawford's classic rodeo novel *The Bronc Rider* (1965) utilizes the classic rodeo subgenre themes in its portrayal of the rodeo-cowboy *contemporary ancestor*. But *The Bronc Rider* is a very different book by a very different author. Unlike his fellow Texan McMurtry, Crawford was a rodeo insider and a zealous promoter of the sport. A Marine Corps combat veteran of the Korean War, Crawford rodeoed in roughstock events for twenty years while simultaneously pursuing a college degree and a career as a writer; politically, he was a Goldwater Republican. His longtime affiliation with the Professional Rodeo Cowboys Association is apparent in the number of books from his personal collection in its archives. As noted, many of these books are the obscure early attempts at rodeo fiction by Bower, Lamb, and Noyes, authors Crawford evidently knew well and whose artistic goals he aimed to fulfill.

Ultimately he far surpassed their efforts, yet his work remains rough around the edges and can never compare to the literary sophistication of a McMurtry or a McFadden. *The Bronc Rider* is far too true to its oral roots to ascend into the high realm of polished literature.[39]

The Bronc Rider, portraying a tumultuous season in the rodeo career of Texas roughstock rider Ernest Cameron, is a book for rodeo purists; it remains today the most widely read rodeo novel among actual rodeo folk. There are no McMurtrian paradoxes in Crawford's portrait of rodeo life; truths are readily apparent to his rodeo men. *The Bronc Rider* is an uncomplicated celebration of frontier individualism, featuring rodeo cowboys who are truly wild. Ernest Cameron ("Cam") is the literary equivalent of Peckinpah's Junior Bonner—stoic, determined, and driven by absolutely nothing but rodeo. Crawford is especially good at conveying the technical details of rodeo competition to his readers, and the book is no doubt the most realistic of the rodeo novels. This realism, however, combines with other factors to contribute to a general lack of subtlety and artistic nuance. Crawford balances this weakness with an ideological purity and a firm adherence to the oral traditions of rodeo.[40]

Rodeo oral traditions are evident in Cam's superstitions—he grows uneasy whenever some greenhorn throws a hat on his bed or eats peanuts in the arena. His Texan speech is peppered with cowboy vernacular and Mexican phrases. He hears and relates rodeo jokes and tall tales, including an interesting variant of the Bob Crosby gangrene-and-manure story. The injury motif is ubiquitous in *The Bronc Rider*, and Cam's "wreck" aboard the bronc Cape Canaveral serves as a pivotal incident, instilling in him a fear that he must overcome in order to prove again that he is truly a cowboy.[41]

The most important oral tradition in *The Bronc Rider* is Cam's continual articulation of and adherence to the tenets of the Cowboy Code. Crawford carefully weaves the Cowboy Code into his narrative, writing reverently of "this way of life, the code by which men live . . . a code of behavior no less rigid for being informal and unwritten." Cam adheres to the Code throughout his rodeo travels, speaking always in reticent understatement, shunning dudes and complainers, and competing in roughstock events despite serious and painful injuries. He freely gives inside information to his fellow bronc riders and is always a gentleman until "bad" women cross his path. Cam is such a Code purist that much of *The Bronc Rider*'s drama stems from his temporary *disregard* of the Code following his ride on Cape Canaveral. Cam temporarily loses his nerve, takes to drinking and fighting in unmanly fashion, behaves rudely in the presence of ladies, and resultantly suffers the ostracism of his fellow rodeo men. Only the story's finale, a return match with and final taming of Cape Canaveral, brings Cam back into adherence to the Code and thus back into the fold of cowboy culture. After conquering the bronc, he "had himself, whole again. He was a bronc rider. That was all he ever wanted."[42]

For liberal post-1960s readers, Cam's (and Crawford's) devotion to Code behavior can no doubt wear a bit thin. Like Junior Bonner, Cam is so devout in his cowboy religion that he sometimes lacks a humanness with which readers can identify. Crawford celebrates Cam's inability to interact with other human beings as a point of honor, but the rugged individualism becomes a little boring at times, and sometimes it is downright offensive. For example, like a host of western heroes before him, Cam is incapable of having a loving relationship with a woman. He practices Code behavior toward "ladies"—but Crawford makes sure that there are very few "ladies" around to enjoy the courtesy. The women of *The Bronc Rider* are, at best, buckle bunnies, rodeo groupies who serve Cam in one-night stands in cheap motel rooms or perform fellatio in the backseats of automobiles. At worst they are like Rita, the "crummy rodeo tramp" who betrays Cam's partner Pierce. "That lousy slut . . . that filthy whore!" Cam remarks in a typical aside. "I swear, if I thought it'd help Pierce, I'd gut and butcher her like a hog." Thankfully, Crawford spares us the gutting and butchering of Rita, though Cam does manage to swindle her out of her insurance money (after she supposedly drives Pierce to a violent arena death).[43]

The liberal critique could also focus on Cam's (and Crawford's) "conservatism." Cam is a Marine combat veteran and a self-styled patriot who hates intellectuals and the "thin, virtually useless brand of education" they represent. He despises the federal government, a government that "summoned him to the courthouse, slapped a tax lien on his herd and impounded his bank account." He leaves ranching for rodeo because there are too many "damned taxes and rules" in the nonrodeo world. He curses the "shiftless loafers" on welfare and foreign aid, all supported by the tax dollars of American workingmen. Like the Goldwaterites, whose rise in the Republican Party corresponded with the writing and publication of *The Bronc Rider*, Crawford's rodeo men feel America is in decline, suffering from a loss of courage and frontier individualism. They blame this decline on the "liberals," the bureaucracy, and the all-powerful state. They shun the "steel squeeze in the soft glove of socialism" to pursue the freedom and independence of rodeo.[44]

But as with the Goldwaterites, there is a libertarian strain in Cam's cowboy individualism that precludes any simplistic "conservative" label. Besides hating the government, he shuns the evangelical Christian church of his Texas upbringing and despises the workaday world of good, Christian, taxpaying Americans. On a rare visit to his Texas hometown, he is repulsed by his parents' respectable, blue-collar life. The petroleum-company houses are "as precise and regularly ordered as a military compound," and an "utter absence of individuality," an "absolute sameness," is reflected in the faces of his parents and his brother Angus, an evangelical prohibitionist Cam rightly sees as a hypocrite and coward. "I don't want to be like you," he yells at Angus in a climactic shouting match (a scene probably borrowed by the screenwriters of *Junior Bonner*). "I'd shrivel up and die. The God you shout about put no man on earth for that."[45]

Cam's (and Crawford's) libertarianism accents the fact that critics should be careful before condemning rodeo cowboys (both mythic and historic) for insensitivity to post-1960s liberal values. Crawford's ultimate strength is his grounding in rodeo folk culture, and that culture is undoubtedly a violent and sexist one. Although he was no Mark Twain, Crawford faced artistic dilemmas (and opportunities) very similar to those Twain faced. He knew that censoring the crudities of American folk speech would produce a bland rodeo literature divorced from its salty oral tradition. Moreover, he knew that a portrayal of the world of Ernest Cameron—like that of Huckleberry Finn—must be decidedly multiethnic (Cam embraces cowboys of any color, so long as they adhere to the Code). As a result, Cam has much more in common with Huck Finn (who also hated being "sivilized") than he has with some contemporary "conservatives." William Crawford emerges as a cowboy purist and articulator of the Cowboy Code who cannot be pegged into modern political categories. He weaves radical social, cultural, economic, and political views from both right and left into a rich cowboy fabric, a fabric characterized by the classical liberal thread of individualism: "Ernest Cameron . . . was a determined individualist in a society equally determined that he should not be and casting him out for the attempt. He was marvelously equipped for complete manhood in a society bound to castrate him. He had to rodeo."[46]

Thus, by the early 1970s, Larry McMurtry and William Crawford had established the basis for an engaging western fiction rodeo subgenre, a subgenre that Hal Borland, Michael Dorris, Craig Lesley, Ken Kesey, and others expanded in the following decades. In addition to these later authors who used rodeo as a means to explore racial and gender themes, a score of minor and unremarkable rodeo novelists, and even some comic book writers, published works in the 1970s and 1980s. The most challenging and important book of that era, however, was Cyra McFadden's 1986 rodeo memoir *Rain or Shine,* a book that reinforces the classic Cowboy Code themes of McMurtry and Crawford.[47]

Although *Rain or Shine* might be classed as a rodeo reminiscence, its artistic achievements so far surpass the reminiscence genre that it is more appropriately discussed alongside the novels of McMurtry and Crawford. McFadden, a noted San Francisco journalist and author of *The Serial* (1977), tells the engaging story of her 1930s childhood on the rodeo road and, later, her volatile relationship with her estranged father, Cy Taillon, the "Dean of American Rodeo Announcers." Taillon and his rodeo trick-rider wife, Pat (Cyra's mother), cut a pretty wide swath in the early days of rodeo. The Taillons were "two peacocks in a sea of mudhens," drinking, dancing, squabbling, and rodeoing their way across the West. Cyra shared this life in the backseat of her parents' Packard, in countless rodeo-town motel rooms, and in the "crow's nest" where her father announced the rodeo contests with his booming, patrician voice. However, by the time Cyra reached age five, her parents' "tempestuous" marriage had destructed in a painful, alcohol-fueled finale.[48]

Cyra then began a long and difficult separation from her father, growing up in Missoula, Montana, with her remarried and mentally unstable mother. Meanwhile, Cy quit drinking, remarried and raised a new family, pursued his rodeo career, and rose to become one of the most famous and beloved of all North American rodeo announcers. McFadden eventually married and left Montana for the San Francisco Bay Area, where she divorced, remarried, pursued a successful writing career, and finally reconciled with Cy nine years before his 1980 death from cancer. She published *Rain or Shine* in 1986. Her memoir intertwines the complex story of a troubled family with that of American rodeo, the myth of a "West once wild and now paved over, once free-spirited and now tame," and the freedom of the rodeo road:

This book is a memoir of my father's life on the rodeo circuit, his marriage to my mother and my effort to understand the ways in which I am their daughter, who left the West and the world of rodeo behind, full of fear and loathing, to find that Cy Taillon's imprint was indelible. . . . Like my father, I love the road show, packing a bag, heading off somewhere or nowhere, traveling light, never looking back over my shoulder. . . . Like him and like my mother, I prefer the night lights and the bright lights to the daylight, moving down the road to staying put. It's hereditary.[49]

McFadden begins by establishing that, despite his role as a rodeo announcer, Cy Taillon was in fact a *real cowboy*. She makes this giant leap over logic effortlessly, noting that rodeo men universally acknowledged Cy's status as a "working cowboy, though he earned his living with his mouth rather than his muscle." The reason for this status was, quite simply, that Cy Taillon espoused and followed the Cowboy Code. Like the rodeo cowboys whose exploits he narrated over the loudspeaker, he lived a hard, itinerant life, working in all kinds of weather and never complaining. He was always generous to his fellow rodeo men. "If he had extra money, everybody drank," and cowboys regularly bunked on Cy and Pat's motel room floor, "with their saddles for pillows." Moreover, Cy was a scrapper, "light on his feet and fast with his fists," who "never hesitated about piling in when there was a fight." An elegant dresser and smooth talker, he was gallant to ladyfolk, and he treated Pat like a rodeo queen (when he wasn't abusing her).[50]

"Westerners love a hero," McFadden continues, "and when the hero is one of their own, a cowboy, their pride does not diminish." Like Pete Knight, Freckles Brown, and Casey Tibbs, Cy Taillon is the subject of oral legends among rodeo folk. The most famous tale, based on a historical incident, relates how Cy single-handedly saved 10,000 rodeo fans when three Air Force planes somehow collided over the Great Falls, Montana, fair and rodeo grounds, exploding, hurling flames and metal shards through the air, and crashing, killing bystanders only three hundred yards from the grandstands. Enshrouded in smoke, Cy Taillon employed his voice, not cowboy ranch skills, to save the day. He calmed the huge, panicky crowd, assuring them the danger was past and somehow persuading them to sit quietly until firemen and ambulances arrived. McFadden, hearing the umpteenth version of her father's heroism "over a whiskey ditch at the Cowboy Bar" in Great Falls, admits to some skepticism: "I size up the fairgrounds and wonder how such a small place could have held ten thousand people. I listen to eyewitness accounts of that afternoon and ponder the discrepancies. As the bourbon flows, the number of people killed increases, the explosion virtually wipes out Great Falls and my father remains at the mike while flames lick at the wooden announcer's stand. I swallow my skepticism, along with the drink I am never allowed to pay for. As my father's daughter, I should know that myth making has its own logic."[51]

Since Cy Taillon never bulldogged a steer or mounted a bucking bronc, McFadden turns to her half brothers Terry and Tommy Taillon to portray the rodeo genre's injury theme. Traveling the rodeo road with their dad and mother (Cy's second wife, Dorothy) during the 1950s and 1960s, Terry and Tommy became roughstock riders as teenagers and, during careers as rodeo cowboys, endured their share of wrecks and broken bones, "held together with steel pins and Super Glue." Tommy carried his rodeo bravado with him into a Colorado bartending job, where he was "shot in a fight he was trying to break up." When McFadden queried him years later about his injuries, Tommy drawled that they were "no big deal"—the bullet "missed all his vital organs and the helicopter that evacuated him to the nearest hospital got there right away."[52]

Throughout her memoir, McFadden incorporates the dialectic of frontier and civilization, wild and tame, into her narrative in fascinating and contradictory ways. She complicates the paradox by adding her simultaneous love and hate of her father and the wild and/or tame values he represents. For example, she disparagingly counters Cy's reactionary political views and support of the Vietnam War with her own enlightened Bay Area liberalism, feminism, and membership in the ACLU. On the other hand, she is strangely (and consistently) nostalgic for her dad's redneck ways, his persona before he quit drinking and settled down to respectability: "Our problem with each other was that I loved the hell-raising gypsy who had disappeared, as the years went by, behind reputation and money, the stability of his second marriage and his increasingly John Wayne–like views of how the world should work."[53]

The negative reference to John Wayne in this context is interesting. It implies, indirectly, of course, that the Duke (not to mention the Ringo Kid and Sergeant Stryker) would not fit into the 1930s rodeo world of Cy Taillon, the "hell-raising gypsy." This is not necessarily true. It seems that McFadden also confuses libertarianism and conservatism here and, understandably, puzzles over the conundrum. Was Cy really wild and free and virtuous when, as McFadden remembers, he was the "dazzling, reckless . . . drunk" who gave her mother black eyes on a regular basis? Was Cy really a tame conformist when, much later in his life, he told the *Denver Post* that he would "shoot first and argue later" if his Denver home were ever again burglarized? Was Cy Taillon wild or tame, or both, or neither? "Inside him, beneath his custom-tailored Western jackets, beat the heart of a cowboy," McFadden writes, as if real cowboys never wore their fancy duds into Dodge City on Saturday night.[54]

Although no one has ever unraveled this paradox of wild and tame, Cyra McFadden attains high art as she attempts to resolve it in her evocative memoir. The significance of *Rain or Shine* lies in McFadden's struggle with Cy Taillon's contradictory western mystique. As a youth Cy was a wild, violent, and irresponsible "rakehell," yet he was also somehow a compelling and romantic western character. As a mature adult, he quit his wild ways yet came to symbolize the Code of the West; he was, the *Miles City Star* (Montana) observed at the time of his death, "an embodiment of an ideal, a spokesman for a quality of life and a way of living it." At both stages in his life, then, Cy Taillon represents viewpoints that McFadden either condemns or celebrates: violence and freedom as a youth, bourgeois respectability and the Code of the West as a mature adult. To make things even more confusing, there is inevitably some overlap between the two Cy Taillons. Moreover, some of Cy's traits are no doubt nonexistent, mythical creations. Finally, if Cy ever was a cowboy (which is certainly debatable), he was a cowboy with a microphone, an electronically amplified *contemporary ancestor* to his family, friends, and admirers.[55]

All of these paradoxes become strikingly clear to McFadden when, with her half brother Terry in 1982, she revisits the Miles City Bucking Horse Sale and Rodeo because "Cy's ghost would be there." Amid the Montana rodeo crowd, the smell of broncs and bulls, the mud and cow dung, the liquor, and the "amorphous roar" of the barroom crowds, McFadden searches without success for the real Cy Taillon. She at last gives up, concluding only that when Cy died, "it marked not only the end of a man, but the end of an era." Yet McFadden exits *Rain or Shine* on a positive note, somehow content with memories of her father and a "West once wild . . . and now tame." At the book's end she writes: "Whoever the man with the golden voice was, . . . I go right on missing him, even as he continues to elude me again."[56]

The poetry of rodeo, like its reminiscences and novels, is strongly rooted in the oral folk traditions of working cowboys and early rodeo men. Much has been made of the so-called "singing cowboys" of the Great Plains cattle frontier, yet as we have seen, storytelling was also an important oral folkway. So was poetry recitation. Folklorists John Lomax, Jack Thorp, Glenn Ohrlin, John White, Hal Cannon, James Hoy, Guy Logsdon, and others have documented the ubiquitous folk-poetry traditions of nineteenth-century cowboys. To be sure, T. S. Eliot and Emily Dickinson would probably not have wanted to saunter in, pull up a horse blanket, and join in a campfire poetry session. Yet most working cowboys either listened to or themselves recited coarse folk verse at some time or other. Any nineteenth-century North American with a few years of public school under his belt had been exposed to memorized, recited British and American poetry. Cowboys combined this scant literary background with the powerful themes brought to mind in their daily work—the danger and excitement of herding cattle in a rugged wilderness, the loneliness of life on the trail, the Code of behavior by which they lived, and the stark beauty of their natural world. These important motifs made plenty of grist for the folk poet's mill. Finally, and very importantly, these aspiring cowboy poets had plenty of time to pursue their craft. As James Hoy has written, the solitary lifestyle of the line camp, trailing cattle, and riding nightherd all demanded folktales, songs, and poetry to break the monotony: "What else was there to do but make up verse?"[57]

Although there are important variants, the standard form of cowboy poetry was and is the four-line ballad form of rhymed couplets. This is the same form of some of the classic poems of Rudyard Kipling and Henry Wadsworth Longfellow, poems that late-nineteenth-century American schoolchildren read, memorized, and recited in the classroom. Using this framework, cowboys added their own penchant for taletelling, folk vernacular, and profanity, as well as a tendency to strain for rhymes and cram too many syllables into a poetic line. The result was a salty, unlearned, and vital folk poetry that was, above all, a poetry of cowboy storytellers.[58]

Of particular importance to later rodeo poems was the "bronc-busting" theme of cowboy folk poetry, folktales, and songs. This classic taming motif appears in many folk poems, but the most famous is "The Zebra Dun," a.k.a. "Educated Fellow," an anonymously authored trickster poem. Jack Thorp first heard it recited or sung as early as 1890. The poem tells the story of a greenhorn who wanders into cow camp one day and immediately violates the Cowboy Code by bragging and putting on airs:

Such an educated feller, his thoughts just came in herds
He astonished all them cowboys with them jawbreaking words
He just kept on talking till he made the boys all sick
And they began to look around just how to play a trick.

The trick they decide upon is an old one—they mount the greenhorn on Zebra Dun (named for its buckskin coat and striped markings), a "rocky outlaw that had grown awful wild." At first the trick goes as planned, for

When the stranger hit the saddle, Ol' Dunny quit the earth
And traveled right straight up for all that he was worth
A-pitching and a-squealing, a-having wall-eyed fits
His hind feet perpendicular, his front ones in the bits.

But then the tables turn: The "educated feller," to the cowboys' amazement, sticks to the saddle. He endures an incredible ride, breaks the bronc, and is ultimately acknowledged by all to be a "top hand." Thus the tricksters are outtricked, and the boss immediately offers the stranger a job cowboying for their outfit. By poem's end the narrator can reflect, "One thing and a shore thing I've learned since I've been born / Every educated feller ain't a plumb greenhorn."[59]

This classic bronc-busting poem is still recited at cowboy poetry gatherings. Lively and entertaining, it contains important motifs that we have seen in cowboy and rodeo folklore, reminiscences, and literature: anti-intellectualism, Code behavior, the taming of wild animals, and the trickster theme, here with the twist that the tricksters are foiled. As a result, "The Zebra Dun" traveled from cowboy oral traditions quite naturally into rodeo folkways and, ultimately, popular culture and country music.

Curley Fletcher, an early rodeo roughstock rider and cowboy poet, is a pivotal figure in the evolution of cowboy folk poetry into rodeo poetry and popular song. Descended from Italian and British immigrants, Fletcher grew up in California's rugged Inyo County, east of the Sierra Nevada, where as a young man he was steeped in cowboy workways and folkways. Riding the rodeo circuit in 1914 with his cowgirl wife, Minnie, Curley penned the first of a number of poems that would bring him only fleeting national fame but enduring renown among cowboys and rodeo folk. "The Strawberry Roan," Fletcher's most beloved work, is not a rodeo poem per se but rather a cowboy bronc-busting poem ranking alongside "The Zebra Dun." It even begins a little like the poem about Dunny, with a "bronk fighter" bragging "the bronk never lived, that I couldn't fan." Unlike the "educated feller," however, this bronc rider finds himself outdone by the Strawberry Roan (also named for the color of his coat), "a reg'lar outlaw" who is quite a trickster himself. The Roan gives the cowboy the wildest ride of his life and then throws him to the earth, "cussin' the day of his birth." The bronc wins the day; the bronc buster is himself "busted."[60]

After quitting rodeo for show business and, later, mining, Curley Fletcher continued to write cowboy poetry, including the bronc-busting standards "The Ridge Running Roan," "The Flyin' U Twister," and "The Flyin' Outlaw." Although Fletcher preferred to recite "The Strawberry Roan" as poetry, an unknown singer adapted the poem into a song that took on a remarkable life of its own. The song version (chapter 5) made the rounds quite literally from cowboy campfires to Hollywood, with Fletcher close behind in numerous doomed attempts to gain author recognition and collect royalties. In the meantime, the poem "The Strawberry Roan" trickled back down into oral tradition, where, at Fletcher's impetus, it was reinvented in widespread, vulgar renditions of "The Castration of the Strawberry Roan." In these variants the cow-boys try to get even with the Roan—"the worst fuckin' outlaw that's ever been foaled"—for taming one of their own. The boss finds a top "bucka-roo" at a local whorehouse and hires him to castrate the horse. The cow-boy manages to rope the Roan:

> The boss held his head and I hog tied his legs
> Got out my jackknife and went for his eggs
> When I carved on his bag, he let out a squall
> And squealed like a pig when I whittled one ball.

However, as in the original poem, the Strawberry Roan triumphs. Fish-ing for the bronc's remaining testicle, the buckaroo is startled by "blood-curdlin' squalls" emanating, not from the Roan, but from the boss, whose testicles the horse is biting off. The chorus concludes,

> Oh! the Strawberry Roan, how many colts has he thrown?
> He's got gonorrhea, the cankers, and syph,
> He's strictured with clap but his cock is still stiff,
> Oh! that renegade Strawberry Roan.
> . . .
> Oh! The Strawberry Roan, I advise you to leave him alone,
> He's a knot-headed cayuse with only one ball,
> And the boss he's a eunuch with no balls at all,
> Lay off of the Strawberry Roan.[61]

Because Curley Fletcher was himself a working cowboy and rodeo rider, his career documents the migration of cowboy poetry off the range and into the rodeo arena as early as 1914. Fletcher represents authen-tic cowboy-poetry folk traditions and, later, the commercialization of those traditions in published poetry collections and popular song. As we will see in Chapter 5, rodeo men also sustained cowboy folksong tradi-tions. But storytelling and poetry were no doubt their strongest inher-itances from ranching culture. Folk poetry remained embedded in rodeo folkways throughout the 1940s, 1950s, and 1960s, with rodeo men and women reciting and even publishing earthy rhymes in local newspapers and the "poetry corners" of *Hoof and Horns, Western Horseman,* and other rural magazines. The poems collected by Glenn Ohrlin and the rhymes of Johnny Baker are good examples of rodeo poetry during the post–World War II decades. This was an authentic folk poetry that never really became commercialized until the first Cowboy Poetry Gathering in Elko, Nevada, in 1985.[62]

The degree to which cowboy poetry and its rodeo-poetry subgenre have today strayed from authentic oral tradition toward commercialization is, of course, a hot topic for debate. Elko's now-famous Cowboy Poetry Gathering has produced results that both gratify and concern professional folklorists. On the one hand, the event has directly and indirectly enabled millions of North Americans to learn about and enjoy what was, until 1985, an obscure regional folkway. Thanks to the Elko gathering, scores of Western communities now stage their own cowboy-poetry festivals, the long-dormant poems of Curley Fletcher are available in a new paperback edition, and cowboy poets Baxter Black, Wally McRae, Red Steagall, Paul Zarzyski, and others perform regularly on radio and television shows (Black even appeared on the *Tonight* show with Johnny Carson). On the other hand, folklore purists would argue that this kind of commercial exposure waters down and compromises any folk genre, inevitably turning it from folklore to fakelore.[63]

An application of Richard Dorson's criteria for distinguishing folklore from fakelore produces a more evenhanded assessment of the cowboy-poetry revival. Dorson called for use of both biographical and internal evidence to determine folkloric authenticity, and modern cowboy poetry thus far withstands both of those tests quite well. Biographical analysis proves that poets like Baxter Black, Wally McRae, Red Steagall, Shadd Piehl, and Paul Zarzyski all undoubtedly possess intimate firsthand knowledge of ranching and rodeo folk and their oral traditions. And an examination of the new cowboy poets' motifs reveals internal themes we can trace directly back to authentic nineteenth-century folktales, songs, and poetry. Thus, contemporary cowboy poetry and its rodeo subgenre are at the very least *folk-based* poetry, if not a pure folk poetry. Perhaps Wilbur S. Shepperson and Judith K. Winzeler have found the most accurate language in their analysis and labeling of contemporary cowboy poetry. Instead of naming it either folklore or poetry per se, they call it *folk art*, a form they situate somewhere between high and low culture.[44]

Cowboy folklorist Hal Cannon's ground-breaking *Cowboy Poetry*, an edited anthology of poems read at the 1985 Elko Cowboy Poetry Gathering, provides seven good examples of the rodeo subgenre. Cannon begins with the traditional bronc-busting poems "The Zebra Dun" and "The Strawberry Roan." Next, "Murph and McClop," anonymously authored, recounts the tale of two rodeo tricksters who prove, to a young woman's grief, that "the rodeo life has no room for a wife." Oregon rancher and poet Jon Bowerman then offers yet another "Tribute to Freckles and Tornado" in his version of Brown's epic 1967 ride. Bob Schild of Blackfoot, Idaho, puts a bizarre twist on the bronc-busting theme in "Two of a Kind," about two "Old Timers," one a rodeo man and one "a vicious old outlaw [bronc], by name Alley Cat." At the end of a memorable ride, the horse dies, but so does the cowboy straddling his back. The rodeo men finally decide to bury the old-timers together, "just the way they had gone / Old cowboy aboard an' his saddle strapped on." Lucky Whipple, a fifth-generation cowboy poet, relates the story of an Arizona cowboy's harrowing, unsuccessful ride on the "Chookaloski Mare." And finally, in "Young Fellers," R. O. Munn of Baker, Oregon, tells an autobiographical tale of a roving cowboy and his buddy who enter the Jordan Valley Fourth of July Rodeo. Mounting a bad Brahma bull, the young cowboy says,

I pulled my hat down
Took a big chew of snoose

Last wrap, nodded my head, and
They turned the old boy loose.

However, in the tradition of "The Strawberry Roan," this cowboy sails "through the air / Like I had been shot from a gun" and then runs for his life to escape the beast he has failed to ride:

I rubbed a few sore spots,
Thinking there must be better ways.
I'd had enough bull ridin'
To last all my days.
Well I guess I survived,
But please believe this narrator:
The next rodeo I attend,
I'll be a paying spectator.[65]

Red Steagall is one of the most accomplished of today's cowboy and rodeo poets. A native of Texas—the state legislature has officially designated him "Cowboy Poet of Texas"—Steagall is, like Curley Fletcher before him, a pivotal artist whose work is situated between the folk and commercial worlds. He publishes and records poetry and songs firmly rooted in the oral traditions of the cowboys and rodeo folk with whom he has had a lifelong association. For example, *Ride for the Brand*, the title poem of his anthology and audiocassette, is an evocative statement of the Cowboy Code and the steadfast loyalty of ranchmen to their outfit. In other poems, Steagall writes movingly and authentically of Plains cattle-country culture past and present. Although his most important rodeo works are musical (his seminal rodeo album *For All Our Cowboy Friends* is discussed in chapter 5), two important poems in *Ride for the Brand* honor rodeo roughstock heroes Freckles Brown and Casey Tibbs. "To Casey" pays tribute to the Code values of courage and resolve that Tibbs exhibited as he unsuccessfully fought cancer "the same way he rode broncs—with a smile." "Your spirit was undaunted till the end," Steagall concludes, "And wherever cowboys gather / And remember golden times / We'll drink a toast and think of you, old friend."[66]

In form as well as in commercial viability, Red Steagall's poems and songs transcend the folk idiom yet strive to maintain a tie to folk origins. Steagall experiments with rhyme and meter, straying far at times from the engaging yet predictable four-line couplets of traditional cowboy verse. In this journey into the sphere of high art he is joined by Montana rodeo-poet Paul Zarzyski, who has also combined Cowboy Code themes and other rodeo oral traditions with more artistically ambitious forms of rhyme, meter, and language. Like Steagall, Zarzyski writes poems that derive their ultimate strength from the earthy folk culture from which they originate.

A Polish-Italian American from the Iron Range of northern Wisconsin, Zarzyski worked his way west to Montana in the mid-1970s, rodeoing for thirteen years as a bronc rider. Like Larry McMurtry, he complemented his cowboy ways with an artistic and academic bent, earning a master of fine arts degree in creative writing from the University of Montana, teaching, and eventually settling into a career as a full-time cowboy poet. Today Zarzyski travels the "cowboy-poetry trail" reading his poems from Nevada to England and even Australia at the many gatherings spawned by the cowboy-poetry movement.[67]

Not surprisingly, Zarzyski's strongest poems are those based on his rodeo experiences. They are featured in his book *Roughstock Sonnets* and audiocassette *Ain't No Life after Rodeo*. Zarzyski has been described as an "economical and extremely visual" writer whose words touch readers' emotions while simultaneously conjuring up strong (and at times outrageous) images of cowboys, the rodeo circuit, and the North American West. "The Bucking Horse Moon," for example, paints a vivid picture of the night heavens in the Big Sky country. "Two rodeoin' lovers," a cowboy roughstock rider and cowgirl barrel racer, view this awesome sight during a summer spent riding the rodeo road, winning prize money, camping out, reveling in nature, and making love "beneath Montana's blue roan bucking horse moon." In this poem Zarzyski, unlike some moviemakers and novelists, finds a strong role for women on the rodeo road. But these women are *real cowgirls*, not civilizers. In this sense they resemble Sissy in *Urban Cowboy*, rather than Louise in *The Lusty Men*.[68]

A prime example is "Zarzyski Meets the Copenhagen Angel." Set in a Miles City, Montana, bar on "a rodeo Saturday night," this poem tells the autobiographical story of the love-at-first-sight meeting of Zarzyski and a Copenhagen-snuff-dipping rodeo cowgirl. "Her levis, so tight / I can read the dates on dimes / in her hip pocket," she smiles at him from a corner barstool, her "pigtails braided like bronc reins. / . . . a barrel racer in love with her horse / her snuff, and a 16 second run." Clearly, both cowgirl and cowboy are wild. They dance close to a Chris LeDoux country tune, kindred spirits in a world of rodeo renegades:

I'm Zarzyski, rhymes with whiskey,
I tell her—a lover, a fighter,
a Polish bareback bronc rider.
And these Copenhagen kisses jump and kick
higher than ol' Moonshine, himself.[69]

On a much more somber note, Zarzyski takes the rodeo folktale and prose themes of injury and death into high art in "All This Way for the Short Ride," the title poem to his and Barbara Van Cleve's 1996 book. Zarzyski again uses first person to tell this tale of the arena death of a fellow roughstock rider. From the vantage point of the bucking chutes, where he is preparing for his own ride on a wild bronc, he remembers his friend's grisly death as the rodeo crowd observes a moment of silent prayer "for a cowboy crushed by a ton / of crossbred Brahma." The most gripping feature of this poem is, again, the introduction of a female character, this time a civilizer, "the wife / stunned in a bleacher seat /

and pregnant with their fourth." Alternating between images of the bull, the slain cowboy, and the wife and her unborn child, the poem becomes as strong as any work ever written about rodeo:

> I know the instant
> that bull's flanks tipped beyond
> return, how the child inside
> fought with his mother for air
> and hope, his heart with hers
> pumping in pandemonium—in shock,
> how she maundered in the arena
> to gather her husband's bullrope and hat, bells
> clanking to the murmur of crowd
> and siren's mewl.

The unborn rodeo child thus learns firsthand, "through capillaries of the placenta, the sheer / peril of living with a passion," and Zarzyski, in the roughstock chutes, reflects on the pain and beauty of rodeo, ultimately embracing both, exploding from the chute aboard his bronc just as his friend, on a bull, had done, "flesh and destiny up / for grabs, a bride's bouquet / pitched blind."[70]

From the perspective of this chapter's survey of rodeo folklore, reminiscences, novels, and poetry, Zarzyski emerges as a writer who has taken the rodeo motifs into high art while somehow retaining their rough-hewn folk vitality. All of the classic rodeo themes appear in his poems. There are individualism, the freedom of the road, and the pull between frontier and civilization, the wild and the tame. Tricksters abound, and so do cowboy vernacular, rodeo folkways, the Cowboy Code, and the themes of injury, death, and what it means to be a *real cowboy.* Yet Zarzyski's experimentation with language and form, his forays into free verse and alternative methods of rhyming, and the physical appearance (often with unusual indentations) of his poems, not to mention his introduction of wild rodeo women, all add new and vital dimensions to rodeo art. It is this combination of old and new, of folklore, folk art, and high art, that makes Paul Zarzyski a strong and important rodeo poet.

"Ain't No Life after Rodeo," the title poem of an audiocassette by Zarzyski and the musical duet Horse Sense, sums up many of these themes in rowdy, rhymed cowboy couplets. Although the folk vernacular is thick enough to scare off most greenhorns, any *real* North American can understand the themes of independence and freedom. In this poem — subtitled "The Polish Hobo Rodeo Poet's Commencement Address to the Chagrin of Every Graduate's Mother at the College of Buckaroo Knowledge"—Zarzyski comes about as close as anyone ever will to making a definitive artistic statement about rodeo cowboys.

"There ain't no life after rodeo," he begins. "So when you feel your spur-lick weaken / And your bareback riggin' goes to leakin'" there is only one solution for a *real cowboy*: to keep on 'dogging and roping steers and riding bucking broncs and bulls, of course. "To hell with lookin' before you leap!" Zarzyski tells his fellow hands. "Fight for those holts, sight down that mane / Spit in the face of age and pain." In rhymed couplets of cowboy lingo, the poet calls for Cowboy Code grit in the face of injury, adversity, and in this case, advancing age. The rodeo cowboy must continue to ride. Indeed, he *has* to ride:

Insanity, love, plus aggression,
Call it passion, call it obsession,

Adrenalined fury, 200-proof,
Like guzzlin' moonshine up on the roof.

Running on Bute, LeDoux-songs, and caffeine,
You rollickin', rosined-up spurring machine,

Too lazy to work, too scared to steal,
Slavin' for wages bushwacks your zeal.[71]

Like Jeff McCloud, Junior Bonner, J. W. Coop, Sonny Shanks, Ernest Cameron, and Cy Taillon, Zarzyski's buckaroos see clearly that there "ain't no life after rodeo." They have a special calling; they cannot fit into the mundane workaday world. Like Gay in *The Misfits,* they pity those mere mortals "slavin' for wages" at nine-to-five jobs. The rodeo cowboys must hit the road, and ride and rope the wild animals. Like Lonnie Bannon in *Horseman, Pass By,* they have to search for what Hank Williams once called the "wild side of life." In telling their tales, the rodeo storytellers, reminiscence writers, novelists, and poets embark on their own quest, their own trip down the rodeo road. At their best, these writers trek on the wild side of art.

CHAPTER FOUR

"Getting It Right"
The Rodeo Cowboy in Art

I was no longer one of the countless, insignificant spectators, I was on
the "inside." . . . I traveled with the cowboys—to the Cheyenne Frontier
Days, the Boulder Pow Wow, the Greeley Spud Rodeo, the Monte Vista
Ski-Hi Stampede, the Pendleton Roundup, and the Calgary Stampede.
—Clifford P. Westermeier, *Man, Beast, Dust* (1947)

There is a story about Clifford P. Westermeier that travels the oral-tale
circuit among professional scholars, artists, and rodeo cowboys alike.
When Westermeier completed his Ph.D. dissertation, "A History of
Rodeo," at Colorado University in 1946, the history department scheduled the traditional oral dissertation defense before a committee of his
major professors. However, Cliff Westermeier put a unique twist on this
rather stodgy academic rite of passage. He told some of his rodeo pals—
men who had helped him in his research—about the dissertation defense, and being experts on the subject themselves, several of the cowboys elected to attend. Thus, when the learned professors of the doctoral
committee walked into the examination room, they found not only the
candidate and his wife seated there but also an array of booted and
Stetsoned rodeo hands.

The dissertation defense proceeded, the cowboys listening earnestly.
Finally, when the professors had finished with Westermeier, the rodeo
men jumped in, asking questions and offering comments and sugges-
tions of their own to the candidate and his professors. Then, after giving Cliff their congratulations, the cowboys sauntered on out of the

university, returning to their work 'dogging steers and busting broncs on the professional rodeo circuit. As one of them remembered later, "We just wanted to make sure all those professors got it right." Evidently Westermeier "got it right." The published version of the dissertation, *Man, Beast, Dust: The Story of Rodeo* (1947), and his second book, *Trailing the Cowboy* (1955), have become bibles to rodeo and cattle folk, who have always counted Westermeier as one of their own.[1]

Westermeier's association with rodeo and rodeo cowboys began long before his Colorado University days and involved yet another of his many talents—that of the pictorial artist. Westermeier was not only among the most important historians of cowboy and rodeo culture, he was also an important painter and illustrator of North American cowboys and rodeo cowboys. Born in 1910 in New York State, where he spent the first three decades of his life, Westermeier seemed an unlikely candidate to embrace and portray the story of the North American cowboy. A talent for drawing and painting led to formal study at the Buffalo School of Fine Arts, the Pratt Institute in Brooklyn, and the New York School of Fine and Applied Arts in Paris. With this training, he secured an appointment as assistant professor of fine arts at the University of Buffalo, a position he held from 1935 to 1944. He seemed destined for a career as a northeastern painter and art professor—before the American West and cowboy culture lit in him a flame that would burn throughout his remaining fifty-year career as an artist, scholar, and teacher.[2]

During the 1930s Westermeier made his first trip west and, in Sidney, Nebraska, witnessed his first rodeo. Immediately drawn to the sport, he left the rodeo arena that day with a full pad of sketches that, later, in his studio, he "completed as paintings." During his tenure at the University of Buffalo, he continued to travel west whenever he could, drawing scenes of the region in general and the American cowboy and rodeo cowboy in particular. Soon his artistic bent was complemented by a historical interest in the subjects of his drawings, and he began the serious study of western history. "In order to enrich my background for this type of painting," he wrote, "I began to investigate the origin of rodeo." In 1939 he earned a master's degree in history from Colorado University in Boulder. Resigning his art professorship at Buffalo in 1944, he moved west for good, beginning work on a doctorate in history at CU. One year later he married Therese Stengel, a CU professor of German who was descended from Boulder pioneer miners. Together they hit the rodeo road, traveling for more than ten years and 100,000 miles as Cliff gathered material for his dissertation and books on rodeo cowboys.[3]

During the decades that followed, Clifford Westermeier served as professor of history at the University of Arkansas (where he was department chair) and, ultimately, at his alma mater in Boulder, where he finished a long and distinguished career, retiring in 1978. He died November 13, 1986. During the post–World War II decades, Westermeier became one of the preeminent historians of the North American cowboy, publishing four books and continuing to sketch and paint the subjects of his scholarly interest. He used his own sketches to illustrate *Trailing the Cowboy,* and he staged numerous one-man shows of oil paintings and watercolors in New York City, Buffalo, Boulder, Denver, Santa Fe, Tucson, and Austin.[4]

In 1954, Westermeier delivered a lecture, "Art and Artists of the Cowboy," before the Texas State Historical Association in Austin. The lecture stands today as one of the most successful attempts to discuss and analyze in essay form this important artistic genre. He traced the long (and now familiar) story of western cowboy art from early-nineteenth-century magazine illustrations through the works of Frederic Remington, Charlie Russell, Will James, Ross Santee, and contemporary cowboy artists. His theme was realism and the contribution of cowboy art to American realism. At the conclusion of his talk, however, Westermeier raised an interesting issue that had not until that time been addressed by western artists and scholars. "It is surprising," he said, "that the most recent, and certainly the best-known, cowboy activity, namely rodeo, has not as yet become a widespread theme for artistic expression." He then proceeded, in brief space, to describe and analyze the work of rodeo artists Frederick Allen Williams and Peter Hurd, and illustrators J. R. Williams and Walt LaRue.[5]

Bostonian Frederick Allen Williams, Westermeier noted, "has devoted more years to a portrayal of the cowboy sport, rodeo, in the media of clay and bronze than any other sculptor" and "has a special interest in the Brahma bull which he so often uses as a model." Peter Hurd's painting *Bob Crosby* portrays the 1930s rodeo champion in a "blunt, forceful, and rugged study" evincing the "impact of the elements and time" on the New Mexico roper. *Sunday Afternoon in New Mexico,* a black-and-white drawing by Hurd, interprets rodeo through the image of a group of local cowboys watching a bull-riding event. Newspaper cartoonist J. R. Williams sometimes featured rodeo men in his syndicated *Out Our Way* comic series. Finally, Walt LaRue, perhaps the most noted rodeo cartoonist, took what Westermeier described as "sly jabs at the strength and weaknesses, the joys and sorrows, the fun and seriousness of the modern rodeo performer" (Ill. 14).[6]

Although Westermeier was partially correct in pointing to the relative paucity of rodeo art, he was unaware of and neglected to mention several pre-1950s rodeo artists. The very first rodeo artists may have been Paul Frenzeny and Jules Tavernier. Tavernier's *Rodeo, or Rounding Up Cattle* accompanied an 1874 *Harper's Weekly* article entitled "The Texas Cattle Trade." This illustration, like his painting *El Rodeo—Santa Magarita, California* (1884), portrays ranch-based, working-cowboy roundups at exactly the time rodeo was making its way to the arena spectator-sport venue. In a parallel artistic development, the garish yet gorgeous works of the Wild West show and rodeo-poster artists of the late nineteenth and early twentieth centuries fit on the edges of the rodeo-art subgenre. Posters advertising the 101 Ranch, Colonel Tim McCoy, and Pawnee Bill Wild West shows (and of course Buffalo Bill Cody's Wild West) form striking examples of this colorful medium (Ill. 17).[7]

The bronco-buster (or bucking-horse) motif, so popular among rodeo storytellers, writers, moviemakers, and singers, proved ubiquitous in early rodeo pictorial art and sculpture. Folk-based cowboy artist Charlie Russell depicted the theme in his 1899 watercolor *Bucking Bronco,* as did turn-of-the-century sculptors Frederic Remington (Ill. 10) and Bob Scriver in their own bronco-buster works. Sometime around World War I, artists added the rodeo milieu to the bronc motif, and rodeo bronco-buster pieces have appeared frequently ever since (indeed, they have probably appeared a little too frequently). Valona Varnum Crowell's *The Artist and the Bucking Horse,* the catalog to the contemporary ProRodeo Hall of Fame show of the same title, provides a definitive collection of bucking-horse art. Crowell gathers forty-three images of this classic pose, ranging from the rough sketches of rodeo folk artists to full-blown, professionally painted watercolors. The twenty-seven artists include Will James ("the bucking-horse artist"), Walt LaRue, Nancy McLaughlin, Ross Santee, and Robert Meyers. Some of the artists, writes Crowell, "were working cowboys or rodeo riders. All were observers of the sport and knew the situation well." She summarizes broadly: "Every Western Artist has done his or her version of the bucking horse."[8]

A late 1920s Ellensburg Rodeo poster (Ill. 16) provides an excellent example of the bucking-horse motif in commercial art. Here the rodeo cowboy and bronc take center stage, with advertising for the rodeo appearing at the top and bottom of the poster. The color scheme is simple yet attractive, with a blue-shirted, buckskin-chapped cowboy mounted atop a sorrel horse. The leather roughstock riggin', saddle, rope, boots, and spurs are accurately depicted. The bronc is in a classic *sunfish* pose, his body contorted into the shape of a crescent as he strains (and fails) to throw the cowboy. A 1925 Pendleton Roundup poster by Wallace Smith features an even more pronounced sunfishing (the horse is truly airborne) and more detailed saddlery. The sorrel bronc and white-shirted rider (with burnt-orange scarf) are superimposed on a red background for dramatic effect. Below, in black letters, Smith has written in rodeo vernacular, "Let 'er Buck."[9]

In the 1920s and 1930s, artists Mary Bonner, Charles Simpson, and Jo Mora crafted rodeo art in the media of printmaking, graphic arts, sketches, and paintings. Born in 1887, Mary Bonner spent a formative part of her youth on her family's Uvalde County, Texas, cattle ranch. After attending the University of Texas in Austin, she traveled in Europe, studied art, and in 1922 joined a Woodstock, New York, artists' colony to study etching and lithography. Bonner never forgot her native Texas, however, even when she traveled to Paris (France) to live and work in the mid-1920s. There her knowledge of the cowboy way made for a minor splash via four etchings that hung in Salon d'Automne—*Bucking Broncos* (1924), *Calf Roping* (1924), *Les Cowboys* (1924), and *Le Taureau au Rodeo* (1926)—and resonated with her Texas ranch and rodeo roots. Meanwhile, across the English Channel, Charles Simpson's 1925 portfolio, published in limited edition as *El Rodeo,* consisted of one hundred sketches and paintings of London's 1924 "Great International Contest." Simpson's work stands as the most complete artistic depiction of the rodeo genre prior to World War II.[10]

Another important pre– (and post–) World War II artist specializing in cowboy and rodeo themes was Joseph Jacinto "Jo" Mora. Born in Uruguay in 1876, Mora worked with and closely observed vaqueros and cowboys from Latin America to Canada before launching a career devoted largely to the narration and illustration of cowboy culture. Mora described "the various tools and accoutrements of the cowboy, with their genesis and evolution" in a series of illustrated books, including *Trail Dust and Saddle Leather* (1946) and *Californios* (1949). His depiction of cowboy clothing, tack, gear, mounts, and herding techniques had taken a rodeo bent in *Evolution of the American Cowboy* (1933), a series of drawings dedicated to the Salinas (California) Rodeo and "chronicling the Western horsemen from Conquistadores and Hacendados to Vaqueros and Texas Cowmen." These drawings all feature a centerpiece rodeo cowboy (or cowgirl) surrounded by smaller and more detailed sketches of cowboys and their gear. Mora's *Sweetheart of the Rodeo,* the most famous of the *Evolution* series, features a cowgirl in a yellow, pink, blue, and white outfit, encircled in a heart of yellow flowers. On the picture's border are a score of tiny illustrations with captions accenting the Hispanic influence on cowboy and rodeo culture. (Millions of contemporary North Americans first viewed *Sweetheart of the Rodeo* in 1968, when the Byrds chose it to illustrate their landmark country-rock album of the same title.)[11]

Jo Mora's focus on cowboy gear raises the interesting topic of cowboy costume and rodeo clothing as art. Highly stylized and colorful, twentieth-century rodeo clothing is closely tied to the folk-art motifs of traditional cowboy clothing. Late-nineteenth-century working cowboys adopted clothing peculiar to their life and work. Broad hats, bandanna handkerchiefs, leather chaps, pointy-toed high-heeled boots, and jingling metal spurs all served specific purposes: protecting cowboys from burning sun and pouring rain, keeping trail dust from entering the shirt collar, shielding the legs in thick brush, securing feet in stirrups, and facilitating a fast getaway on horseback. On special occasions such as a dance or trip to town, cowboys embellished this ensemble considerably, exhibiting a pronounced flair for gaudy fashion and an apparent desire to cultivate a cowboy mystique. They donned colorful shirts, silver buckles, hand-tooled belts and gun holsters, and fancy boots that they carried with them solely for the purpose of show. This fondness for "fancy duds" took on an even more pronounced expression among rodeo cowboys and cowgirls. In the early twentieth century, rodeo performers became famous for their colorful garb, which obviously served aesthetic as well as practical purposes. In the 1920s and 1930s cowgirls like Ruth Roach, Vera McGinnis, and Mabel Strickland dazzled rodeo audiences with their stunning outfits of colored hats, satin tops with bloused sleeves, split skirts, and multicolored boots, complemented with silver jewelry, hand-tooled belts, bright scarves, and other accessories (Ill. 15).[12]

The career of an eastern tailor known simply as "Rodeo Ben" marks the point where cowboy folk costume became commercial art. Born in Philadelphia in 1894, Rodeo Ben (whose surname, perhaps Jewish, is unknown) began tailoring for rodeo men and women in 1930. "Rodeo Ben's, the East's Most Western Store," catered to thousands of rodeo cowboys and western movie and singing stars, hosting a special Belvedere Hotel showroom during New York City's annual Madison Square Garden Rodeo. Later, Ben and his son—Rodeo Ben Jr.—worked with Blue Bell jeans and world-champion rodeo cowboy Jim Shoulders to produce the first "five-pocket, straight-legged, fitted blue jeans targeted at rodeo cowboys." But Rodeo Ben's greatest artistic legacy is his line of western shirts and suits, the preferred "fancy duds" for professional rodeo cowboys and cowgirls throughout the 1930s, 1940s, and 1950s.

A sampling of Rodeo Ben's gorgeous work is preserved in the Pro-Rodeo Hall of Fame, the Gene Autry Western Heritage Museum, and the Tyler and Teresa Beard Collection. One 1940s suit (valued today at $1,500) is made of kelly-green wool "with longhorns all over the place [and] early painted snaps on the cuffs." Wavy "smiles" (known as "arrow pockets") adorn another Rodeo Ben piece, a light-green-and-cream-colored shirt with embroidered designs "reminiscent of Indian petroglyphs" and topstitching around the cuffs, collar, and pearl-snap placket. Simpler, yet just as beautiful, is a "red, white, and blue Rodeo Ben shirt in red gabardine and cotton twill with three-snap and candy-strip whipcord trim." And finally, collector Tyler Beard notes a stunning 1940s shirt Ben made for Flying A Rodeo producer and singing-cowboy movie star Gene Autry. Because of its dazzling colors, Beard says, "Rodeo Ben must have had a time concentrating on this fuchsia silk-satin shirt with multiple Indian heads and full feather headdresses in chain-stitch embroidery."[13]

Reviewing the work of the early Wild West show and bucking-horse artists, and of Mary Bonner, Charles Simpson, Jo Mora, Rodeo Ben, and several others, it is obvious that Clifford Westermeier inadvertently omitted several artists from his 1954 "Art and Artists of the Cowboy" speech. And he omitted yet one more pioneer in the field, for in fact Westermeier was *himself* one of the first and foremost artists of the North American rodeo cowboy. From that first Nebraska rodeo onward, he sketched and painted rodeo cowboys and rodeo scenes. Although he never published his rodeo sketches, he displayed them in his one-man shows and left a few of them to posterity. The Clifford P. and Therese S. Westermeier Collection in the University of Colorado Library contains fifteen of these rodeo paintings, sketches, and illustrations. They include portraits of Westermeier's rodeo compatriots, illustrations of famed rodeo bucking broncs, and a series of drawings interpreting each of the events that form the classic rodeo program.[14]

The collection also contains much of Westermeier's nonrodeo cowboy art (including the original illustrations for *Trailing the Cowboy*), but it is the rodeo pieces that concern us here. These fifteen works, all black-and-white sketches and illustrations, address nearly every facet of the rodeo subgenre (Ills. 11, 12, 13). In testament to the role of realism in cowboy art, drawings like *High Skip* and *Bull #55* graphically depict the rodeo roughstock events of bronc and bull riding. The timed events of calf roping and bulldogging appear vividly in *Closing the Gap* and *Hold That Ox*. Adding variety are *5 Minutes to Midnight* and *Midnight's Grave*, pictorial tributes to the famed and feared father-son bucking-bronc duo now buried on the grounds of Oklahoma City's National Cowboy Hall of Fame and Western Heritage Center. Finally, Westermeier's *Doff Aber* and *Homer Pettigrew* complement Peter Hurd's *Bob Crosby* and form what might be described as a rodeo folk-hero portrait subgenre.[15]

Clifford Westermeier thus joined Paul Frenzeny, Jules Tavernier, the Wild West show poster artists, Frederic Remington, Bob Scriver, Frederick Allen Williams, Peter Hurd, cartoonists J. R. Williams and

Walt LaRue, Mary Bonner, Charles Simpson, Jo Mora, Rodeo Ben, and others to create the rodeo subgenre of cowboy art. Although, as Westermeier stated in "Art and Artists of the Cowboy," rodeo art has never been particularly widespread, it was in retrospect more plentiful than he knew. Moreover, in the years following Westermeier's 1954 address, more and more artists began to experiment with the themes of the small, sturdy rodeo-art subgenre. Just as moviemakers, novelists, poets, and songwriters discovered the mythic power of the rodeo man, so did artists working in various media. These are the artist-descendants of Clifford P. Westermeier and his colleagues.

As it did in movies, literature, and music, the Vietnam era fostered an interest in rodeo as a subject for art. However, with the exceptions of painter Red Grooms and photographer Garry Winogrand, the counterculture's rodeo artists did not immediately produce works to rival Vietnam-era songs and movies such as Ian and Sylvia's "Someday Soon," Buffy Sainte-Marie's "He's an Indian Cowboy in the Rodeo," and Cliff Robertson's *J. W. Coop*. The rodeo-art subgenre arrived in the world of "pop art" in 1976 when "The Great American Rodeo" opened at the Fort Worth Art Museum. This commissioned show aspired, according to its catalog, to expand the "realist tradition in American Art," complementing and interpreting the Fort Worth Rodeo. By making a record of the rodeo's "sounds, images, moods, and atmosphere" the artists aimed to "increase the museum visitor's visual knowledge and understanding of an important American event." Comprising works by eleven contemporary artists, "The Great American Rodeo" was dominated by Red Grooms. Born in Nashville, Tennessee, in 1937, Grooms left the mid-South for the bohemian art scene of New York City in the 1950s. By the time he was commissioned to do *Ruckus Rodeo* for the Fort Worth gallery, he had a reputation as a wildly innovative painter, sculptor, and moviemaker whose modern and provocative works often were simultaneously playful, good-natured, and humorous.

Beyond Grooms's work, "The Great American Rodeo" ranged from

Garry Winogrand's black-and-white photography to John Alberty and Joe Ferrell Hobbs's multiacre "exterior environment" arranged in the shape of a gigantic western belt buckle.[16] Like many commissioned shows, it encompassed both the sublime and the ridiculous. Contemporary press accounts were very negative, and one need not speculate long on the reactions of Fort Worth rodeo folk who, upon paying a visit to the museum, found themselves standing before Robert Rauschenberg's *Rodeo Palace*. A "room" decorated austerely in the media of cardboard, wooden doors, screens, metal, and paper cutouts, *Rodeo Palace* was "non-associative" and "elusively referential"—the rodeo theme was definitely understated. In a similar vein, Terry Allen's *The Paradise* used a "lurid pink motel and bar," "glaring neon and plastic palms," and a saddled motel bed filled with arena dirt to, in Allen's imagination, "unif[y] the whole life style surrounding the rodeo." George Green followed suit in *Life Lust Cycle*, which portrayed rodeo via an Astroturf graveyard under the watchful eye of a gaily painted horse head with nine reins emanating from the nostrils. Finally, Andy Mann's *Video Rodeo Parade* employed twenty television sets showing alternating images of five separate black-and-white rodeo videotapes—evidently a novel concept in 1976.[17]

Much more engaging was Grooms's *Ruckus Rodeo*—a gaudy and energetic rendering of the modern rodeo arena via a "Sculpto-pictorama" of "wire, elastic, acrylic canvas, and burlap, 14 1/2 × 50 1/2 × 24 1/2 feet" with a hint of danger underneath its playful and colorful exterior. Unlike the brooding, politicized works of Rauschenberg, Allen, Green, and Mann, *Ruckus Rodeo* was, in the words of one critic, "not a cruel spectacle, an unfair slap at rodeo denizens. Grooms' hilarity pushes him beyond any thought of justice or the lack of it." Similarly, Mimi Gross Grooms contributed a colorful plywood and Plexiglas sculpture, *Waitin' behind the Bullpen*, and Ed Blackburn, in *Painted Magazine Rodeo Rider*, offered up rodeo hero Larry Mahan writ as large in art as he is in life. Alberty and Hobbs's *Mobile Ranch* took the viewer on an interesting stroll through a huge museum back lot full of redneckiana—pickup trucks, horse trailers, eighteen-wheelers, cattle guards, and a corral fence in the shape of the state of Texas.[18]

Standing between the polemical antirodeo pieces and the works of Grooms, Blackburn, and Alberty and Hobbs is the remarkable photography of Garry Winogrand, originally commissioned by the Fort Worth Museum and subsequently published as *Stock Photographs* (1980). Winogrand's camera roams the entirety of the Fort Worth Rodeo, capturing images of goings-on both inside and outside the arena: the inaugural parade, youth livestock competitions, rodeo cowboys and cowgirls behind the chutes, socializing rodeo fans, dancing couples, and roughstock riding (there are no timed-event photographs). The combination of an indoor setting and the black-and-white photographic medium makes for images that are at times stark and cold. Yet there is a compelling humanness in the faces of the Texas farm kids, rodeo cowboys and cowgirls, and slow-dancing lovers. Although these photographs stand in marked contrast to the less severe works of John Addison Stryker and Rosamund Norbury (discussed below), they eschew the cynicism of Rauschenberg, Green, Allen, and Mann. Viewers' responses, one critic suggested, would be highly subjective: "In the same picture some will find humor; some will find confirmation of their stereotyped impressions of Texas; others will find excitement and vitality, irony and social commentary." *Stock Photographs*, along with Grooms's *Ruckus Rodeo*, constitutes the most important legacy of the Fort Worth Art Museum's infamous "Great American Rodeo."[19]

In today's booming western art scene, the rodeo subgenre plays an increasingly important role. The 1985 founding of the Professional Rodeo Cowboy Artists Association (PRCAA) has greatly enhanced the vital folk connection to rodeo art, for each of the twenty members is also a former rodeo contestant. Founded for "rodeo cowboy artists only," the PRCAA is dedicated to "faithfully recording and preserving the true spirit and authentic detail of the sport, the show, and the lifestyle of rodeo."

Charter members are Jerry Valdez (bronc rider and silversmith), Tony Chytka (bull rider and sculptor), Tracy Mikes (bronc rider and engraver), Bob Burkhart (bronc rider and sculptor), and Jack Wells (roper and painter). Wells, the PRCAA's director, notes that the association conducts a summer artist-in-residence program at the ProRodeo Hall of Fame and hosts an annual "PRCAA Showcase" at the National Finals Rodeo, awarding gold, silver, and bronze medallions in oil painting, sculpture, watercolor, drawing, and artisan categories. Although many of the PRCAA artists are professionally trained, their techniques and direct personal ties to the subject matter invite comparisons to the folk traditions of rodeo musicians, storytellers, and poets. Works like Boots Reynolds' acrylic *Wild Horses at Pendleton* and Jack Wells's *A Pair of Aces*, for example, evince the gritty folk culture these rodeo cowboy artists know so well. Ultimately, "all of the emotions and excitement conveyed in their art is from a first-hand experience."[20]

At present, the bucking-bronc motif continues to proliferate in rodeo art, appearing in shows, galleries, and western art magazines in forms that range from Lynn Hays's classic rendering of *Cheyenne Frontier Days Rodeo 1902* to Papas' more esoteric *Rodeo*, a watercolor in which horse, rider, and atmosphere blend into one rising, ephemeral image. More realistic, but nevertheless stylized, are the pen-and-ink drawings of Syracuse University art professor Murray Tinkelman. Tinkelman, an artist member of the PRCA, has spent a good deal of time in the rodeo arena, publishing and illustrating several books on the sport, including *Rodeo Drawings of Murray Tinkelman* (1982). Delmas Howe, from Truth or Consequences, New Mexico, is the first painter to portray the cowboys and cowgirls of American gay rodeo. Arizonan Howard Post, an accomplished all-around rodeo hand, features cowboys and rodeo in his traditional western paintings. And Montanan Buckeye Blake, the son of a southwestern rodeo roper and ranch cowboy (Blake's first word was "Buckeye," the name of the Arizona town where his father was then competing), continues to explore individualistic cowboy and rodeo themes in his painting and sculpture. "I'm not thrilled with the hulking, modern world," Blake confesses. "Society is going fast, and we have to go fast ... to survive in a high-tech world. So a painting of the West is like a slow song, something that gets your heart down to the proper speed."[21]

Walter Piehl, undoubtedly one of the most innovative contemporary rodeo painters, has direct ties to the worlds of both rodeo and high art. Born in Marion, North Dakota, in the mid-1940s, Piehl grew up in a ranch/rodeo family and as a youth produced, announced, and rode broncs in numerous northern Plains rodeo contests. He also aspired to being an artist, studying painting at the graduate level and ultimately securing an art professorship at North Dakota's Minot State University. There, since 1970, he has taught painting and drawing, helped his wife raise four children (two of whom are rodeo roughstock riders and one— Shadd Piehl—a rodeo-cowboy poet), raised horses, and roped in weekend rodeo competitions. Throughout, he has continued to paint, producing an important body of work evincing western and rodeo themes in sophisticated and contemporary abstract forms. His paradoxical wild/ tame (nature/culture) background makes him something of an anomaly in both the rodeo and the art worlds. "People a lot of times ask, 'If you're such a cowboy, why'd you go to college?' Well," Piehl replies, "I can be ... a cowboy, but life on a haystack wore thin. I wanted to see more than just a [hay] rake." Very few rodeo hands know of Piehl's work—"those guys don't hang around in galleries and museums," he notes—and the literati and "art people sometimes have a hard time getting past the subject matter" of his western paintings. But Piehl has steadily built a regional audience, with his engaging expressionistic paintings displayed in galleries in Montana, Idaho, Wyoming, Nevada, Colorado, and Arizona.[22]

In discussing his radical approach to the old bucking-horse motif, Piehl answers Cliff Westermeier's 1954 query as to why so few artists have pursued the rodeo subgenre. Piehl believes that serious artists have tended to shy away from rodeo art because the arena action proves to be "too formidable a subject. It cannot be captured or really have justice done to it by paint or photo that merely stops/freezes the action . . . it is intimidating to the point of [artists'] being overwhelmed by it." Piehl was inspired to take on the bucking horse not only by his own rodeo roots but also by his study of the Italian futurist school (circa 1909–1920) of painters. The futurists "dedicated their art movement to action, chaos, anarchy, and the dynamic of the fourth dimension," he writes. "They vowed never to paint their subjects as static objects again."[23]

Thus, incongruously, Italian futurism found its way to Minot, North Dakota. One result was Piehl's *Sweethearts of the Rodeo*—a pivotal late-1980s show of thirty mixed-media paintings in acrylic, charcoal, water-color, and pencil that take the classic bucking-horse motif to its most ambitious representation to date. The signature pieces are bright acryl-ics on great sheets of white paper, presenting multiple images of buck-ing broncs (the "Sweethearts") with cowboys and cowgirls mounted atop their backs, hanging on for dear life (Ills. 18, 19, 20). Piehl's "splash, dash, and splatter" painting technique evokes the fleeting, swirling motion of horse and rider that is the very essence of the roughstock competition—"swift kicks of color, broncs and determined riders; heads, hooves, hands, boots, spurs jerking about, dust kicking up, ten-sion, exhilaration" characterize the paintings. The constant presence of bronc and rider, however abstract, places the works paradoxically yet firmly in the realist tradition. Piehl considers the word *realism* "most descriptive when it speaks to the *underlying* characteristics of the sub-ject." And of course, bronc and rider portray a theme stemming from the western genre and its frontier/civilization juxtaposition.[24]

Photographers, working almost exclusively in black-and-white, have produced an important and evocative body of contemporary rodeo art. Like other rodeo arts, rodeo photography began early in the twentieth century. Among its pioneers were two Canadians, A. D. Kean and Rob-ert A. Bird. Kean, a British Columbian cowboy and rodeo competitor turned photographer, moved quickly from high-speed, stop-action still photography to live-action cinematography in the opening decades of the century. His work often featured the heroes of Canadian folk culture—trappers, Mounties, ranchmen, and of course, rodeo cowboys. Rodeo was the focus of his early theatrical short *The Calgary Stampede* (date unknown) and his 1913 documentary film of Vancouver's Minoru Park Provincial Rodeo Championship, during which Kean was reportedly "knocked over several times during the bronco-busting competitions. . . . Once a bull knocked him off his horse and trampled all over him, the horse, and the camera." Meanwhile, in neighboring Calgary, Alberta, R. A. Bird built a 1916–1959 career in black-and-white photography that included much rodeo work, especially action shots of the Calgary Stampede.[25]

Due south on the United States Great Plains, the rodeo photography of Kean and Bird was paralleled by that of Ralph R. Doubleday, Erwin E. Smith, DeVere Helfrich, and John Addison Stryker. Born on July 4, 1881, South Dakotan Doubleday was a pioneer in rodeo photography. After a brief stint as a working cowboy, young "Dub" learned photography and, in Cheyenne in 1910, shot his first rodeo. "Up to then," he remembered, "no one had ever taken a picture of a man flying through the air off a bucking horse." Doubleday decided to earn a living doing exactly that. He literally created a market for his rodeo photographs, developing and selling them on-site to cowboys, fans, and collectors as postcards at three cents apiece or $30 per thousand (or, later, as objets d'art at $300 each). Dub specialized in the bucking-bronc and bucking-bull motifs, usually naming the photographs in honor of the rider and his mount: *Leonard Stroud on Indian Tom* (1919), *Tex Crockett on South Dakota* (1919), and *Smoky Branch on Glass Eye* (1921) were some of his favorites. When he was not dodging broncs and bulls in the rodeo arena, Doubleday dodged bullets and other dangers throughout the world, shooting pictures of World War I military action, the ouster of Mexican president Porfirio Diaz, Florida's Seminole Indians, Teddy Roosevelt's African hunting expeditions, and even Congress' Teapot Dome hearings. But

10. The bronc-busting motif is ubiquitous in rodeo painting, drawing, sculpture, and graphic arts. The folk-based motif began to appear in professional works, like Frederic Remington's *Bronco Buster* (bronze, lost-wax process; 23" x 7" x 20"; 1900–1918). Photo by Richard Nicol. Collection Tacoma Art Museum. Gift of Mr. and Mrs. W. H. Lindberg, 1983.1.34.

11. Noted rodeo historian Clifford P. Westermeier combined a scholarly career with a talent for drawing and painting. These three rodeo drawings are part of a substantial portfolio of rodeo art that Westermeier bequeathed to the University of Colorado. *Sports on the Range* (n.d.). Reproduced with the permission of the Archives, University of Colorado at Boulder Libraries (Westermeier Collection).

12. Clifford P. Westermeier, *Behind the Chutes* (n.d.). Reproduced with the permission of the Archives, University of Colorado at Boulder Libraries (Westermeier Collection).

13. Clifford P. Westermeier, *Taking Off* (n.d.). Reproduced with the permission of the Archives, University of Colorado at Boulder Libraries (Westermeier Collection).

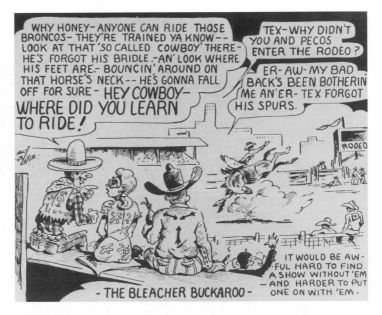

14. Walt LaRue traveled the rodeo road as a roughstock rider before turning to a career in the pictorial arts. Among many career accomplishments, LaRue pioneered the rodeo cartoon genre with numerous works like *The Bleacher Buckaroo* (1948). Courtesy, Walt LaRue.

15. Rodeo duds are an important folk-based subgenre of rodeo art. This picture of Pauline Nesbitt, a famed post–World War I cowgirl, shows a flair for style in her hand-tooled boot tops, silky sash and scarf, and ten-gallon hat. Reproduced with the permission of the National Cowgirl Hall of Fame, Hereford, Texas.

16. *(above)* The bucking bronc motif is a mainstay in rodeo poster art. This Ellensburg Rodeo poster (artist and date unknown) is typical of those used immediately preceding and following World War II. Courtesy, Joel Smith.

17. *(right)* Rodeo poster art descended from the Wild West show posters of the late nineteenth and early twentieth centuries. *Buffalo Ranch Real Wild West* (artist unknown; chromolithograph, n.d.; 1966.54) is typical of the genre. Courtesy, Amon Carter Museum, Fort Worth, Texas.

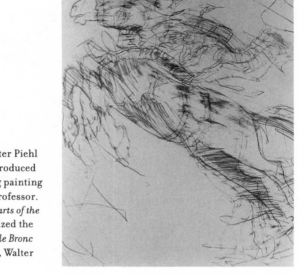

18. North Dakotan Walter Piehl rode roughstock and produced rodeos before studying painting and becoming an art professor. His late 1980s *Sweethearts of the Rodeo* show revolutionized the field of rodeo art. *Saddle Bronc Study* (1987). Courtesy, Walter Piehl.

19. Sky Pilot (n.d.) from *Sweethearts of the Rodeo* by Walter Piehl. Courtesy, Walter Piehl.

20. She Flesh (n.d.) from *Sweethearts of the Rodeo* by Walter Piehl. Courtesy, Walter Piehl.

21, 22. New York City photographer Rob Fraser returned to his hometown of Ellensburg, Washington, to shoot these scenes "behind the chutes." Both of these photographs were featured in his 1996 show, *Bulls, Broncs, and Buckaroos*. (top) *Under the Grandstand* (1996). (bottom) *Taping Up* (1996). Both courtesy, Rob Fraser.

rodeo was Doubleday's first and truest love. When he died in 1959, he left a legacy of more than 20,000 black-and-white negatives.[26]

Nebraskan John Addison Stryker found his way to rodeo art during an intriguing life that began on his parents' midwestern homestead in 1883 and included, along the way, high school and college teaching, calligraphy, circus announcing (he worked for Ringling Brothers in 1928), and rodeo production and announcing. Stryker began to snap black-and-white photographs professionally during the 1920s—the formative years of North American rodeo. Although he photographed rodeo hands at rest and behind the scenes, his most famous pictures are those of live arena action. In this work Stryker developed a technique that was unusual, effective, and dangerous. The prize-winning 1920 photograph *Rose Smith on Easy Money* was shot, according to old-time rodeo announcer Foghorn Clancy, as "Stryker lay flat on the ground . . . it made the horse appear ten feet in the air." Clancy described this picture as "one of the greatest cowgirl bronc-riding shots ever." It launched Stryker on a long career that would include a rodeo picture-postcard cottage industry, numerous book, magazine, and newspaper publications, one-man shows, and following his 1974 death, a retrospective photographic anthology, *The Rodeo of John Addison Stryker* (1977).[27]

As Stryker's, Bird's, and Doubleday's careers concluded in the 1960s and 1970s, a new generation of rodeo photographers emerged. In 1962, Louise Serpa, a Vassar graduate, former nightclub singer, and photography novice, became the first woman granted a press pass by *Rodeo Sports News*. Serpa eventually won that magazine's prestigious Silver Buckle Award for rodeo photographs that, as evidenced in her collection *Rodeo* (1994), "threaten to spin, buck, or race right off the page." She has, as one critic observes, "a wonderful sense of composition and design and uses light and atmosphere to give the best of her images depth and texture." Whereas Serpa most often aims her camera at arena (especially roughstock) action scenes, other photographers also roam behind the chutes. Garry Winogrand, as already mentioned, surveyed the Fort Worth Rodeo and Stock Show in all of its variety in *Stock Photographs*. Geoff Winningham shot and narrated a remarkable variety of scenes in his 1972 *Going Texan: The Days of the Houston Livestock Show and Rodeo*. "What I sought," Winningham writes in the introduction to *Going Texan*, "was a clear, personal description of the show and the people who are involved, as I explored it with my camera and tape recorder. Evidence, so to speak, of a contemporary, adopted Texan looking at a celebration of Texas' past and a program for its future."[28]

Douglas Kent Hall added great splashes of color to the repertoire of the rodeo photographer in *Rodeo* (1976). Although Hall's work is composed mostly of black-and-white rodeo imagery, *Rodeo* is noteworthy for its multi-imaged color collages focusing on clowns, rodeo animals, and cowgirls. Other sections center on specific rodeo events, youth rodeo, judging, rodeo school, and life behind the chutes. Hall concludes that "rodeo has inherited all that the Old West had to offer." More recently, photographer Rob Fraser has returned to sepia-toned black-and-white images in his rodeo work. Fraser, a native of Ellensburg, Washington, whose studio is in New York City, recently staged *Broncs, Bulls, and Buckaroos* (Ills. 21, 22). The show, featuring roughstock contestants at work, aims at capturing "the classic confrontation between man and beast that accents, metaphorically, the old-time cowboys' 'winning of the West' from the wild forces of nature."[29]

Rosamund Norbury is Canada's latest photographic interpreter of rodeo and rodeo cowboys. Born in the foothills of the Himalayas and schooled in Paris, she resides now in Vancouver, from whence she hit the Pacific Northwest rodeo road in the 1980s with camera in hand. The result was a series of rodeo-specific shows leading to an important published collection of her photographs, *Behind the Chutes: The Mystique of the Rodeo Cowboy* (1993). Unlike some of the photographers who preceded her (with the notable exceptions of Winogrand and Winningham), Norbury is not so interested in arena action shots as in the backstage social and cultural milieu; hence the title of her collection. Norbury's camera swirls all around the rodeo scene, clicking on cowboys poised for competition or at rest, recording their lifestyle and material culture, focusing on family and interpersonal relationships. *Behind the Chutes* aspires to tell the story of "real people making a hard living at a very difficult and dangerous job."[30]

The sturdy narrative and well-crafted black-and-white photography of *Behind the Chutes* evince myriad facets of North American rodeo. First, Norbury's plentiful helping of Canadian rodeo images helps balance a too-frequent artistic focus on rodeo men south of the forty-ninth parallel. Her work includes the usual shots of roughstock and timed events, while injury and Cowboy Code folk motifs appear in photographs of hurt competitors who nevertheless "'suck it up' and go on to the next ride." There are motel-room images of "wild" beer-swilling bachelor rodeo men who ramble from town to town. Yet family scenes, complete with children and in-laws, portray a less isolated, less individualistic rodeo lifestyle. Unlike the work of some artists, Norbury's rodeo world shows women often and in various poses: marrying rodeo men, keeping house in camper trailers, or participating themselves in mounted rodeo competitions. Photographs of cowboys, hats off, standing at attention for their national anthem, alongside images of churchgoing cowboy members of the Fellowship of Christian Athletes, offer a view of patriotic and devout rodeo men. Thus, in *Behind the Chutes,* Rosamund Norbury blends wild and tame, frontier and civilization, inviting readers to "see through the stereotype of hard drinking, heavy-handed men to meet their families and share the friendships that develop between the bouts on the backs of half-wild animals."[31]

Rodeo art, like cowboy art, occupies a small niche in the history of North American realism. Clifford Westermeier summed this up in his 1954 discussion of cowboy art: "Realism, in its purest form has been the keynote in this school of painting; the approach is one of order and, in most cases, of serenity. Shadow and light, texture, space, and the intricacy of multiple reflection on forms in action and repose are, with imagination and originality, the aims of these artists." Yet Westermeier would no doubt be surprised (and pleased) at the elastic boundaries that realism has, in the past forty years, afforded the rodeo artist. Rodeo Ben's stunning shirts, Red Grooms' *Ruckus Rodeo*, Garry Winogrand's *Stock Photographs*, and of course, Walter Piehl's *Sweethearts of the Rodeo*, to name a few examples, amply demonstrate the great range of possibilities for the contemporary rodeo artist working in the realist tradition.[32]

In the work of rodeo artists as in that of rodeo writers, poets, and singers, the folk connection is apparent, although in different ways. Early rodeo artists were less influenced by folk traditions than were their poet, singer, and novelist counterparts, who could trace their origins directly back to oral folkways, tall-tale sessions, and campfire balladry. The bucking broncs of Charlie Russell and Will James come as close to folk art as any early rodeo art, and there are not many 1920s and 1930s examples of rodeo folk artists. One obvious exception here is Walt LaRue, who is self-trained and drew pictures when he was a rodeo competitor in the pre–World War II years; perhaps Rodeo Ben's work also qualifies, because rodeo-costume art has some direct connections to cowboy folk clothing motifs. Clifford Westermeier fully embraced rodeo folk culture, but he was nevertheless a studio-trained New York painter. Thus rodeo art began on a more or less professional basis, founded upon the work of artists like Russell and Remington and expanded through the efforts of Simpson, Williams, Hurd, Wild West show and rodeo poster artists and cartoonists, Bonner, Mora, Simpson, and Westermeier.

This artistic professionalism has continued, but with interesting and important exceptions. The formation of the PRCAA in 1985 reintroduced powerful folk elements into the emerging field of professional rodeo art. All of the PRCAA artists have been rodeo cowboys, and they bring vital firsthand rodeo experiences to their work. Some are folk artisans, working in media such as silversmithing and producing spurs, fancy tack, and other artifacts in a new rodeo folk art. And although some PRCAA artists are studio trained, many are not. (This fact does not in any way imply that the PRCAA works are unambitious; in fact, the opposite is true.) The PRCAA artists paint and sculpt works that evince a powerful and sometimes coarse aesthetic particularly appropriate and effective in rodeo art.

Today rodeo art grows and matures as a full-fledged subgenre of professional western art, yet it does so with important folk motifs intact. Verbal and nonverbal folklore is obvious in the work of folk and studio-trained rodeo artists. The taming theme is of course ubiquitous, as evidenced in bronco-buster works that descend from oral tales and folksongs such as "The Zebra Dun," "The Strawberry Roan," and "Flyin' U Twister." The danger, injury, and death themes of oral tradition are ever-present in rodeo paintings and sculpture and in the images of photographers such as Winogrand and Norbury. The rodeo folktales (and literature and poetry) about Pete Knight, Casey Tibbs, Freckles Brown, Larry Mahan, and others echo in rodeo folk-hero portraits, dozens of which now hang in the National Cowboy Hall of Fame's R. J. Reynolds Gallery and the ProRodeo Hall of Fame. Rodeo-hero paintings such as Hurd's *Bob Crosby* and Westermeier's *Doff Aber* exude the strength and stoicism of the Cowboy Code—although they do so as professionally composed works of art. Thus, even if the rodeo artists cannot claim direct descent from folk artists, they have incorporated the important verbal and nonverbal rodeo folk themes into their work.

Perhaps a good place to conclude this discussion of rodeo art is where we began it—with the story of Clifford Westermeier's defense of his doctoral dissertation, a tale that sheds considerable light on the paradoxical relationship of high and low art in the rodeo country of the North American West. What makes this anecdote so compelling? What interests us in a bunch of rodeo cowboys attending and participating in a doctoral candidate's dissertation defense? I think it is not overintellectualizing to say the tale is driven by the frontier/civilization theme of cowboy and rodeo oral tradition. In this analysis, the rodeo cowboys of the Westermeier tale represent the forces of the frontier entering the placid halls of academe, which represent the taming forces of civilization. The resulting dialectic is a classic western, but without the violent edge. Between the rodeo cowboys and the Colorado University professors stands Cliff Westermeier, the hero. Westermeier has staked out an intellectual endeavor, but he has done so in good, all-American, anti-intellectual fashion—his dissertation addresses, of all things, cowboy folk culture. In one defining moment the folk and the intellectuals—the frontier and civilization—come together in the seminar room. The intellectuals do their stuff, and then the cowboys show the intellectuals a thing or two, making sure they "get it right." Westermeier mediates all of this, for he is, after all, the anti-intellectual intellectual. Then all parties depart on friendly terms. Civilization has prevailed (Westermeier earned his Ph.D.), but not without a heavy dose of the "Old West" thrown in to help him along the way.

In his sketches and paintings, as in his historical scholarship, Clifford P. Westermeier mediated between the wild and the tame. With all his professional training in New York and Paris, he devoted his artistic talents to painting folk themes of the North American West. He combined his cosmopolitan talents with his love of cowboy folk culture. The result was a rodeo-art subgenre that somehow combines low and high art, folkways and sophistication, the frontier and civilization.

CHAPTER FIVE

"I Ain't Rich but Lord I'm Free"
The Rodeo Cowboy in Country Music

He loves his damned old rodeo as much as he loves me.
—Ian and Sylvia, "Someday Soon" (1964)

Raised on a farm in western Canada, Ian Tyson traversed Saskatchewan, Alberta, and British Columbia as a teenaged migrant laborer and lumberjack in the late 1940s and early 1950s. He hit the rodeo road, competing in roughstock events until 1952, when he was seriously injured at age nineteen. It was after his brief rodeo stint that Tyson turned to art and, ultimately, to folk music, moving to Toronto to pursue a career as a songwriter and singer. There he met Sylvia Fricker, who joined him as artistic collaborator and then in marriage. Their famed folk duo, Ian and Sylvia, made very significant contributions to the folk, folk-rock, and country-rock revivals of the 1960s and 1970s. In some of his best songs, Tyson turned back to his youthful roving through western Canada—for example, in the evocative "Four Strong Winds," a song of migrant Canadian farm laborers. But among Tyson's most compelling songs is one grounded in his experience as a rodeo rider: his country-western ballad "Someday Soon."[1]

First recorded by Ian and Sylvia in 1964, "Someday Soon" has been covered successfully by country and folk artists Judy Collins, Linda Ronstadt, Judy Lynn, Moe Bandy, Chris LeDoux, and Suzy Boggus. It has appeared on the *Billboard* charts on at least three occasions. This popularity can be attributed in part to the compelling melody and to the arrangement and instrumentation (which, interestingly, are very similar in nearly all of the recordings). But equally important to the success of "Someday Soon" is the story it tells.

The song paints a classic picture of the romantic, wandering rodeo cowboy as seen from the perspective of his young lover,. "There's a young man that I know," the sweetheart tells us, "Just turned 21 / Comes from down in southern Colorado." The cowboy, "Just out of the service / and lookin' for his fun," is as infatuated with rodeo as he is with the young woman—indeed, "He loves his damned old rodeo as much as he loves me." But she is a determined girl and is not about to lose him: "Someday soon, goin' with him, someday soon," she promises herself again and again in the song's chorus. In addition to the pull of rodeo on her lover, however, she faces a problem with her parents, who "cannot stand" the cowboy "'cause he works the rodeo." Her father refuses to welcome him when he comes to call (she speculates on this behavior: "Got a hunch he was just as wild / back in the early days"). Her parents warn of the cowboy that "he's not your kind, he'll leave you cryin'," but she remains true to her sweetheart. "So blow you old blue norther / Blow him back to me / He's likely drivin' back from California." At the end of the song she can still sing, "I'll follow him down the toughest row to hoe / Someday soon, goin' with him, someday soon."[2]

"Someday Soon" stands as a classic rodeo song alongside Tyson's "Leaving Cheyenne" and creations by country-and-western songwriters and singers Chris LeDoux, Red Steagall, Garth Brooks, George Strait, and many others. Although rodeo music is not a dominant force in country-music history, it has enlivened the country genre from the earliest times onward. There is an important connection between working cowboys, rodeo cowboys, and country music, and rodeo songs form a subgenre within country music that features certain themes. Like the rodeo movies, folktales, novels, poetry, and art that we have examined, these themes are Turnerian—they draw upon archetypal Cowboy Code traits to portray a rodeo-cowboy hero, this time in the folk-based artistic medium of country music. Nearly all of the rodeo songs emphasize in some way or another the individualistic traits of the rodeo-cowboy folk hero: his wanderlust, stoicism, courage, pride, humor, attitudes toward rodeo animals and the wild, and ambivalence toward women. Thus, as do other artistic and popular-culture forms, rodeo music addresses the frontier/civilization dialectic and the role of the rodeo cowboy as a forceful but ultimately ambivalent "civilizer."[3]

To fully investigate rodeo music we must return to the cattle frontier of the last half of the nineteenth century and to Anglo-American and Celtic American folk-music traditions. The origins of contemporary rodeo music lie in the folk songs and poetry of American cowboys. American cowboy life was steeped in an oral tradition, which included a small but interesting cowboy-music genre. Today folklorists agree with Guy Logsdon that poems and tales dominated cowboy oral traditions and that images of "singing cowboys" have been romanticized and overdrawn by twentieth-century popularizers. Nevertheless, during the height of the cattle kingdom of the 1870s and 1880s, working cowboys incorporated and adapted some traditional Anglo-American and Celtic American poetry and folk songs to form a cowboy-music tradition. Again, one should avoid here notions of Autry/Rogers "singing cowboys" and emphasize instead a small, coarse, and untutored folk-music tradition. Cowboys did sing on occasion for diverse reasons. After a long day in the saddle, hands relaxed and entertained one another with songs, poems, and stories around the campfire. Singing also served the practical purpose of preventing runaways and stampedes by soothing restless cattle as they grazed at night. So cowboys relaxing around the campfire or at work circling the herd during night watch sang, without instrumental accompaniment, the refrains of "Streets of Laredo," "Sam Bass," and "Bucking Bronco."[4]

Rodeo songs stem from a motif in cowboy poetry and folk songs relating specifically to bronc busters—that special breed of cowboys who excelled in the art of riding and subduing wild horses. One of the earliest of these songs is "Bucking Bronco." Sung from a supposedly female perspective, the lyrics celebrate the bronc buster for his horsemanship and his prowess with women. In language much saltier than most rodeo songs that would follow, cowboy minstrels sang, "Lie still ye young bastard, don't bother me so / Your father's off bucking, another broncho." Even more explicit is a subsequent verse, "He will rope you and throw you, and when you're fast tied / Down on your bare belly, Lord God how he'll ride."[5]

One of the most respected cowboy-folksong collectors was Glenn Ohrlin, a working cowboy who also competed in professional rodeo during the late 1940s and 1950s. In Ohrlin's collections we can see the presence of cowboy bronco-busting folk songs in an emerging rodeo music of the first half of the twentieth century. A good example of this connection is "The Strawberry Roan," a nonrodeo song based on cowboy and rodeo rider Curley Fletcher's famous 1914 poem (see chapter 3) about a "bronc fighter" looking for some "bad ones to tame." The cowboy gets his wish and finds his match in a "regular outlaw" horse that "ain't never been rode." The bronc rider enters the fray confidently, "For the bronc never lived or ever drew breath / That I couldn't ride till he starved plumb to death," but he soon finds he has bitten off more than he can chew:

> He turned his old belly right up to the sun.
> He sure is a sunfishin' son of a gun.
> He was the worst bucker I seen on the range,
> He can turn on a nickel and give you some change.

The bronco buster soon finds himself "a-settin' up there in the sky," and when he comes back to earth he is a much humbled cowboy: "I bet all my money the man ain't alive / Can ride old Strawberry when he makes his high drive."[6]

Interestingly, "The Strawberry Roan" celebrates the bronc more than the bronc buster—an attitude that appears in several rodeo songs that followed. But Ohrlin also collected folk songs and poems lionizing early rodeo roughstock riders, for example, "Fritz Truan, a Great Cowboy" and "Kenny Madland." The words to these songs circulated by word of mouth and/or appeared in rodeo trade journals such as *Hoof and Horns* and *Western Horseman*. Pete Knight, a world-champion bronc rider from 1932 through 1935 is celebrated in "Pete Knight," a song of the folk genre that mourns that fallen hero. The song touts Knight as "a rider of horses / The best that I ever did see," and then warns: "But often a life in the saddle / Is not what it's cracked up to be." After the bronc Duster trampled Pete Knight, "Ten thousand fans saw him carried / Away from the field and the horse."[7]

"The Strawberry Roan" and "Pete Knight" spanned folk and commercial music traditions as they spawned 1920s, 1930s, and 1940s covers and spinoffs that form a rodeo-music subgenre of country-and-western music. Curley Fletcher's "Bad Brahma Bull" took the motif of "The Strawberry Roan" off the range and into the rodeo arena, as our bronc buster turned bull rider finds himself catapulted from a Brahma who has "got big horns that looks pretty bad / He weighs a good ton and that whole ton is mad." "Bad Brahma Bull" and Everett Cheatham's "Blood on the Saddle" were both popular and important rodeo tunes of this era. Meanwhile, Kenneth S. Clark collected and published a 1930s song folio, *Songs for the Rodeo*, and Dakotan George P. German and Canadian country artist Wilf Carter (a.k.a. "Montana Slim") became pioneers in the field of commercial rodeo music, regularly performing and recording the songs of Curley Fletcher and others. They were joined by a very small number of country artists who performed and recorded rodeo songs in the post–World War II years.[8]

In the 1950s, bronc rider Johnny Baker became the first musician to dedicate his career solely to rodeo music. Baker eventually wrote, produced, recorded, and marketed at least four rodeo albums, *Songs of the Rodeo* (1964), *Let 'er Buck* (1965), *Rodeoin' with Johnny Baker* (1966), and *The Rodeo in the Sky* (1974). These obscure albums explore the bronc-buster motif in such songs as "Son, Don't Ride the Buckin' Bronco," "Ballad of Billy the Bull Rider," and "Don't Hang off the Side." Baker expanded the rodeo-music genre, exploring the mystique of non-roughstock events, the nomadic lifestyle of rodeo men, their view of animals, and their shifting attitudes toward women. Songs like "Rodeo Widow," "Small Town Show," "Timed Event Blues," "Microphone Bandit," and "Easy Rider" are based on the oral traditions and taletypes in which Baker was himself immersed during his rodeo-cowboy years. These songs greatly expanded the number of themes available to future rodeo-music artists.[9]

Meanwhile, the noncommercial folk song tradition continued among rodeo cowboys, although in much reduced form. Scattered throughout modern rodeo cowboys' reminiscences are references to songfests behind the chutes and late-night singing in motel rooms. Bronc rider Chris LeDoux writes of "six or seven of us riders . . . in a motel room, passing a guitar around for hours" in the 1970s. But just as all occupational folk groups saw folk song traditions greatly diminished by the introduction of phonographs, tape players, and mass-marketed country-western music, the rodeo cowboy also turned to the new electronic media. Thus the important rodeo songs of the last half of the twentieth century are found on records and tapes of a burgeoning and diverse country-western rodeo-music subgenre.[10]

Ironically, it was the long-haired folk, folk-rock, and country-rock musicians[11] of the Vietnam War era—the 1960s and early 1970s—who first successfully tapped and marketed the rodeo mystique. In so doing, they demonstrated the counterculture's pronounced fascination with rural mystique—a hippie fascination that manifested itself also in rodeo movies, literature, and art. Ian and Sylvia recorded "Someday Soon" on their 1964 folk LP *Northern Journey,* and the song flourished in 1968 when Colorado folksinger Judy Collins covered it on *Who Knows Where the Time Goes.* Collins wisely chose to add drums, bass, and pedal steel guitar on "Someday Soon," thus completing the transition from folk music to country. This was no coincidence, as 1968 marked the birth of country-rock music with the Byrds' landmark album *Sweetheart of the Rodeo.* Although the album does not feature any rodeo songs per se, its striking Jo Mora cover illustration bathed country rock in the rodeo myth. When the Byrds followed with "Chestnut Mare," perhaps the most effective (albeit psychedelic!) bronco-busting song in the country-rock genre, these hippies laid permanent claim to a piece of the symbolism of rodeo. "Chestnut Mare" directly addressed traditional folk bronco-busting songs like "The Strawberry Roan." Sung by Byrd Roger McGuinn, it showed the Cowboy Code bond between man and horse, and used the bronc chase as a metaphor for the quest for meaning in life:

> I lost my hold, and she got away,
> but I'm going to catch her again some day.
> I'm going to catch that horse if I can,
> and when I do I'll give her my brand.
> And we'll be friends for life.
> She'll be just like a wife.
> I'm going to catch that horse if I can.[12]

The Byrds were followed by scores of country rockers, including Great Speckled Bird (Ian and Sylvia Tyson's group), Poco, the Flying Burrito Brothers, Gram Parsons, Emmylou Harris, Linda Ronstadt and the Eagles, Mason Proffit, Commander Cody and the Lost Planet Airmen, and the Nitty Gritty Dirt Band. All of these musicians were enamored of western imagery and the cowboy mystique, as evidenced by Great Speckled Bird's live performances of "Someday Soon," their fellow Canadian Buffy Sainte-Marie's recording of "He's an Indian Cowboy in the

Rodeo," the Burrito Brothers' cover of the Rolling Stones' "Wild Horses,"
and Mason Proffit's double album *Bareback Rider.* It was the Nitty Gritty
Dirt Band that covered Michael Martin Murphey's "Cosmic Cowboy,"
singing in a long-haired country-boy vein:

> I just want to be a Cosmic Cowboy
> I just want to ride and rope and shoot
> Wahoo!
> I just want to be a Cosmic Cowboy
> A supernatural, country rockin' galoot![13]

The sight of the long-haired Byrds performing selections from
Sweetheart of the Rodeo in their late-1960s Grand Ole Opry appearance
must have deeply disconcerted country-western diehards, and certainly
rodeo cowboys. But in "The Cowboy and the Hippie," the singer/
songwriter tells an autobiographical tale that reaches a different conclusion about the relationship between cowboy culture and the counterculture. True, the singer notes, most rodeo folks believe that "cowboys and
hippies ain't never got along," but he relates an experience that changed
his mind on that count. "Down on his luck" on a lonely desert highway,
a rodeo cowboy finds himself hitchhiking alongside a hippie. The cowboy is initially repulsed by this "long-haired freak" and does not hesitate to comment on his "stinking" aroma, adding, "Boy, you're a disgrace
to the human race." But the hippie counters with some jibes of his own
concerning "the green stuff" on the cowboy's boots and jeans—"it's
enough to make a buzzard belch!" Then, refusing to fight, the hippie
voices what amounts to a soliloquy celebrating the free, wandering
lifestyle that the two, in parallel, enjoy:

> You know, man, in a lot of ways we're an awful lot alike,
> once you get down beneath the skin.
> Like two books with different covers but the same words inside,
> we're both brothers of the wind.

Now we both love our freedom and we'll answer to no man,
and you've heard it said, 'to thine own self be true.'
We're just a couple of free spirits driftin' across the land.
Doin' exactly what we wanta do.

"I don't see why we can't get along," the hippie observes, and the rodeo cowboy finds himself shaking hands, drawn to the hippie's down-home philosophy. Although they soon leave the desert and go their separate ways, the cowboy has come to understand in a broader sense the Cowboy Code to which all rodeo cowboys subscribe: "The closest thing to freedom is livin' on the road / in a country where freedom's almost gone."[14]

The author of "The Cowboy and the Hippie" was Chris LeDoux, former world-champion saddle bronc rider and North America's foremost rodeo-song composer and singer. LeDoux is the best example of what Elizabeth Atwood Lawrence describes as a close association between country music and the rodeo community. Born in 1948 into an Air Force family, LeDoux became interested in horses when his father was stationed near Austin, Texas, in the early 1960s. He soon took up rodeoing as an arena-trained cowboy; he won a rodeo scholarship to Casper College in Wyoming but dropped out to join the Professional Rodeo Cowboys Association and pursue a career as a bronc rider. LeDoux married Peggy Rhoads in 1972, and they had five children while he continued to pursue an elusive gold buckle in bareback bronc riding. He won the world championship in 1976. LeDoux continued to compete sporadically until 1984, but as he recalls, "I didn't quite have the same fire, so I decided to move on to something else." Rodeo had lost a bronc rider but gained its most gifted country-western singer-composer.[15]

Chris LeDoux had written and performed rodeo songs throughout his stint as an active rodeo contestant—selling cassettes through his family's Wyoming mail-order business and playing dances to supplement his income. In the 1980s, as a full-time professional musician, he developed a cult following among rodeo aficionados and savvy country-western music fans. In the early 1990s he was at last thrust into the national entertainment spotlight. Although LeDoux is now branching out into nonrodeo songs, his career is nevertheless anchored in his rodeo music. To date, he has written and recorded so many songs about rodeo (his mail-order catalog lists over twenty-five separately titled cassette recordings) that he is easily the world's foremost rodeo song stylist.[16]

"The Cowboy and the Hippie" is not Chris LeDoux's most famous or popular song, but it shows his innovative style—his ability to blend important new motifs and variants while maintaining the integrity of the country-western rodeo-song subgenre. This is an essential talent, for the rodeo subgenre could easily become redundant for a performer like LeDoux, devoting entire long-play recordings exclusively to rodeo songs. He avoids redundancy also by pacing his albums with fast and slow tunes, including some rock and roll, balanced by traditional country motifs, as well as by incorporating a variety of thematic interpretations of rodeo. For example, on every one of LeDoux's albums there are at the very least two songs (one is always the leadoff tune—side one, number one) that directly address the mystique of the rodeo cowboy and define for the listener the central themes of the Cowboy Code and the rodeo-cowboy myth. "Lord, I've Got to Be a Rodeo Man," "Born to Follow Rodeo," "He Rides the Wild Horses," "Goin' and a' Blowin',", and "A Cowboy's Got to Ride" are all signature tunes that define the rodeo man, his lifestyle, his state of mind, and the Cowboy Code tenets to which he adheres.

"Don't everybody know? A cowboy's got to ride," LeDoux tells his listeners in one of these archetypal tunes. "Lord, I ain't really a bum," he explains in another, "But this rodeo life's got its hold on me / And there ain't no way it'll set me free / You know I've got to be—a rodeo man." Thus we see that from LeDoux's artistic perspective, the rodeo cowboy is driven by powerful forces—spiritual forces—to follow the rodeo life: "There's a great big world just waitin' out there for you." But a cowboy has to hurt and disappoint friends and loved ones when he opts to hit the rodeo road. "Your mamma finds it hard to understand / Why her lovin' son wants to be a rodeo man," and "Your best girl thinks it's time you settled down . . . she's ready for a wedding gown." According to LeDoux, these steady, unadventurous folk have "a whole lot of great big plans" for their rodeo man but don't "really know how you feel inside." They don't understand why a rodeo cowboy must give up home, marriage, and financial security to do what he does. They can only shake their heads and say, "Man, you've gone insane."[17]

Yet, Chris LeDoux sings, the rodeo man knows that these people can *never* understand, and that some of them are really only jealous. "They're all working nine to five," while the cowboy is "foot-loose and fancy-free." Once the cowboy has made his choice to hit the rodeo road, he separates himself physically and spiritually from the drudgerous life of the common North American workingman. LeDoux's archetypal rodeo man rejects the twentieth century and its rush-hour traffic and materialism, and returns instead to the world of his Plains cowboy ancestors. Free at last, he becomes one of the chosen, one of the special breed of men "a-headin' down the road," down the "highways and backroads" of America. Bound for the next rodeo, he is "drivin' all night 'neath the pale moonlight . . . flying high on caffeine and Copenhagen / And breathin' that cool night air." LeDoux concludes: "It's a mighty tough life, but I like it all right / You know I wouldn't have it any other way."[18]

Like the best of the rodeo moviemakers, writers, poets, and painters, Chris LeDoux confronts the relationship of man and animal. And like these other artists, he shows an ambivalent strain in his attitude. On the one hand, he sings of wild broncs as dangerous beasts whose only purpose in life is to be ridden by the rodeo cowboy. A note of apprehension is always evident. A bronc "comes boiling out and blows up at the roof"; another emerges "kicking like a curly wolf." The broncs are clearly formidable, fearsome adversaries, but the rodeo cowboy who can ride and rope them is the song's only hero. On the other hand, LeDoux sometimes expresses admiration and even a feeling of kinship for the wild critters of rodeo. Although the cowboy's job is to ride and rope, he cannot help respecting these wild animal remnants of the Old West. Indeed, if all the broncs were broken, the cowboy would be out of a job, and this can never be. Thus "He Rides the Wild Horses" paints a picture that stresses the common wildness of cowboy and bronc. The "rodeo drifter" has a spirit "as wild as the horses he rides." LeDoux extends the metaphor of the wild horse in sounding the themes of freedom and mobility: the rodeo man will "never be broke—he won't be tied down / He'll never wear no man's brand." Thus a more reverent attitude toward the rodeo animals emerges, because they share traits with their cowboy adversary:

> And he rides the wild horses.
> The same blood flows through their veins.
> Yes, he rides the wild horses.
> And like the horses, he'll never be tamed.[19]

LeDoux's interpretation of women in his rodeo songs also shows some ambivalence and, resultantly, some innovation in the rodeo-music subgenre. The rodeo-cowboy mystique, like that of the Plains cowboy, has traditionally held precious little space for women. Women represent tameness and civilization, bad news for any true cowboy, and most writers, moviemakers, and songwriters have made sure that their rodeo men steer clear of females. LeDoux certainly hews to this tradition in songs like "Born to Follow Rodeo" and "A Cowboy's Got to Ride," which describe an itinerant rodeo life that leaves no room for a wife and family. Yet LeDoux's 1972 marriage to Peggy Rhoads, who traveled with him during much of his career, has obviously made a deep impression on a handful of songs that show a different attitude. In some of these sentimental songs, it seems that there might be room for a woman in a cowboy's life—but only for the *right* woman, i.e., one who will let him rodeo and support him in his rambling ways *temporarily* while they save enough to buy some land and settle down to a life of cattle ranching. Thus, like the hero and heroine in *The Virginian,* Bud and Sissy in *Urban Cowboy,* and (as we will see) Lane Frost and his wife, Kellie, in *8 Seconds,* some of LeDoux's rodeo couples search for a middle road between the frontier and civilization—a home on the range. These rodeo couples are truly *contemporary ancestors.*

In "Our First Year," LeDoux describes a newly married rodeo couple "headed down the road," making the rodeo circuit in an old truck, camping each night beside a stream, and cooking meals outdoors. "She cheered me on at every rodeo" and "never complained when the winnings didn't come." Even when "the baby started showin'," this cowboy's bride stood by her man, wore his oversized clothes in lieu of the maternity outfits they could not afford, and fried him eggs for breakfast over an open fire (morning sickness evidently notwithstanding). But there is some light at the end of the tunnel for "that little girl I married." At the end of this cowboy's rodeo road lies "the house we planned down there beside the stream" and a stable family life in which "all those hard times" will be "just cherished memories." Another song written for Peggy, "The Greatest Prize," echoes a similar message as a rodeo champion praises the wife who "stuck by me through thick and thin." When "the lights were shining on me and me alone / You stood back in the shadows," but again this loyalty is repaid:

> Of all the things I've ever done
> I have to tell you true.
> The greatest prize I've ever won,
> Is the love I won from you.[20]

In making some place for women and marriage in the rodeo man's life, LeDoux injects a healthy dose of historical reality into the rodeo-song subgenre, for the happy, swashbuckling, rambling rodeo man is, arguably, largely a figment of the male imagination. LeDoux describes two different kinds of rodeo men in his music—the rambling bachelors and the more stable married men—but that is not the only paradox he creates. The myth of the hard-drinking, self-destructive rodeo man is also debunked. In "So You Want to Be a Cowboy," LeDoux implores would-be rodeo contestants to "lay off hard liquor, and leave them pills alone / They'll only dull the senses and leave you weak and stoned." If you want to be a top hand, LeDoux warns, you had better make "caffeine and Copenhagen" your mind-altering substances of choice.[21]

This temperance theme is unique to LeDoux and conspicuously absent from other artists' rodeo songs. Yet it is based on reality, for although there are many exceptions (Casey Tibbs comes immediately to mind), most rodeo champions have to play it straight. But like the appearance of a married cowboy in some LeDoux songs, the temperance theme adds reality at the expense of the music's virility. One of rodeo music's great strengths has always been its heavy reliance on the cowboy myth, including woman avoidance and substance abuse. These "qualities" are part and parcel of the Cowboy Code and the rodeo-cowboy mystique. In introducing a dash of reality into a few of his tunes, LeDoux ultimately waters down the message of his more numerous songs promoting that myth. These thematic contradictions weaken his work but ultimately do not, I think, decrease its importance. In his songwriting, as in his rodeo career, LeDoux has always been a gambler and an innovator. He is the most prolific and accomplished rodeo singer-songwriter to date.

The Texan cowboy poet Red Steagall is also a singer-songwriter, one whose rodeo songs, although not as numerous as those of Chris LeDoux, are every bit as authentic, polished, and ambitious. Steagall has produced only one rodeo album, but what an album it is. Steagall and the Coleman County Cowboys' *For All Our Cowboy Friends* serves up some of the most powerful and evocative music in the rodeo subgenre. Its authenticity comes from a very close connection with the rodeo world. Born in Gainesville, Texas, Red Steagall, like Chris LeDoux, cultivated an interest in rodeo simultaneously with a talent for singing and writing folk and country music. Steagall enjoyed a very brief stint as a bull rider, but the effects of childhood polio made a rodeo career impossible. He studied animal husbandry at West Texas State University in Canyon while simultaneously working the coffeehouse folk-music circuit. He first became involved in country music as a songwriter but in 1969 signed a recording contract. He helped to spearhead the western-swing revival with a 1976 album, *Lone Star Beer and Bob Wills Music*. Throughout this time, however, he remained interested in rodeo and pursued professional opportunities as a rodeo musician, playing numerous concerts and dances held in conjunction with North America's top rodeos. He became a favorite among the rodeo men and women and satisfied a lifelong ambition by meeting and becoming close friends with many top hands. Indeed, he was as much a part of the rodeo world as a noncompetitor can ever be. The culmination of this passion for rodeo was *For All Our Cowboy Friends*, a recording that I believe is—Chris LeDoux's fine work notwithstanding—the definitive rodeo album.[22]

Steagall's lyrics, instrumentation, and arrangements are more complex and engaging than those of most rodeo musicians, probably because of his western-swing origins, which place him a little closer to jazz in the country-music spectrum. Then too, there is a pronounced Hispanic—"Tex-Mex"—guitar influence in his songs. Combined with a savvy for arrangement and pacing of album cuts, all of this makes *Cowboy Friends* a genuine work of folk-based musical art. The album opens with a prologue—"Rodeo"—which introduces the listener to the rodeo folk festival and the themes and aims of the album. "Rodeo, you're a part of America," Steagall sings, imploring Americans, "don't let the cowboy be a dyin' breed." In the next selection, "For All Our Cowboy Friends," Steagall hones his description of the rodeo mystique and goes on to dedicate the album to the professional rodeo men of North America, mentioning prominent competitors—Larry Mahan, Roy Cooper, Donnie Gay, "Hawkeye," and many more—by name. Thus Steagall literally includes the men of rodeo in the music in a very unusual, recorded public tribute. At the same time, he lets nonrodeo listeners know that he is on a first-name basis with all of the rodeo greats and is thus himself an authoritative spokesman for rodeo.[23]

Using his grounding in cowboy poetry, Steagall relies heavily on oral narrative in *Cowboy Friends,* often talking in traditional cowboy vernacular with musical accompaniment. "The Night the Copenhagen Saved the Day" is an entirely spoken folktale that portrays rodeo cowboys as hard-drinking, snuff-chewing, boisterous tricksters. A bunch of cowboys are on a spree in a rodeo town, "shootin' pool and drinkin' tubs of beer" and, of course, courting the local women. The frolic turns dangerous when a local man—a fellow as big as "Genghis Khan"—arrives unexpectedly to find his girlfriend partying with the cowboys. Things look mighty grim until one of the rodeo hands fixes "that dude a drink" made up of the spit from all of the cowboys' snoose cups. "Well that big ol' boy took one big gulp and looked like he was shot / and a bunch of cowboys grabbed a batch of gone." Thus the cowboys use trickery, not violence, to outfox a tough noncowboy foe who "still can't believe we got away." And "there's a bunch of cowboys that ain't likely to forget / the night the Copenhagen saved the day."[24]

Steagall exploits, in unique and entertaining ways, the classic rodeo themes of wild animals and cowboys' relationships with women. The former are the subject of "Bandito Gold," sung in first-person narrative. For nearly its entirety, the song seems to be only about a young boy and the colt, Bandito Gold, that he raises and loves during their youths on the Texas Plains. Then a drought strikes and the boy's father is forced to sell Bandito Gold. There follow two verses in which Steagall moves his human protagonist ahead in time ten years; the memory of Bandito Gold fades as the boy grows up to be a rodeo roughstock rider. The song's last verse creates an abrupt and startling climax:

It's my turn to ride, my horse is in chute 5,
and I've checked the rein and pulled my saddle tight.

Way out in Idaho, at the Twin Falls Rodeo,
I've drawn the outlaw horse, Bandito Gold.

The colt that he lost as a boy has ended up in a rodeo roughstock string, and the two old friends have become adversaries. As in LeDoux's "He Rides the Wild Horses," the rodeo cowboy's ambivalence toward the wild and the tame is presented in dramatic fashion.[25]

Ambivalence is also apparent regarding women in Steagall's songs. In "Tight Levis and Yellow Ribbons," much as in the folk song "Bucking Bronco," women are likened to bucking stock, and the process of breaking the bronc is used as a metaphor for a sexual liaison. Interestingly, women in this song represent forces of the wild, mares that the cowboy "knows he'll never break to ride." By contrast, "Two Pairs of Levis and a Pair of Justin Boots" is an archetypal statement of the principle that cowboys and stable female relationships don't mix. Here the rodeo man is abandoned by a mate who has run completely out of patience with his unorthodox lifestyle. She leaves, taking with her everything in the house save the jeans and boots of the song's title, but the cowboy is glad to see her go.[26]

More complex and more successful is Steagall's tender love story of the rodeo cowboy Dawson Legate and his long-suffering but loyal wife. Set on the High Plains of North America and performed with evocative Spanish guitar work underneath, "Dawson Legate" tells the tragic story of a rodeo man who tries to settle down with his true love to a life of ranching, only to be drawn irresistibly back to the arena. As the song begins, Legate, a bronc-riding champ, has returned to his wife and their small cattle ranch and "hung his old [rodeo] saddle up high in the barn." Promising his wife that "his cowboyin' is done," he begins to improve the ranch, plant crops, and herd cattle, resolving to "spend my last years here with you." But he ranches only until after their first harvest. Then his feet start "itchin'" and he secretly enters the Calgary Stampede. Even though he wins first prize in bronc riding,

> She cried when he showed her the money he'd won
> She knew by the first light of day he'd be gone
> But he promised he'd quit when the season was through
> He'd be home to plant wheat 'fore winter winds blew.

The song continues: "Now the summer went fast, he was ridin' them all / He placed high at Cheyenne and a first at Sioux Falls." Things are going well for Dawson; he is sending money home. "But then life for a cowboy don't go like it should"; he draws "a bad one at 'Frisco that Fall / A mean one to ride, he was a chute fightin' hoss." Exploding out into the arena, the bronc stumbles, falls, and rolls. "As his neck snapped like straw, Dawson's body grew cold." Thus, in the tradition of "Pete Knight" and countless rodeo movies, folktales, ballads, novels, poems, and artworks, Steagall tells the story of a brave rodeo cowboy who meets a tragic death while challenging a wild bronc.

Folk origins are only one component of the power of "Dawson Legate." The song imparts an evocative image of the North American High Plains moving through the planting, harvest, and winter seasons. Evincing an intimate knowledge of ranching life, Steagall sings of the workaday world of the Plains ranch families, the wheat and white oats that they raise, the cattle ("Baldies") they "run in the hills," and the "bad weeds" that grow up there. This picture of the land combines with another important theme of the song—the role of a woman in the rodeo cowboy's life—to provide a lyrical chorus and, ultimately, a profoundly moving conclusion to "Dawson Legate." Throughout the song we hear of the harsh high-country winters that "get long up out our way" and the clouds "so dark at times there's no light of day." These vivid images form a backdrop for another image, that of the rodeo man's lonely but loyal woman. In this dark, blue, brooding winter, the young wife spends long nights patiently waiting, waiting "as she dreams of a cowboy named Dawson Legate." This chorus is repeated until the cowboy's death, when the music suddenly stops. Then the chorus is reintroduced in a slow, spoken narrative, stripped of all instrumental background except the Spanish guitar and reworded to provide a compelling epilogue to the piece:

> Now the bad weeds have taken the flatlands again.
> There's a few strands of wire where the fences have been.
> The Baldies are starvin' in the hills where they graze,
> While she's rockin' the first son of Dawson Legate.[27]

Side one of *For All Our Cowboy Friends* ends with yet another bronc-busting/bull-riding song, but "Freckles Brown" possesses none of the somber qualities of "Dawson Legate." Like its folk song predecessors "Fritz Truan, a Great Cowboy" and "Kenny Madland," this is a tale in which the cowboy triumphs and becomes a hero to the rodeo community. The song is based on Brown's epic 1967 ride on Tornado, and although not so ambitious and lyrical as "Dawson Legate," it is nevertheless an exciting and tightly woven portrait of the rodeo-cowboy folk hero. Musically, it is a hard-driving western-swing tune decorated by the Spanish acoustic guitar that characterizes much of Steagall's work. But in addition there is an up-tempo acoustic rhythm guitar driving constantly underneath, and a pedal steel guitar providing striking transitions and responses throughout. Steagall does not quite *sing* the song— rather, the lyrics are half sung and half spoken, resembling the spoken narrative folktale and cowboy poem. The exception is the chorus, which Steagall sings joined by a tight harmony voice underneath. Finally, the arrangement is effectively peppered with the roar of an actual rodeo crowd, fading in and reaching a crescendo at the moment when Freckles successfully rides Tornado. The overall effect is very exciting, recreating the atmosphere of Brown's famed ride.

In the first verse Steagall introduces the National Finals Rodeo and the night of December 1, 1967:

> In Chute 2 is a cowboy we all know
> He's a young man now of 46 and he's made a mighty draw

The bull is from Jim Shoulders' string
Tornado's how he's known
Yes Freckles Brown has drawn a bull no one has ever rode.

From this point Steagall taps his intimate knowledge of rodeo, carefully narrating Brown's preparations in the chute, his lowering himself on "dark red hide," his intricate wrapping of the bull rope, and the moment of truth as the gate swings open and Freckles says, "Let's ride!" Suddenly "2,000 pounds of boilin' hell was turnin' inside out / And showin' four feet to the Lord." With the roar of "8,000 fans" rising underneath, the buzzer sounds; it "seemed the whole world exploded as Freckles hit the ground." "A cowboy hero born that day and Freckles totes the load / 200 times that bull had bucked, the first time he'd been rode!"

On the surface "Freckles Brown" appears simple enough: rodeo cowboy rides wild beast. Yet there is an epilogue to the song that shows a much more complex relationship between man and bull. Steagall reminds us that the cowboy is not the only hero of this piece; "you know, Tornado gets some [credit] too / 'Cause without the bull to show him off / no cowboy's got a call." Interestingly, Steagall then borrows a motif from cowboy poetry and balladry and paints a picture of life after death— heaven after the range—but this time a heaven for rodeo critters as well as rodeo cowboys. He sings that he is sure that "bulls have got a heaven" and hopes that "Tornado's up there, and the Lord has let him through." Then, tapping his knowledge of animal husbandry and ranch workways for just the right touch, he concludes:

I hope his pasture is the greenest,
and his stock tank's never dry.
I hope there ain't a single spur
to gouge his ugly hide.
And I hope the cowboys up there
keep him fat and treat him kind.

And I hope he lives forever,
on bunch grass belly-high.[28]

Reviewing the many rodeo songs of Chris LeDoux and Red Steagall, it is obvious, again, that LeDoux is the foremost rodeo songwriter and singer, while Steagall has produced what is arguably the finest long-play recording about rodeo. Together, they weave into their music the rodeo Cowboy Code themes of courage, freedom, wanderlust, individualism, plain talk, stoicism in the face of physical pain, respect for animals, and ambivalence toward women and romantic relationships. Like other artists portraying rodeo-cowboy heroes from Jeff McCloud to Sonny Shanks to Junior Bonner, LeDoux and Steagall paint a portrait of a rodeo-cowboy *contemporary ancestor*—a Plains cowboy born a century too late, drifting along the twentieth-century North American rodeo road.

Although LeDoux and Steagall are the best-known contemporary rodeo songwriters and performers, the themes of rodeo appear in many other works of contemporary country music. This not to say that rodeo music is a dominant force in country music—rodeo songs have always been and no doubt will always be only a small accoutrement to the repertoire of country-music songwriters and entertainers. Yet rodeo songs form a persistent subgenre that continually appears in country musicians' repertoires. Elizabeth Atwood Lawrence has examined in some detail the connection between rodeo and country music, and especially the rodeo songs of contemporary country artists. Although focusing on Chris LeDoux, she also interprets the work of Red Steagall, Michael Burton, Michael S. McGinnis, Lealand Dwayne Pack, Duke Benson Pack, Gary McMahan, Chimp Robertson, Bill Staines, Frank Dycus, and many others who have written and performed rodeo songs. More recently, the Sweethearts of the Rodeo have surfaced as a popular country female duo, borrowing their name (and, with it, the power of the rodeo mystique) from the Byrds' album. North of the forty-ninth parallel, the Canadian group Blue Rodeo has tapped the rodeo myth, and there are many other examples of the rodeo influence on the contemporary country-music scene. Bruce Ford, five-time PRCA bareback-riding champion, has recorded a country album; so has Libby Hurley, a nationally ranked barrel racer from Alaska. In a 1988 episode of television's *48 Hours* documenting rodeo, Americans heard the songs of Monty "Hawkeye" Henson, a world-champion saddle bronc rider turned country singer. (Hawkeye's riding feats and quick wit have made him a legendary figure among rodeo cowboys; his name surfaces several times in Steagall's *For All Our Cowboy Friends.*) Finally, country singer Reba McEntire is a former barrel racer who boasts a father, grandfather, and ex-husband who are all former world-champion steer wrestlers and ropers. Reminiscing about a childhood spent "rodeoin'" and traveling the rodeo road, McEntire today reflects that "we were on the road so much that it kind of trained me to be on the road now. That's why I don't mind it so much."[29]

Garth Brooks, one of the giant stars of 1990s country music, did not make his meteoric rise without recording an important rodeo song. On *Ropin' the Wind* (1991) Brooks performed Larry Bastian's "Rodeo." The song ultimately climbed to the top of the country and pop singles charts. "Rodeo" utilizes the motif of many other rodeo songs in its interpretation of women; the story is the classic one of a woman whose cowboy lover finds rodeo more compelling than her. Bastian even borrows a lyric lick from Ian Tyson in saying that "damned old rodeo" is taking the cowboy away:

> [H]is need for it controls him
> and her back's against the wall
> And it's 'So long girl, I'll see you'
> when it's time for him to go.

Although "Rodeo" relies on this tried-and-true motif, it is nevertheless a very atypical rodeo song. For one thing, it is not performed in tra-

ditional country style, but as a bluesy rock number devoid of country
vocal and instrumental stylings. But the really striking feature of "Rodeo" is its lyrics, which are sensuous while at times flirting with violence. As sung by Brooks, the song has a much more dangerous tone than
"Someday Soon" or the early rodeo road tunes of Chris LeDoux. Rodeo
is here portrayed as a powerful addiction—"his need for it controls
him"—that will "drive the man insane." Indeed, this rodeo cowboy will
sell everything he owns just to play the game:

> And a broken home and some broken bones
> is all he'll have to show
> for all the years he spent chasin'
> this dream they call Rodeo.

This rough edge is blended with a mood that must be described as, in
a strange way, sexual. Rodeo is cast in the female persona, a competitor
for the cowboy's love. Moreover, images of physiological substances, the
human and animal bodies, the earth, and the roaring crowd all combine
in a sensuous chorus:

> Well, it's bulls and blood,
> it's dust and mud,
> it's the roar of the Sunday crowd.
> It's the white in the knuckles,
> the gold in the buckle.
> He'll win the next go 'round.
> It's boots and chaps,
> it's cowboy hats,
> it's spurs and latigo.
> It's the rope and the reins,
> and the joy and the pain.
> And they call the thing Rodeo.[30]

A rock-and-roll arrangement thus combines with earthy lyrics to create a rodeo song that approaches an old motif in a striking new way. But bold as it is, most rodeo-song aficionados will not remember Brooks's "Rodeo" as the signature rodeo song of the post—*For All Our Cowboy Friends* era. That honor falls to George Strait's "Amarillo by Morning."

"Amarillo by Morning" is simple and pure, and it serves as a fitting conclusion to this discussion. The introductory notes of the lone fiddle are the mark of the Texas western-swing revivalist George Strait, a steer roper and PRCA member. Strait goes right to work in this classic rodeo song, adding a full country ensemble, including pedal steel guitar, to tell a now-familiar story. We meet our cowboy at night, traveling across the expanse of West Texas, bound for a rodeo in Amarillo. Not surprisingly, he is alone and broke—"Everything that I got / is just what I got on." Characteristically, he believes his luck could turn: When the "sun is high in that Texas sky / I'll be buckin' at the County fair / Amarillo by mornin'/ Amarillo I'll be there."

With the haunting fiddle and western-swing beat and volume escalating gradually underneath, the cowboy continues his story. Out of money, he sold his saddle in Houston, and then broke a leg in Santa Fe. Then too, of course, he has lost a "wife and a girlfriend / somewhere along the way." A win in Amarillo could turn it around, though, and he is "lookin' for eight when they pull that gate / and I'll hope that judge ain't blind / Amarillo by mornin' / Amarillo on my mind." As the chorus repeats, the fiddle comes up, the drums, tempo, and volume increase, and we head for the musical rodeo gate, as it were. Typically, this cowboy saves his best lick for the end. "I ain't got a dime / but what I've got is mine," he reminds his listeners; "I ain't rich but Lord I'm free / Amarillo by mornin' / Amarillo's where I'll be."[31]

CHAPTER SIX

"If You're a Cowboy, You're a Cowboy"
Rainbow Rodeo Riders and the Archetypal Anti-Archetype

Politics is for people who have a passion for changing life
but lack a passion for living it.
—Bonanza to Sissy in Tom Robbins' *Even Cowgirls
Get the Blues* (1976)

On the evening of August 25, 1988, the rodeo-cowboy hero rode into
millions of North American living rooms via a television documentary.
CBS's *48 Hours* aired "Showdown at Cheyenne," a one-hour look at professional rodeo through the lens of Wyoming's famed Cheyenne Frontier Days Rodeo. Correspondents Dan Rather, Bernard Goldberg, John
Blackstone, Victoria Corderi, and Harry Smith presented a colorful
portrait, with segments featuring live arena action, flamboyant rodeo
personalities, country-music entertainers, western clothiers, community volunteers and entrepreneurs, and even a trip to a nearby dude
ranch specializing in trail drive reenactments. The general tone of the
show was celebratory and romantic. In his introduction, Rather im-
plored those Americans who believe the days of the Wild West "are gone
forever" to "come along with us to Frontier Days in Cheyenne, Wyoming," where "the men and women you are about to meet aren't playing games. Other people's dreams are for them everyday reality."[1]

Yet, like all good post-1960s television journalists, the *48 Hours* crew
took the opportunity to politicize its portrayal of North American rodeo.
Avoiding animal-rights questions and finding no basis for a class cri-

tique of rodeo culture, *48 Hours* took aim at race and gender issues in the all-American sport. To pursue these themes, correspondents Goldberg and Corderi interviewed two respected rodeo roughstock riders, Brian Riley—an African American cowboy—and bull-riding cowgirl Johnnie Jancowski.

Bull rider Riley was visibly taken aback when Goldberg immediately raised the issue of race, asking if "being black matters" and if there is "any name-calling or anything" like that on the rodeo circuit. Riley responded with a healthy dose of Cowboy Code behavior. "No," he drawled in Plains cowboy vernacular identical to that of all rodeo folk. "I been riding for eight years and I've never really run into nothing." If Riley had ever "run into" some "name-calling"—an occurrence that seems entirely possible—we can be sure he was not going to share his feelings or vent his anger on *48 Hours.* "Cowboys, they're really just one big family, you know," he informed Goldberg. He might also have told the interviewer that cowboys do not let greenhorns in on their secrets. To a black rodeo man, other cowboys, whatever their race, are more trustworthy than a CBS reporter and his audience of dudes. Riley summed up his rodeo experiences in typical fashion: "You got to prove yourself just like anybody else does before you get your breaks, and once you prove yourself, then you're all right. . . . If you're a cowboy, you're a cowboy."[2]

Champion woman bull rider Johnnie Jancowski of Montana was less reticent in discussing equal rights in rodeo but no less true to the cowboy way. She had come to Cheyenne to spearhead a historic undertaking: a women's bull-riding exhibition in the Frontier Days arena for the "first time in fifty-two years." Jancowski was outspoken about her desire to overturn professional rodeo's half-century segregation of men's and women's competitions and "to let this opportunity be there for the other girls to do it." Yet Jancowski's deportment on the documentary was steeped in cowboy tradition and behavior. In answer to reporter Corderi's queries, she spoke in a Plains accent, using lingo like that of Riley and the rest of their rodeo compatriots. During the filming, she exhib-

ited stoicism in the face of severe injury and extreme loyalty to her fellow cowgirls and cowboys. She referred to the rodeo "people and the
lifestyle" as "something that I love . . . this opportunity to compete, and
have this be a little bit of fantasy part of our lives." When Corderi asked
why she had shed tears during the playing of the American national anthem, Jancowski stated, "I guess because I'm out here doing what I want
to do, and I can." By rodeo's end, she could say: "The guys, a lot of the
guys, you know, are coming up and going 'God,' you know. They know
what we've taken this week, you know, and they're realizing we're not
trying to steal their show. We just want to ride bulls, we want to ride
broncs."[3]

"Showdown at Cheyenne" is just one example of the significance of
rodeo cowboys and the Cowboy Code in the contemporary American
debate over "multiculturalism" and "diversity." The principals in this
documentary represent opposite poles in that debate. Although Goldberg (who has recently attacked the abuses of politically correct journalism) may be playing devil's advocate here, both he and Corderi nevertheless adhere to the multiculturalist point of view throughout their
interviews. Both correspondents' comments evidence the presupposi-
tion that racial and gender differences divide and cause conflict among
rodeo folk. Goldberg and Corderi are stymied, however, when Riley and
Jancowski politely resist their attempts to uncover and focus upon strife
within the rodeo community. Instead of pointing to diversity within a
cowboy "multiculture," Riley and Jancowski instead reiterate their loyalty to a shared Cowboy Code of behavior. In so doing they directly con-
tradict the multiculturalist notion of race- and gender-based "identity."
Riley's and Jancowski's self-professed "identities" are closely tied, not
to their race or gender, but instead to the "rodeo people and lifestyle"
and their status as *real cowboys and cowgirls.* Race and gender are no
doubt important to them, but not all-important.[4]

I do not know if the distinguished historian Arthur Schlesinger Jr.
has ever attended a rodeo or studied rodeo cowboys and the Cowboy

Code, but I am struck by the relevance of historic rodeo and the portrayal of rodeo cowboys in popular culture to his recent and important critique of multiculturalism, *The Disuniting of America: Reflections on a Multi-cultural Society* (1992).[5] I will further discuss Schlesinger's book at the conclusion of this chapter. Meanwhile, a survey of the history of black, Hispanic, and Indian cowboys and rodeo cowboys, as well as female, gay, and prison cowboys, will document the fact that cowboy "identity" has never revolved around an individual cowboy's ethnicity or gender. Moreover, the cohesive historic cowboy culture has directly impacted artistic and pop-culture portrayals of black, Hispanic, Indian, female, gay, and prison rodeo cowboys. In art, as in life, if you're a cowboy, you're a cowboy.

Cowboys working the nineteenth-century Great Plains cattle frontier came from a wide variety of backgrounds, and this pattern has been replicated among rodeo folk. But even though cowboys "always consisted of a varied mix of ethnic backgrounds," as Hal Cannon writes in the introduction to *Songs of the Sage* (1986), the cowboy lifestyle/ethos dramatically affects all who embraced it, regardless of race or former identity. It is "so charged with cultural elements that it pervades the life of anyone who participates in it," Cannon continues. Having "its own creed, dress, fancy gear, language, poetry, and songs," cowboy culture "often outwardly replaces ethnicity altogether. For many ethnic Americans, being a cowboy represents the ultimate American dream—a new identity on the American frontier."[6]

Although European American cowboys dominated the cow camps of the northern and southern Great Plains, they were joined by large numbers of Mexican American and African American cowboys, especially in Texas and the Southwest. Later in the nineteenth century and in the early twentieth century, Indian cowboys began to work their own spreads and those of their neighbors throughout the West. Cajun (Acadian) French cowboys in east Texas and south Louisiana exemplify the great variety found among European American cowboys. This variety is also shown in the differentiated cultures and herding techniques of English American and Celtic American cowboys. In the Hawaiian Islands, the paniolos, Hawaiian cowboys, added yet another ingredient to the brew. Moreover, while it is not known to what extent, there were some homosexual cowboys. And on many working cattle ranches, women regularly demonstrated their cowgirl skills and horsemanship. This wide assortment of cowboys and cowgirls, bound together by cowboy culture and the Code of the West, made for a fascinating melting pot within the larger American melting pot.[7]

From its very beginnings, North American rodeo echoed this ethnic, sexual, and cultural variety. This is not to say that rodeo was immune to prejudice or segregation. Many old-timers can point to instances of prejudice against cowgirls and Indian, black, and Hispanic cowboys. The elimination of nearly all women's events in RCA rodeos during and after World War II and the existence of segregated black, Indian, and Hispanic festivals throughout the West are proof that rodeo, like all of American culture, exhibited (and exhibits) racial and sexual barriers. Today, cowgirls can still only race barrels in most PRCA rodeos. Many Indians still prefer to compete in "all-Indian" rodeos, and it is safe to say that gay rodeo will not be accepted into mainstream cowboy culture in the near future. On the other hand, there has never been a time when North American rodeo was *consistently segregated across the board* like, for example, professional American baseball. If one can point to specific examples of segregated rodeos in specific western towns, there are always many counterexamples of nearby towns with rodeo shows open to all. There was *never* an all-white-male rodeo era—a time of definitively racially and sexually segregated continental rodeo. Thus, despite the existence of sexual and racial barriers, rodeo, rooted in folk traditions, has ultimately proved far too decentralized, localized, and uncontrollable to encompass systematic segregation.[8]

After all, Mexican American cowboys played a pivotal role in the creation of the rodeo folk festival and have remained important and skilled rodeo riders throughout the twentieth century. A list of North American rodeo greats is peppered with surnames such as Camarillo, Airola, Oropeza, Castro, Trujillo, and Carillo. Similarly, 1982 world-champion bull rider Charles Sampson inherited an African American rodeo tradition established by Nat Love, Bill Pickett, George Fletcher, Marvel Rogers, and other black cowboys during the first half of the century. Rodeo cowgirls Tad Lucas, Fern Sawyer, Fox Hastings, Ruth Roach, the Greenough sisters, Mabel Strickland, and six hundred more rode in their own special events and exhibitions at pre–World War II professional rodeos, sometimes competing against the men. Indian cowboys began riding in Pendleton, Calgary, and Cheyenne in the nineteen-teens, when horsemen like the Nez Percé bronc buster Jackson Sundown gained renown for their cowboy skills. Later, prison-convict cowboys and the cowboys and cowgirls of the post-1970s gay rodeo circuit added a varied and controversial social and sexual dimension to the rodeo rainbow.[9]

This documented variety of ethnic and sexual backgrounds among historical rodeo folk was early reflected in rodeo movies, literature, art, and music, but it took on special importance during the Vietnam era. Although the serious portrayal of rodeo cowboys in popular culture began with Robert Mitchum's *The Lusty Men* in 1952, we have seen that it was during the Vietnam and post-Vietnam decades that moviemakers, authors, songwriters, poets, and artists produced a substantial body of rodeo movies, literature, music, poetry, and art. Those turbulent years brought issues of racial and sexual inequality to the forefront of American debate and politics, and some rodeo writers and artists quite naturally turned to themes of race, sexuality, and social status as they built upon and expanded the rodeo genre. In so doing they aimed to establish a new kind of rodeo-cowboy hero, an *anti-archetype* of the rodeo-cowboy archetype. I call this new anti-archetypal rodeo hero the "rainbow rodeo rider."

My thesis is that the artistic portrayal of rainbow rodeo riders as anti-archetypes is in fact an archetypal portrayal. The rainbow rodeo hero is an *archetypal anti-archetype.* By this I mean that artists and popularizers of the rainbow rodeo rider, no matter how radical their initial political motivations, ultimately adopted a very traditional, culture-based approach in painting their "new" hero. Just as historic cowboys and rodeo folk subordinated their ethnicity and sexuality to embrace a common cowboy vision, so too did the artistic portrayers of rainbow rodeo men and women. Thus all of the artists and popularizers have themselves been drawn toward the shared values of the Cowboy Code.

Inevitably, the portrayers of the rainbow rodeo rider initially encountered the same complexities that the *48 Hours* reporters found in Cheyenne in 1988. Artists approaching rodeo and rodeo cowboys with aims that included political and social protest faced a challenging, yet potentially energizing, prospect. Cowboys and rodeo are, as we have seen, quintessentially American; they represent the forces of westward migration, Manifest Destiny, and the civilizing of the North American West. Thus, from some radical 1960s anti-American perspectives, rodeo cowboys, like cowboys in general, represented American imperialism, cultural genocide, and other unsavory aspects of westward expansion (one thinks of the abuse and ridicule the 1960s left heaped on John Wayne). From the point of view of 1960s and post-1960s feminists and animal-rights activists, for example, rodeo men might seem excellent candidates for the role of villain in rodeo art.

Yet could a viable rodeo art encompass a denigration of cowboys, the cowboy way, and the failings of "white America" while at the same celebrating the heroic rainbow rodeo hero? If, as history shows, the rainbow rider had been part of the winning of the West, as well as an important presence in professional rodeo from its earliest beginnings, how would that history be presented? What characteristics would artists ascribe to the rainbow rodeo hero? Would these traits differ from those ascribed to the white male cowboy, and if so, in what ways? What role would racism and sexism play in these artists' works? How, if at all, would animal-rights themes be incorporated? In other words, what themes and motifs would provide dramatic force for the rainbow rider subgenre of rodeo art?

The agrarian ideology of the 1960s counterculture eventually played an important role, though certainly not the only one, in resolving this artistic dilemma. Perhaps one of the most important facets of the social history of the 1960s is the huge difference between the hippie and the new-left segments of the "counterculture." Although the groups certainly overlapped, the hippies were much more numerous, influential, artistic, and apolitical than the neo-Marxists. Most important for the purposes of this study, the hippie counterculture, as opposed to the new left, was deeply imbued with an almost Jeffersonian vision of an agrarian republic—hence the anti-industrialism of the commune movement, long hair, buckskin, beads, and all of the many "natural" trappings of hippieana. The predominant counterculture vision—that of a "greening of America"—was a vision of Arcadia that could quite easily be transcribed into a variant of the Cowboy Code.[10]

A strong segment of the hippie counterculture's artistic community became fascinated with the rural mystique, and they influenced other artists with less direct countercultural leanings. The country-rock movement was born of this folk romanticism, as the Byrds, Linda Ronstadt, Poco, Commander Cody and the Lost Planet Airmen, Rick Nelson and the Stone Canyon Band, the Nitty Gritty Dirt Band, and many others rediscovered and reveled in the sounds of steel guitars, fiddles, and nasal redneck vocal stylings. We have already seen the importance of rodeo imagery in the songs of 1960s and 1970s folk and country-rock musicians Ian and Sylvia, Buffy Sainte-Marie, and the Byrds. Chris

LeDoux's song "The Cowboy and the Hippie" explores the ironic yet undeniable Kerouacian connection between 1970s hippies "on the road" and their rodeo-cowboy counterparts following their own road across America. Thus when literary and cinematic artists established the rainbow rodeo genre in the post-1965 era, they did so in a frame of mind strongly and positively drawn to the mystique of rodeo-cowboy culture.

A novel by Ken Kesey will serve as the first example of this literary blending of countercultural beliefs in racial and sexual equality, rural virtue, and the Cowboy Code. Kesey's respect for the rugged individualism of the rural folk of his native Oregon provides much of the energy and art of his acclaimed novels *One Flew over the Cuckoo's Nest* (1962) and *Sometimes a Great Notion* (1964). The rural-culture theme is evident in much of Kesey's later work, including his recent rodeo book, *Last Go Round* (1994). Coauthored with Ken Babbs, *Last Go Round* does not rank with Kesey's earlier classics. Nevertheless, it provides a case study in the possibilities and pitfalls awaiting the artist who seeks to weave an egalitarian racial and gender message into the rodeo genre via depictions of rainbow cowboys.[11]

Last Go Round is based loosely on an oral tale about a historical incident of the 1911 Pendleton Roundup, which ended with a three-way tie for all-round champion among George Fletcher (a black Oregonian), Jackson Sundown (a Nez Percé Indian), and Johnathan E. Lee Spain (a seventeen-year-old white Tennesseean). A final "go-round" in saddle bronc riding (an event in which judging can, arguably, be subjective) resulted in Spain's victory. With that bare framework of historical information, Kesey and Babbs take over. Choosing "to conjure our riders out of the old tall tales . . . instead of the cold facts," they have their first-person narrator, an aged John Spain, tell his version of the story, "Take it or leave it." And Spain's version is that the "last go-round" was fixed—that white racism, not superior cowboy skills, caused his victory.[12]

The cast of characters represents nearly every hue of the rodeo rainbow. There is George Fletcher, the "Black King of the Broncobusters," and Jackson Sundown, the famed "Rough Riding Redskin." With the feisty Sarah Meyerhoff representing the rodeo-cowgirl contingent, Kesey provides Spain a love interest while adding a unique dimension— a Jewish cowgirl from the "Lost Tribe of Levis." This potpourri is further varied by Sue Lin (a Chinese noncontestant), Prairie Rose Henderson (a cowgirl who doubles as a feminist firebrand), and a young John Muir in his alleged preconservationist cowboy phase(!). Conspicuous by their absence in this presentist historical fiction are Hispanic Americans (with the exception of one "bloat-bellied Mexican migrant" who impersonates Sundown) and Humane Society activists (even Muir toes the rodeo line here). White America is represented by the youthful Spain (an admirable fellow), a diabolical Buffalo Bill Cody, wrestler Frank Gotch, robber baron Oliver Nordstrum and his Pinkerton henchmen, and their business associates and friends in Pendleton. The only persons underrepresented in this cast, then, are the plain white folk who make up the core of Pendleton rodeo culture.[13]

As literature, Spain's first-person narration succeeds, but his movement back and forth through time via flashbacks does not. The Frank Gotch wrestling sequences, while evincing former Oregon State champ Kesey's love of the sport, seem just a bit incongruous in a rodeo book. Moreover, the presentist egalitarian political tone of the novel is at times overdrawn and detracts from the historical feel. Yet despite these problems, the story of the 1911 Roundup is a good one, and Kesey has adapted it ably if not brilliantly.

The themes of racism and prejudice are threads that help hold *Last Go Round* together. Racist language and behavior punctuate the story line. Buffalo Bill and his entourage call George Fletcher "nigger George," the "coal-skinned cowboy." A friend warns George that locals might "dance a do-se-do on your fool black face." Jackson Sundown fares a little better—"cowboys and Injens go together," George jokes, whereas nobody "ever heard of cowboys and niggers"—yet whites still call him

"Indian Jack" and denigrate his "wild Indian talk" and native ways. All of this racism comes to a head when Cody, Nordstrum, Gotch, and their Pinkertons try to "fix" the Roundup so as to ensure a white "fair-haired All-American" victor. When Fletcher and Sundown resist, the bad guys complain that "our nigger and our Indian is proved uncooperative," beat up Fletcher, and, adding insult to injury, steal his hat. Meanwhile, young Johnathan Spain becomes extremely disillusioned with this unfolding of events, concluding that "my frontier Camelot was turning out to be infested with rats and riddled with weakness and greed."[14]

Yet while Kesey portrays greedy, hegemonic European American "rats," the white cowboy Spain, a Jim Crow—era Tennessean, escapes his aim; so do the rest of Spain's cowboy crowd. Indeed, as it turns out, all of the villains in this piece are dudes and *noncowboys* (unless you count Wild Bill Cody a cowboy, as Sundown, Spain, and Fletcher most certainly do not). From the first pages of *Last Go Round,* the cowboy trio of Jackson Sundown, Johnathan Spain, and George Fletcher—red, white, and black Americans—symbolize the archetypal cowboy way and its overall goodness. Their backdrop is Pendleton and its rural environs. The trio camp and ride the banks of the Umatilla River between rodeo events, and their ties to this stark and beautiful eastern Oregon landscape form an important subtheme. The author makes no distinction between working cowboys and rodeo men, and we come to view the tricolored trio as *real* *cowboys.*[15]

Sundown and Fletcher take young Spain under their wing, initiating him into their world. After his "greenhorn" baptism in hard liquor, the two sages mentor him and teach him the Cowboy Code. They extend hospitality to him, providing food, sleeping quarters, liquor, and prime information about the roughstock they know well. All three men show great respect for their horses, treating them with care and affection. Johnathan's midland drawl is enhanced by exposure to George's and Jackson's cowboy lingo. He borrows George's prized "cream-colored Stetson," an honor that teaches him proper respect for a good cowboy hat.

He describes the "poky and gimpy" way the two cowboys walk "out of the saddle" and the marked reticence of Sundown's Indian/cowboy persona. Spain treats Sarah Meyerhoff to all the overdrawn courtesies he has learned in cowboy company, and she reciprocates with heaping portions of her own Cowgirl Code demeanor.[16]

In short, the Cowboy Code is as important a theme in *Last Go Round* as racism and prejudice. Indeed, archetypal cowboy values stand in stark contrast to the valueless "rats" who have invaded Spain's "frontier Camelot." Only the cowboys can prevent this perversion of the West, and Fletcher's and Sundown's rainbow status seems to make them almost doubly qualified. In a conversation with Fletcher and Spain, Mr. Meyerhoff (Sarah's father and a Pendleton shopkeeper) calls George "our hero. Our *champion,*" a title which George disclaims, describing himself instead as a "wu'thless cowhand." Meyerhoff retorts: "Though he may have been the fool sometimes, and occasionally wild, he was never worthless. George and men like him are the hand the Master is using to tame this wicked country. That hand sometimes *has* to be wild, you see? To tame a wicked land."[17]

Last Go Round is a recent example of artists' addressing issues of racial and sexual equality via the rainbow rodeo theme, but it follows patterns established two decades earlier in the movie *J. W. Coop.* Like Kesey and Babbs's novel, Cliff Robertson's film provides abundant examples of the counterculture's antimodernist message that influenced Hollywood in the late 1960s and early 1970s. Moreover, the movie features a varied array of rodeo folk—convict, black, female, and hippie—that equals even Kesey's wild rainbow.

J. W. Coop opens with J.W. (Robertson) competing in a Texas prison rodeo, on the final leg of a ten-year stint for "bad penmanship" (writing hot checks). Prison "wasn't no county fair," Coop concedes, and he is eager to restart his once-promising rodeo career. Broke and reduced to hitchhiking, he has an experience similar to that described in LeDoux's "The Cowboy and the Hippie." J.W. meets Bean (Christina Ferrare), a hippie girl bedecked in beads, bell-bottoms, and wool poncho, dispensing granola, soybeans (J.W. calls them "hippie seeds"), and peace signs to Coop, now a late-1960s Rip van Winkle. The two fall in love and hit the rodeo road, driving an old army ambulance in lieu of a VW van. Along the way they meet a host of J.W.'s old rodeo pals, including "Big Martha" (Marjorie Durant Dye), a stock-truck driver who is a modern-day Calamity Jane, and Myrtis "Merc" Dightman (played by himself), an African American rodeo man. Together, the "old hands" of J.W.'s circle bemoan the commercialization and declining authenticity of modern-day rodeo. Yet in the end J.W. is swept up in this frantic materialism, a development that costs him his lover and his life.

Myrtis Dightman's self-portrayal stands as the most developed portrait of a black rodeo man in American movies. Despite J.W.'s criminal record, Merc shows no hesitation in welcoming him back and assisting him in his rodeo comeback try. Their shared status as cowboys, not the color of their skins, is the source of their identities and their friendship. In order to renew that friendship and catch up on old times, Merc and J.W. retreat to a local watering hole, the Branding Iron, against Merc's better judgment. A racist waitress harasses them and asks them to leave: "We ain't runnin' no NAACP teahouse here." Two local toughs try to beat up Merc in the bathroom, only to feel the combined wrath of Merc and J.W. The two rodeo men prove their loyalty to each other by beating the bigots severely, shoving one into the urinal headfirst. When the sheriff arrives and demands to know what has happened, J.W. says simply, "Oh, nothin', sheriff. Just a couple of old boys in here makin' weird advances." The lawman counters, "What's that fellow doin' in there [the urinal]?" Merc and J.W. appear perplexed until J.W. finally replies, "I don't know. Just washin' up." Then he and Merc return to the rodeo.[18]

The prison theme expounded in *J. W. Coop* has continued to prove an effective tool for artists seeking to portray alternative rodeo cowboys. This usage in rodeo art parallels the employment of the outlaw motif (à la Jesse James, Billy the Kid, etc.) as a strong variant in artistic portrayals of nineteenth-century working cowboys. As in the traditional western, the introduction of prison riders adds an even wilder, "outlaw" component to the mystique of the rodeo man. This is why the opening scene of *J. W. Coop*, with Coop bronc-riding in striped prison fatigues and cowboy hat, proves so gripping visually and emotionally. And it is why William Crawford, in his novel *The Bronc Rider* (1965), introduces Ernest Cameron's mentor, Barlow Plane, a drifting outlaw who has ridden in the "prison rodeo in Huntsville." In the movie *Urban Cowboy* (1980), Bud and Sissy are at first awed by the prowess of Huntsville inmate and rodeo champ Wes Hightower (although by movie's end, the former convict has clearly revealed a persona so evil that it is the very antithesis of the cowboy mores that Bud and Sissy represent). Most recently, John Voigt ably plays the outlaw role of a Montana prison cowboy and rodeo man in Showtime's cable movie *Convict Cowboy* (1995).[19]

The best-known prison-rodeo movie puts a unique twist on the subgenre, using the fearsome aspects of prison-rodeo outlaws for ironic and comic effect. Indeed, *Stir Crazy* (1980), directed by Sidney Poitier, is the only comedy ever created around the rodeo theme. *Stir Crazy* begins in New York City, with bosom buddies Skip Donohue (Gene Wilder) and Harry Monroe (Richard Pryor) discontented with their harried urban lives. Fired from their jobs, they decide to "head out West" and relish the freedom of life on the open road. But the West turns out to be a sinister and dangerous place for nice guys like Skip and Harry. Falsely convicted of a bank robbery, they land in Glenboro State Prison, surrounded by a few new friends, a lot of tough hombres, a sadistic warden (Barry Corbin), and a crazed head guard (Craig T. Nelson). Fortunately, Skip exhibits uncanny skill riding Warden Beatty's mechanical bull, explaining "It's just like the merry-go-round at Coney Island" and winning himself a spot on Glenboro's rodeo team. Although Warden Beatty has $50,000 riding on the outcome, Skip, Harry, and their convict friends use the prison rodeo as an opportunity to escape. By movie's end, after a hilarious set of adventures (and an obligatory romantic nod from Wilder to JoBeth Williams), the two New York City dudes set out for Hollywood and new lives in the Golden West.

Stir Crazy spotlights almost every shade of the rodeo rainbow. Skip Donohue, the "New York Yankee," is not identified as a Jew (his name is certainly not Jewish), but Wilder cannot help playing him as one. Sexuality is addressed through a flamingly gay African American convict who falls for Harry, whom he calls "sweet pants." Jesus Ramirez (Miguelangel Suarez), "the champion bull rider of his province," lands in Glenboro and coaches Skip and Harry in rodeo before facilitating their escape. Harry, who gets the job of clown in the rodeo, is one of several black characters, most of whom dress in full cowboy regalia. There are Indian cowboys as well. The rival prison's top hand is César Geronimo, a polyglot character of mestizo ethnicity.[20]

Although at least one scholar has tried to attach deep meaning to this movie,[21] it is safe to say that Bruce Jay Friedman, the writer of *Stir Crazy*, was not trying to send a profound message. Skip and Harry are nice fellows, but their knowledge of the Cowboy Code is limited, filtered through decades of urban living. If there is a message in *Stir Crazy*, it is that prisons (and wardens) are bad news, that prisoners can sometimes prevail (as when Geronimo throws a bag of prize money to the convict crowd), and that easterners can do anything that westerners can do, only better. Indeed, one of the most interesting things about this movie is its creators' overdrawn, villainizing portrayal of the twentieth-century American West (and its "redneck" citizenry) and their celebration of the savvy, forthright easterner Skip Donohue. Skip shows the western bad guys a thing or two, beating them at their own game and ultimately riding the infamous outlaw bronc Untamed. The prison-rodeo announcer, who initially jokes that Skip robbed a bank in order to "help New York City out of its financial bind by usin' our money," ultimately has to confess "that Eastern boy's got a little cowboy in him." Skip and Harry, in the meantime, have flown the coop, leaving the western dunderheads in their dust. Their archetypal dreams of the mythic West are at last realized, not through ethnic or sexual identity but through individual liberty: "For the first time in our lives we're free."[22]

Stir Crazy's inclusion of a gay suitor for Pryor's Harry raises possibilities that might be explored and utilized with great effect in mainstream rodeo arts. There no doubt existed homosexual working cowboys in the nineteenth century, and homosexual rodeo competitors appear regularly today in segregated gay rodeos throughout the West. Nevertheless, homophobia is pronounced in rodeo circles, and gay rodeo cowboys are conspicuous by their absence from most rodeo movies, literature, art, and music. Moreover, the gay literati are for the most part unaware of, or averse to portraying, gay rodeo culture. Many urban-based gay and lesbian literary artists hold strong prejudices against rodeo and rodeo cowboys. Because of the combination of these two forces, it is safe to say that gays will remain excluded from rodeo art, and from rodeo per se, for many years to come.[23]

Since no gay or lesbian cowboy or any other homosexual rodeo insider has ever written on the subject of gay rodeo, the homosexual rodeo cowboy is the least developed of the rainbow riders. The few literary works on gay rodeo are the product of a handful of East or West Coast gay and lesbian artists and activists who have an interest in, but little firsthand knowledge of, gay rodeo. Like gay playwright David Link, they see gay rodeo mainly as evidence that some gays evince "a rather clunky sense of aesthetics." Some of these writers are outright hostile, opposing the "inherent cruelty" of rodeo whether practiced by gay or straight cowboys. They chide gay cowboys, reminding them that the animal-rights movement is akin to the struggles for gays' and women's rights, and they claim that the white male rodeo establishment labels all these movements "ridiculous." Taking to heart the taming imagery and the female pronoun in "let 'er buck!" lesbian essayist Judy Grahn denounces and ridicules rodeo culture in her essay "Boys at the Rodeo" (1981).

Grahn sees only a demeaning status for cowgirls and "rodeo queens" and is apparently unaware of lesbian participation in the sport.[24]

Yet in at least one literary work, the homosexual rainbow rodeo man and woman have nevertheless come out of the closet, or chute, as it were. In his nonfiction "road book" *Heartlands: A Gay Man's Odyssey Across America* (1992), Darrell Yates Rist devotes an important chapter, "The Rodeo's Dry Heat," to his 1987 experience at North America's premier gay rodeo venue, the Denver Gay Rodeo. New Yorker Rist tries his best to understand and portray what, before *Heartlands,* had been to him an essentially foreign aspect of North American gay culture. Arriving in Denver, he is swept up in the romance and western mystique of the festival, referring to every gay man or lesbian he sees in a hat and boots as a "cowboy" or "cowhand." He calls Stetson hats "Tetons" and never quite understands the rodeo program, its rules, and its ritualistic progression of events. When Rist notes the complete absence of gay journalists in Denver, a local organizer explains that "the urban gay press" has "never taken much interest in such 'uncultivated' gay life." Thus, in "The Rodeo's Dry Heat," Rist has become a pioneer gay artist, leaving New York City behind for the Heartlands, in search of the rest of gay America. He discovers a gay and lesbian cowboy and cowgirl culture that simultaneously adheres to archetypal Cowboy Code traits and homosexual identity.[25]

What Rist describes is a melting pot of homosexuality and straight cowboy folkways. The Denver rodeo is obviously gay, with rodeo clowns in drag, a steer-riding race between "drag queens and dykes in drag," and other "camp" events that set it apart from the "straight circuit." Yet Rist notes that "plenty of disgusted [homosexual] cowboys wanted to butch up the rodeo" because it had become "too gay." He records these contestants' western vernacular phonetically, capturing its rural authenticity. A lesbian cowgirl is seen "raising a paper cup toward her lips," spitting "amber streams of tobacco," and picking "the shreds from her teeth." Many (not all) of these cowboys and cowgirls are devout Christians, praying as a gay minister recites "The Cowboy's Prayer" at the rodeo's beginning. And Rist is particularly struck by the contestants' courage and stoicism in the face of danger and injury. He describes one bull rider, his shoulder bleeding, nestled "in his lover's thighs, to sleep more peacefully." Another roughstock cowboy with a "long, rough wound" successfully rides his bronc and immediately embraces his boyfriend, crying "I damn kicked *ass!*"—to which his cowboy compadre responds, "You damn sure did all right!"[26]

Despite their adherence to the Cowboy Code, these gay and lesbian rainbow cowboys and cowgirls know well that they are caught between two worlds—that they stage their own rodeos because "they're not welcome on the regular circuit—no matter how well they handle a rope or how tough they are in the saddle." "We can ride with the best of them," a gay cowboy explains, "but they don't want us around." On the other hand, Rist's narrative shows that the gay-rodeo crowd is not quite welcome in the cosmopolitan world of urban gays either. Rist arrives and departs Denver in a positive and supportive frame of mind, and he goes farther than any gay artist to date in sympathetically portraying gay rodeo. Yet the New Yorker cannot help but display a lack of knowledge about his rural gay cousins and what he perceives as their lack of a gay identity. He is puzzled by their apolitical ways—for example, they drink Coors beer ("the cowboy's favorite beer"), completely oblivious to the "Coors boycott" and the "problems" Coors represents to politicized urban gays. Rist never mentions animal rights, but he is regularly put off by the cowboys' rough-hewn language and behavior. In one important episode, he winces but holds his tongue as a rodeo man, a self-proclaimed Pentecostal, maligns an effeminate passerby: "Now *here* comes a real queen. It makes me *sick* to see somethin' as nelly as that. . . . People sees that kind of thing and they think all the queers are that way. It's enough to make you stay in the closet. Pro'ly from California anyways." Through much of this conversation, Rist is actually unsure of the cowboy's sexual orientation. "Are *you* gay?" he finally asks, only to hear: "*Hell!* . . . I knowed from the time I was this high . . . I didn't do anything about it, though, till I divorced my wife. That was eight years ago. Took me another four years after to git myself goin' with men."[27]

Ultimately, Rist comes to respect his newly discovered gay-rodeo brothers and sisters. He praises the courage with which they have claimed their Americanness. His conclusion is, if unintentionally, nothing less than an ode to archetypal Jeffersonianism, Turnerian values, and the cowboy way:

> There was a magic for me at the gay rodeo—in this crowd of alienated men and women reclaiming their past. Many of the homosexuals I knew [in urban America] had fled their heritage, as I had, because "queers" were not allowed a part in it. The cost of remaining in our hometowns was the brutal threat of discovery. Both fear and the bitterness of exile soured a life. . . . The cowboys and cowgirls at the rodeo were flaunting their banishment. . . . If many of the gay rodeo folks were still "closeted" by gay urban standards, they were closer to healing their lives, it seemed to me, than a host of us homosexuals who had escaped to the cities to scoff at everything we grew up with and still live exiled in secrecy. The men and women at the rodeo taught me the joy of wider possibilities.[28]

The question of sexual identity among rodeo folk brings to mind Bonanza Jellybean, the lesbian cowgirl heroine of Tom Robbins' *Even Cowgirls Get the Blues* (1976). Unfortunately, for the purposes of this study, Bonanza is a *real cowgirl*, not a rodeo cowgirl. She works the Rubber Rose Ranch, her own Dakota spread, and helps cowgirl initiates learn how to ride and rope and hoot on the northern range. In answer to Sissy Hankshaw's query, "Tell me about . . . being a cowgirl. What's it all about?" Bonanza expresses an interesting and important afeminist cowgirl philosophy: "I'm a cowgirl. I've always been a cowgirl," she insists. "But don't get the notion I'm trying to create a movement or contribute to one . . . I'm too happy just being a cowgirl to worry about stuff like that. Politics is for people who have a passion for changing life but lack a passion for living it."[29]

Although there are documented accounts of hundreds of working cowgirls and rodeo cowgirls,[30] this historic evidence has never been fully translated into cowgirl movies, literature, art, and songs. The artistic portrayers of rainbow rodeo cowgirls face a sticky proposition. Historian William Savage Jr. has outlined some of the obstacles to treating cowgirl heroes like Annie Oakley in pop-culture media. Certainly one of the most important problems has been predominantly male artists' preconceptions. We have seen that, in the classic American western, women usually play the tame role in the frontier/civilization dialectic. This makes them unsuitable, or at the very least problematic, in the role of the wild hero. Since the wild side of the western hero persona is laden with violent and virulent masculine traits, how can a cowgirl be a western hero and a woman too?[31]

Western artists portraying the cowgirl have thus been forced to be very creative. For example, some of the most successful portrayals of cowgirl folk heroes in popular culture are based on oral folk traditions in which the cowgirl hero simply acts like a man. In this way Calamity Jane and Belle Starr carry on in the tradition of Sal Fink and other frontier amazons before them, setting the stage for Ma Barker, Bonnie Parker, and even the 1990s movie heroines Thelma and Louise. They become pop-culture icons because they behave like cow*boys*, riding, shooting, cussing, drinking, and chewing with the best of them. An exception was Annie Oakley, who feminized the archetype considerably. But in real life Annie was a circus performer, not a *real cowgirl.*[32]

The title of "I Want to Be a Real Cowboy Girl," an anonymously authored turn-of-the-century popular song, exhibits the dual wild/tame symbolism of the rainbow rodeo-cowgirl hero. She wants to be a cow*girl* but views her ambition through the male lens, hence the title "Cowboy Girl" (those who sang the song did not yet have the term *cowgirl,* but they were headed in that direction). The singer "is always happy / at the rodeo." She wants "to be a real cowboy girl" and "bulldog a steer at the fair every year / And jump on my pony and ride." Ken Kesey's Sarah Meyerhoff does exactly that in *Last Go Round* and wins the heart of Jonathan Spain as much for her riding skills as for her energetic sexuality. However, in *Urban Cowboy*, Bud and Sissy fight constantly over Sissy's desire to be a cowgirl and ride the mechanical bull at Gilley's. Bud thinks Sissy's place is in the home (trailer home, actually), but she rebels. Although Sissy eventually comes around to Bud's way of thinking, she never does so completely, and then only after logging an unforgettable ride on that bucking machine. More recently, the real-life adventures of roughstock rider Johnnie Jancowski have prompted a celebratory country song by the Nitty Gritty Dirt Band, "The Bullrider Is a Lady." Yet as we have seen, Johnnie might prefer the former label to the latter. It will be interesting to see how Jancowski and her cowgirl status will be portrayed by Hollywood; a production company has recently purchased rights to make her life story the first feature movie ever devoted to the career of a professional rodeo cowgirl.[33]

In only one artistic portrayal does the rodeo cowgirl give up her wild ways and Code behavior completely, and that story is the product of a dude's imagination. Actually, two brilliant dudes — choreographer Agnes de Mille and composer Aaron Copland — collaborated to create the only rodeo story in high art, their ballet *Rodeo* (pronounced, in an elitist undermining of cowboy lingo, "ro-day-o," from the Spanish). In 1942 the Ballet de Russe Monte Carlo commissioned a ballet with a "cowboy" theme, and Copland (who had just scored great success with his *Billy the Kid*) wrote the *Rodeo Suite* to accompany de Mille's dances. Together they scored an artistic coup — translating American folk-music and folk-dance motifs into the ballet and symphonic forms of high European culture. Their heroine is a bona fide cowgirl who loves the "Champion Roper." But the western lovers have a big problem. Like Bud and Sissy in *Urban Cowboy* (and I hesitate just a *bit* to use this comparison), the *Rodeo* couple has some real disagreements over the proper role of a woman in a ranch courtship. After being spurned, *Rodeo's* heroine ultimately toes the male line, giving up her boots, dungarees, and cowgirl ways for a pretty party dress. This makes her man happy, and the couple are joined in dance in *Rodeo's* finale, "Hoe Down."[34]

More in keeping with the cowgirl way is rodeo-poet Paul Zarzyski's "Copenhagen Angel," a snoose-dipping Montana barrel racer with "pigtails braided like bronc reins" (see chapter 3). Zarzyski also wrote, with Justin Bishop, "Fannie Sperry Steele (Buckin' Hoss Suffragettes)." The song honors the great Montana roughstock rider of the nineteen-teens North American rodeo circuit and her rodeo-cowgirl contemporaries. It recounts Steele's ranch-raising and her 1912 and 1913 world broncriding championships in Calgary and Winnipeg:

> Sitting pretty in that photo, she's got her toes turned out
> While Blackie's climbin' ladders made of air
> A fraction of a second caught 80 years ago
> When Fanny rode them slick and clean and the pins flew from
>   her hair.

The important allusions to tame images of the pretty cowgirl and her hairpins are ultimately overpowered by wild images of Steele riding the fierce bronc. So, too, the political allusion to "suffragettes" plays second fiddle to its wild modifier in Zarzyski and Bishop's chorus:

> Buckin' hoss suffragettes callin' their own shots
> While the boys cheered 'em on from way back of the chutes
> Buckin' hoss suffragettes like Fannie Sperry Steele,
> Tad Lucas, Ruth Roach, & Kittie Canutt . . .
> Bonnie McCarrol . . . Dorothy Morel, Lucille Mulhall,
> Vera McGinnis, Goldie St. Claire . . .[35]

Like Sarah Meyerhoff, Bonanza Jellybean, Sissy, the Copenhagen Angel, and Johnnie Jancowski, the "buckin' hoss suffragettes" embrace and then transcend noncowgirl feminist stereotypes. Their radicalism is cultural, not political, and it includes both wild and tame, female and male, characteristics. Most important, the cowgirl in rodeo art shows a profound regard for a variant of the archetypal Cowboy Code, the Code of the West *cowgirl*-style.

Portrayers of gay and female rodeo, then, have viewed the rodeo rainbow focusing on only one of its hues—sexuality—but in so doing they have woven Cowboy Code traits of individualism, loyalty, and courage into their vision of the gay or female rodeo hero. Similarly, other artists have focused on only one particular ethnic group in their depictions of the archetypal anti-archetype. Unlike *Last Go Round* and *J. W. Coop*, which serve up cowboys and cowgirls of every conceivable variety, these artists' works explore in depth the role of the Hispanic, African American, and Indian rodeo-cowboy hero.

Interestingly, and despite his importance in the origins and evolution of the rodeo folk festival, the Mexican American cowboy is the one character who lacks a full-scale artistic treatment in English-language popular culture north of the Rio Grande. The language barrier might provide one reason for this absence, yet cowboy and rodeo culture in the American Southwest have always exhibited bilingualism in varying degrees and accents. Racism is certainly a possible factor in the Mexicans' exclusion, yet if so, then why has virtually every other group of minority rodeo folk—black, Indian, prison, gay, and female—found its way into rodeo art, music, literature, and movies? In a completely different vein, the missing Mexican American rodeo cowboy may be the result of assimilation and cross-acculturation. Perhaps Mexican Americans are so thoroughly integrated into southwestern cowboy and rodeo-cowboy culture that artists of the rainbow rodeo do not see them at all—much less see them as subjects for rainbow rodeo arts. Whatever the reason, only Crawford's *Bronc Rider* and the movie *The Cowboy Way* (1994) utilize Hispanic American cowboys and characters, and even then only tangentially.[36]

South of the Rio Grande, however, *charro*—Mexican cowboy and rodeo cowboy—heroes play a lively role in the movies, literature, art, poems, and songs of southernmost North America. In her ground-breaking work *Charrería Mexicana: An Equestrian Folk Tradition*, Kathleen Mullen Sands devotes an entire chapter to artistic portrayals of *charro* heroes on the range and in the arena. Her depiction centers on a *charro* code—courage, stamina, camaraderie, chivalry, virility, patriotism, and love of horses—that of course directly parallels the expressed values of the *charro*'s northern cowboy brethren. Sands points to expressions of *charro* code in art, songs, literature, and movies such as the documentary *Patria y Tradición* (1987). Poets Delfín Sanchez and Luis Tijerina Almaguer have devoted entire poems to descriptions of *charro* equestrian competitions, their events, and the Code qualities of the *charro* and *charra* contestants. Almaguer's *Alma Charra* (*Charro Soul* 1971) includes one poem expressing these attributes in the first-person voice of a proud *charro*, who boasts of his horsemanship, skills, success with women, and his love of the coarse *charro* lifestyle:

> I like to dress as a charro
> Because it's the Mexican suit.
> I like to drink from a jug
> And display my hat.
> To bring my horse to a sliding stop with gusto,
> Fine style and courage,
> In front of my love.

"That's how we are in my land," the *charro* concludes. "And I don't think anyone can change us. / . . . I like to dress charro."[37]

African American cowboys and rodeo men often diminish their ethnic identity in order to embrace what they perceive to be a more important identity—that of a North American rodeo cowboy. A flamboyant reminiscence by cowboy and rodeo star Nat Love provides a case in point. Born and raised a slave in Davidson County, Tennessee, young Nat Love headed West after the Civil War and found work as a cowboy on the northern Plains cattle frontier. He became a top hand and rodeo roper, and he lived an exciting life that earned him respected status among his peers. He tells his intriguing story in *The Life and Adventures of Nat Love, Better Known in Cattle Country as "Deadwood Dick," by Himself.* Love no doubt embellishes upon and concocts some stories of his "unusually adventurous life" in the "wild and wooly West"—he was a self-promoter (and only one of several claimants to the coveted title of "Deadwood Dick"). But he was also an actual working cowboy whose memoirs evidence authentic Plains cowboy culture. He tells of his experiences herding cattle on the Great Plains; fighting Indians; going on drinking sprees; pursuing romantic liaisons; the 1876 Deadwood, South Dakota, "roping contest" where he won his fame and name; and "last but foremost the friends I have made and the friends I have gained," his fellow cowboys.[38]

What is notable for our purposes, however, is not Love's understandable pride in being a cowboy but some telling comments written a century later by the author of the introduction to the 1995 edition of *The Life and Adventures of Nat Love.* This scholar finds it difficult to fathom how Nat could abandon his ethnic loyalties to follow the Cowboy Code and considers Love's reminiscence a "construction" written in a "voice" that "does not prove easily recognizable as an African-American one." It is "a western voice" defying "what modern sensibilities might think a man of color ought to have recorded, felt, and reported": "Perhaps . . . the strangest aspect for many readers will be the fact that his tale paints the picture of an African-American man who seems to seek no solace in contact with African-American communities or in the company of African-American cowboys who are present. The 'boys' to whom Nat Love appears tightly bound and deeply loyal, are a brotherhood of cowboys, defined without regard to race or place."[39]

Bill Pickett, the most famous of the African American rodeo cowboys, pioneered the portrayal of black rodeo men in movies. Pickett, a Texan who achieved notoriety bulldogging steers by biting their lower lips, starred in a 1920s action movie, *The Bull-dogger.* The Norman Film Manufacturing Company, producers of *The Bull-dogger*, billed Pickett as a "Colored Hero" performing "Death Defying Feats of Courage and Skill." Decades later, the first documentary film to portray African American rodeo cowboys appeared. *Black Rodeo* (1972) takes the viewer into the arena of the 1972 New York City Black Rodeo and provides historical background about black working cowboys and early black rodeo greats like Love and Pickett. In *Songs of My People: African-Americans, a Self-Portrait* (1992), contemporary black rodeo men are photographed in archetypal poses. And finally, Bill Pickett himself has recently returned in "Bill Pickett," a country tune sung by Justin Bishop. The song traces the bulldogger's career from beginning to end, telling tales of his legendary courage and prowess over wild steers from Oklahoma to Mexico. In the rodeo folk tradition that celebrates the hero's tragic demise, "Bill Pickett" ends with Pickett's death (in 1932, at age seventy-three) after being thrashed by a bronc in a ranch accident.[40]

Black rodeo cowboys play important supporting roles in *J. W. Coop, Stir Crazy, Last Go Round,* and as we shall see below, *A Yellow Raft in Blue Water* (1987). Interestingly, one of the most ambitious portrayers of multiethnic cowboys and black rodeo men was the most traditionalist of the rodeo authors. William Crawford's *Bronc Rider* includes in-depth portrayals of Celtic American, Anglo-American, Native American, Mexican American, and African American rodeo riders competing on the southwestern rodeo circuit. The racial attitudes of the novel's hero, Ernest Cameron, reflect a blending of cowboy egalitarianism, individualism, and the early-1960s civil rights milieu in which Crawford penned his rodeo novel.[41]

Landing in the hospital after a serious wreck on the bronc Cape Canaveral, Cam is befriended by Sharon Kelly, a "Negro" patient with whom he converses about rodeo and race. On first meeting Sharon, Cam exhibits "the cautious unfounded prejudice all men have toward the unfamiliar and the unknown" and at one point unthinkingly starts to mouth the epithet *nigger,* catching himself just in time. Yet the tension between the two immediately evaporates because of Sharon's thoughtful conviviality, Cam's lifelong isolation from mainstream racist culture, and his strongly held Cowboy Code individualism. Telling Sharon about the rodeo cowboy, Cam explains that "no matter where he's from or how he was raised, he thinks and acts a pretty certain way, has certain beliefs." Cowboys might "think and act alike," but "no two of them're *really* the same. Too danged independent." Thus there is plenty of room for individualism and variety within the shared rodeo-cowboy culture. When Sharon asks if there are many Negro rodeo cowboys, Cam admits that he knows only "a few." But Cam (like Brian Riley thirty years later) stresses that in rodeo every man, regardless of "race, color, creed," has a chance, for only one thing matters: "a man's ability to ride or rope stock in competition." Racism and segregation are fundamental violations of "the entire code of rodeo." When he "searched his heart, Cam knew it had to be that way."[42]

Whether the world of early-1960s Texas rodeo was as egalitarian as Crawford portrays it to be is, of course, open to question. Cam is correct, however, when he notes that the Rodeo Cowboys Association was always a de jure integrated organization, even before the 1960s civil rights era (although he evidently does not consider the exclusion of women from every event except barrel racing to be segregation). Moreover, Cam impresses Sharon Kelly with his profound admiration for the early black rodeo rider Marvel Rogers, "the greatest natural-born saddle bronc rider I ever saw." Indeed, in the finale of *The Bronc Rider,* Cam rides his old nemesis Cape Canaveral to a literal standstill—an incredible feat of horsemanship "he had seen . . . done just once, by the Negro bronc rider, Marvel Rogers." And after meeting Cam, Sharon Kelly is swayed by his espousal of cowboy individualism. "Perhaps you [cowboys] and your kind have the real answer" for "the final emergence of my people," Sharon tells him. "We cannot and *should* not wait for self-

seeking others, especially the government, to rescue us; we should fight
and claw through our own way."[43]

The Indian rodeo cowboy is perhaps the most paradoxical member of
the rainbow rodeo-cowboy group. The reason, quite simply, is that cowboys and Indians have been cast as incompatible foes in both the historic and the mythic North American West. In the folklore, literature,
and popular culture of the American West, Indians have always represented the wild forces standing in opposition to civilization. However,
as we have seen, the classic western cowboy hero veers strongly toward
the wild frontier lifestyle himself, even in his efforts to civilize it. Western heroes from Daniel Boone to the mountain men and from Leatherstocking to Shane have adapted to native dress, speech, and material
culture. Often they are paired in history, folklore, art, and popular culture with "Indian companions"—from Chingachgook to Tonto—to create an even more powerful frontier image."[44]

So both historic and mythic cowboys and Indians have much in common in their love of the land, horses, and the nomadic lifestyle an un-
civilized West affords them. Historically, Plains Indians cross-acculturated early on, learning to ride Spanish horses and adapting European
equestrian skills to the buffalo hunt and warfare. After military defeat
made their former hunting-and-gathering lifestyle impossible, many
Indians actually did become cowboys around the turn of the century.
Their horsemanship made them top ranch hands and, as Peter Iverson
has shown in *When Indians Became Cowboys* (1994), naturally led them
into the rodeo arena in the earliest days of the sport. One hundred years
later, Edison Bitsuie of the American Indian Rodeo Association can
write that "in today's modern setting, there's no such thing as Indians
and Cowboys." And one observer has said, "The cowboys are Indians,
the Indians are cowboys—at Indian rodeo there is no difference."[45]

This extensive Indian cowboying tradition has been ably translated
into movies, literature, poetry, art, and music. For example, in *Winter*

in the Blood (1974), his gripping novel about modern Montana Indian reservation life, Blackfeet–Gros Ventres writer James Welch briefly introduces Raymond Longknife, a shiftless haybuck whose true skill is as a "cowboy" and saddle-bronc "champ." Del Roberts, Ernest Cameron's best friend and traveling buddy in *The Bronc Rider,* is an Indian, and so is the *Rodeo Roper* in the western art of John L. Doyle, one of many artistic portrayers of contemporary Indian cowboys. One of the first Top 40 musical depictions of rodeo was "He's an Indian Cowboy in the Rodeo," a 1970s hit written and performed by Cree Indian folk rocker Buffy Sainte-Marie. Her song tells the classic tale of a girl who falls in love with a wandering rodeo man, but in this case both the cowboy and his smitten girlfriend are Indians, accenting the Native American role in North American rodeo.[46]

Perhaps the most widely read novel about an Indian rodeo man is Hal Borland's *When the Legends Die* (1963), a polished yet ultimately overdrawn work that falls somewhere between the categories of young adult and adult fiction. Borland's novel and its 1972 movie version are set in early-twentieth-century Colorado. The hero, Thomas Black Bull, is a Ute Indian trying to preserve the "old ways" in the face of insurmountable white encroachments. At first, young Thomas and his family hide in the Colorado mountain wilderness, nurturing their spirituality and living as hunter-gatherers. But his parents' deaths force Thomas into a dismal stint in an Indian reservation boarding school, where he resists acculturation and tries to cling to the old ways of his people. Reaching manhood, he hits the rodeo road, traversing Colorado, Wyoming, Idaho, and Utah to become a champion bronc rider. Like all rodeo men, he learns the "code of the arena," but he also cultivates a fatal aberration from that Cowboy Code: Thomas is a bronc hater, and a killer. His rides are "rough, hard, and punishing," exuding a "cold viciousness," literally killing horses ("snorting bloody foam" from their mouths), and earning him the moniker "Killer Tom Black." If at this point *When the Legends Die* loses credibility as a depiction of early-twentieth-century rodeo, it nevertheless effectively sets the stage for the novel's dramatic climax. Injured in the arena, Thomas Black Bull comes full circle. He returns to his Colorado wilderness home and hunts down one of the last grizzly bears in the mountains. Ultimately, he chooses not to shoot the grizzly, letting this symbol of the old ways endure. "There was no question now of who he was," Borland concludes. "He was a Ute, an Indian, a man of his own beginnings, and nothing would ever change that."[47]

Less polished but much more authentic is *Winterkill* (1984), by Oregon novelist Craig Lesley. Set in the 1970s, *Winterkill* introduces us to Danny Kachiah, a thirty-four-year-old Nez Percé living in a trailer house in the semiarid country surrounding Pendleton, Oregon. Danny is eking out a living wrangling a few cattle and winding down an unsuccessful regional rodeo career as a bulldogger and roughstock rider. The story centers on his transition to parenthood as he regains custody of his teenaged boy, Jack, after Danny's drunken ex-wife's death in a car accident. In fits and starts, Danny and Jack—who have not seen each other for a decade—establish a father-son relationship through rodeo competition (in which Danny coaches Jack), cattle herding, fishing, and traversing the eastern Oregon plains and towns in Danny's pickup truck in search of their family roots and Indian heritage. Along the way there is a colorful cast of modern reservation Indian characters; a lot of rodeo action; a couple of pretty good fistfights; much beer and hard liquor; plenty of tales and western lingo (in the region of Oregon where seafood cocktails are made of "tuna fish and mayonnaise" and good old Indian boys say things like "I like my coffee like my women—hot and dark" *all* the time); a romance between Danny and Tenley Adams (a rodeo trick rider turned land developer); a diabolical scheme by developers to appropriate native lands; and graphic incidents of racism and prejudice toward Pacific Northwest Indians. In a compelling finale, Danny takes Jack deer hunting in the Wallowa country of the Blue Mountains, the sacred Nez Percé homeland, to teach him about his grandfather Red Shirt and the Nez Percé people.[48]

Like Thomas Black Bull in *When the Legends Die,* Danny Kachiah is drawn to the "old ways," but he remembers and interprets them from a marked 1970s perspective. Danny learned his heritage from his dad, Red Shirt, and from elder Indian men. He dances the old dances at the Crow Fair; he hears the stories of Chief Joseph and the "Dreamer" tradition- alists who "took up the rifle" against the "bluecoats" in the famed Nez Percé War. One of his most vivid childhood memories is catching and eating salmon at Celilo Falls, a sacred place on the Columbia River. He and Red Shirt returned to Celilo the day the Army Corps of Engineers closed the floodgates on the Bonneville Dam, and Danny is haunted by memories of the "high wail" of the old Celilo Indians "chanting the falls' death chant." Danny Kachiah hunts, traps, and fishes to stay close to the natural world and the spirit of his people. His annual return to Red Shirt's Wallowa elk camp combines all of the elements of his reverence for the old ways. There he tells Jack stories of Chief Joseph and the "Dreamers," Red Shirt, and Red Shirt's father (Jack's great-grandfather), Medicine Bird. And there Danny finds his father's spirit—his *Weyekin*— embodied in a lone, mysterious wolf who roams the Wallowa."

Ironically, Danny also demonstrates his love of the Indians' old ways through rodeo competition and archetypal Cowboy Code behavior, for to be more of an Indian he has become more of a cowboy. He reminds Jack that Nez Percé were the "Horse People," some of the first and fore- most of the mounted Northwest Indians (and he pokes fun at horseless Columbia River "fish Indians"). *Winterkill* is punctuated with descrip- tions of the bulldogging and roughstock-riding feats of this "honest working cowboy," "Indian cowboy," or—as one announcer puts it— "First American rodeo rider." At the Pendleton Roundup, Danny intro- duces Jack to the world of rodeo, noting that it "feels pretty good" to compete in front of a crowd that includes "some fancy dude with spiffy boots" who "practices law or medicine" and "wouldn't climb on a real bronc or bull for anything because he doesn't have it here." A trip to the Pendleton Roundup Hall of Fame enables Danny to tell Jack about Jackson Sundown, the Nez Percé who, in Danny's view, combined the best of the Indian and cowboy worlds. Viewing a photo of Jackson Sundown with "dark bangs under his flat-brimmed hat," Danny explains that at age eleven Sundown (then known as "Blanket of the Sun") fled wounded to Canada with the Dreamers following Chief Joseph's defeat in the Nez Percé War. He returned and began rodeoing in his late forties, winning Pendleton's bronc-riding crown in 1916.[50]

Danny Kachiah is as much cowboy as he is Indian—it is the combination of the two cultures that defines his personality and lifestyle. He talks like an Indian cowboy, evincing the pronounced reticence and understatement that characterize both cultures. He has a cowboy's passion for western clothing ("nice duds," he calls them), Tony Lama boots, red and midnight-blue cowboy shirts with "stitching on the yoke and mother-of-pearl snaps," complemented by Indian-style turquoise jewelry. Although rednecks are sometimes vilified in *Winterkill* (Red Shirt dies after a drunken fray with two bigots), Danny's trailer-home lifestyle, his tastes in food and music, and his periodic drinking sessions are typical of common rural folk throughout the American West. Indeed, in Danny's love of guns, elk hunting, fishing, trapping, four-wheeling, rodeo, and taverns, we see an archetypal depiction of western rural male folk culture—Indian or cowboy or both. Danny's memory of Red Shirt bursting out of a bronc chute, "his chaps flying, his braid swinging under the straw cowboy hat," provides a vivid image—Indian braid and cowboy hat—of the melding of two ways of life. And at "elk camp"—a significant folk ritual prevalent in both modern white and Indian culture—the novel finds its natural conclusion. Danny and Jack find their ancestors, their heritage. Jack kills his first elk, and his "winterkill" makes him a man, an Indian, and a cowboy.[51]

The depiction of rainbow rodeo riders in movies, literature, poetry, songs, and art fits well within the parameters of archetypal depictions of the rodeo-cowboy hero. Artists portraying African American, Mexican American, Indian, gay, female, and prison cowboys and cowgirls naturally place great importance on themes of racism and sexism, but they ultimately frame their portraits in an archetypal and apolitical form. The rainbow rodeo rider that emerges is a *contemporary ancestor*; he or she represents the forces and values of a frontier lifestyle that is surrounded by an encroaching civilization. As a contemporary ancestor, the rainbow rodeo rider adheres to a Turnerian frontier value system, exhibiting classic cowboy traits that include an absolute loyalty to fellow cowboys and the cowboy way. Ethnicity and sexual orientation are important but ultimately secondary. "If you're a cowboy, you're a cowboy."

This depiction of rainbow rodeo cowboys is, as I noted earlier, quite relevant to current heated debates over "multiculturalism." In *The Disuniting of America* (1992), Arthur Schlesinger Jr. warns of an emerging "cult of ethnicity" among American adherents of multiculturalism. Although Schlesinger goes to great lengths to acknowledge the righteousness of attacks on historic and present-day American racism, he expresses great concern over the multiculturalist challenge to the classic belief in an American "melting pot," creating "one people" out of many races: "The cult of ethnicity . . . rejects the unifying vision of individuals from all nations melted into a new race. Its underlying philosophy is that America is not a nation of individuals at all but a nation of groups, that ethnicity is the defining experience for most Americans, that ethnic ties are permanent and indelible, and that division into ethnic communities establishes the basic structure of American society and the basic meaning of American history." Schlesinger believes that multiculturalists threaten a centuries-old equilibrium that has sustained American development and progress. "Unless a common purpose binds [people] together," he warns, "tribal hostilities will drive them apart."[52]

The "common purpose" Schlesinger sees as necessary to keep his people united is what Gunnar Myrdal called "the American Creed." Schlesinger reintroduces, explicates, and enlarges upon Myrdal's

American Creed, relying in part on the words and ideas of Frederick Jackson Turner. "The frontier," Turner wrote, "promoted the formation of a composite nationality. . . . In the crucible of the frontier immigrants were Americanized, liberated, and fused into a mixed race." The result was a set of uniquely American characteristics that include individualism, adaptability, courage, pragmatism, anti-intellectualism, materialism, and a steadfast belief in democracy, equality, and opportunity. "The American Creed," writes Schlesinger, "envisages a nation composed of individuals making their own choices and accountable to themselves, not a nation based on inviolable ethnic communities. The Constitution turns on individual rights, not on group rights." When individuals among "nonwhite minorities" are wronged in this society, Schlesinger, like Myrdal before him, sees the American Creed "as the spur forever goading Americans to live up to their principles."[53]

Although *The Disuniting of America* makes at times for sobering reading, Schlesinger ends his book on an optimistic note. "The historic forces driving towards 'one people' have not lost their power," he concludes. "Whatever their self-appointed spokesmen may claim, most American-born members of minority groups, white or nonwhite, while they may cherish their particular heritages, still see themselves primarily as Americans and not primarily as Irish or Hungarians or Jews or Africans or Asians."[54]

Our brief look at the ideas and behavior of both mythic and historic rainbow rodeo riders certainly confirms Schlesinger's thesis. To be sure, it is safe to surmise that few rodeo cowboys have read Schlesinger and Myrdal, and that neither of those two scholars has spent much time swigging Coors and swapping lies behind the bulldogging chutes. But the intellectuals' and cowboys' sets of ideas, however differently expressed, are nevertheless closely and intriguingly related. The writings of Myrdal and Schlesinger (and Turner) are important high-culture replications of a wisdom strongly embedded in North American rural folk culture.

Myrdal's American Creed is an intellectualized variant of the Cowboy Code.

Michael Dorris' *A Yellow Raft in Blue Water* (1987) reinforces this point while providing an engaging final example of the archetypal anti-archetype hero of the rainbow rodeo subgenre. In *Yellow Raft* Dorris, a noted post-1960s American Indian writer, tells the story of three Montana Indian women: Ida, her daughter Christine, and Christine's teenaged daughter, Rayona. Through these three women's unique perspectives we learn a family secret; at the same time we gain a better understanding of urban Indians, contemporary Montana Indian reservation culture, the strained yet binding ties of familial love, and a young girl's coming of age. Rayona (Ray), born in Tacoma, Washington, to Christine and Elgin, Ray's estranged African American father, is central to the story line of *Yellow Raft*. When she returns with Christine to Ida's Montana reservation home (from which Christine fled two decades earlier), Ray suffers a crisis of identity. The mixed-race adolescent girl from Tacoma now finds herself in a contemporary rural Indian culture that simultaneously is and is not her own. Running away from Ida and Christine, Ray embarks on an odyssey that takes her across eastern Montana. She has many adventures. She meets her aunts and cousins, learns more about her Uncle Lee (a promising rodeo rider who died in Vietnam), narrowly avoids a lovesick priest's advances, learns of Montana redneck ways, and works a summer job at Bearpaw State Park, where she lives in a trailer house with Evelyn and Sky, an eccentric, compassionate, white working-class couple. Yet it is in her final adventure, aboard a bucking bronc in the Havre All-Indian Rodeo, that Ray finally comes to terms with herself and her American heritage and identity.[55]

Ray is constantly, and often cruelly, reminded that her mother married a black man and that she is half Indian and half African American. In Tacoma and Seattle she is aware of people's gossip about her mixed ethnicity, her unique physical features, the color of her skin, and her bilingualism ("She speaks Indian"). "I can read their thoughts," she complains of two old Indian women eyeing her mother: *"That little Indian woman, I don't know what tribe, with a big black man. And a child, a too-tall girl. She looks like him."* On the Montana reservation, nothing changes. The worst verbal abuse comes from Ray's own cousin, a cowardly would-be rodeo rider named "Foxy" Cree. "You're Christine's kid ... whose father is a nigger," are his first words to her, and it gets worse. He asks if she is a *"Blackfeet"* Indian, makes jokes about her "Coppertone tan," and tells her to go back to Africa. It is Foxy's hate that in part drives her to run away, yet ironically, Foxy's cowardice makes it possible for Ray to resolve her personal crisis.[56]

Surrounding Ray's confusion about her identity are countless pieces of evidence that, once collected, will lead to her triumph—evidence proving that, in spite of racism, nothing in her world can be seen in terms of black or white (or red). Ida, Christine, and Ray, in their respective lives, reflect nearly each and every hue of the ethnic and gender rainbow. Each of the three speaks her native tongue fluently, and Ida and Christine are well aware of, if not steeped in, their Indian tribal culture. Yet all three have cross-acculturated, in varying degrees, to homogenized American lifestyles. We first meet Ida mowing her lawn, wearing Walkman earphones, and singing along to Johnny Lee's "Looking for Love (In All the Wrong Places)" in her "craggy, accented voice." Ida watches *As the World Turns* daily (along with *People's Court*) and on Sunday tunes in a live mass "broadcast from the Catholic cathedral in Denver." When Ray explores Christine's old bedroom (which Ida has left intact for twenty years), she finds evidence of a seemingly typical early 1960s adolescence: "green pedal pushers and ... a Bobby Rydell sweat shirt ... pictures of Elvis Presley, Jacqueline Kennedy, and Connie Francis," and piles of high-school yearbooks and photo albums. Christine brags at one point, "I'm American all the way." Like Ida, Christine is a country-music fan; she lives her life to the accompaniment of Patsy Cline, Kenny Rogers, and the Oak Ridge Boys. Christine's brother, Lee,

was also fully Americanized. Although for a time in the 1960s Lee embraced native folkways and tried out "red power" politics, ultimately,
like many other Indians, he joined the army and fought (and died) for
his country in Vietnam.[57]

And, of course, Lee was a rodeo cowboy, and it is the importance of
rodeo in his life, and finally in Ray's life, that weaves together all of the
disparate red, black, white, and female American strands in *A Yellow
Raft in Blue Water*. "The one thing that was pure Lee was rodeo," Christine remembers. "All over eastern Montana he was getting known. . . .
Lee was on his way to All-Around [champion cowboy] . . . poised to enter the big ones at Cheyenne and Calgary" before the army and Vietnam
intervened. Many Montana reservation Indians followed the rodeo road,
readily adapting rodeo-cowboy lifestyle to their tribes' former nomadic
Indian ways. Foxy Cree aspires to his uncle's rodeo stature, sporting
cowboy shirts, boots, and a "black Navajo hat with a beadwork band"
atop his long black hair in "leather-wrapped braids." But Foxy is too
cowardly to follow in Lee's footsteps. Entering the Havre All-Indian
Rodeo, he proceeds to drink himself into a stupor and cannot ride. Fear-
ing loss of a year's rodeo eligibility, he pulls a knife on Ray and orders
her to disguise herself as a man and ride in his place.[58]

Michael Dorris' account of Ray's ride on the bucking bronc Babe is
only a little short of spectacular. Pushing Foxy's hat over her "long frizzy
hair in . . . a herringbone braid," she mounts Babe and breaks from the
chute. Suddenly the "crowd is color, the whirl of a spun top," her "legs
flap like wings" and she flies off Babe "like a bird coasting . . . spiraling
into a place without bones or weight." Amazingly, Ray picks herself up
and *remounts* Babe, "And bang! We're off again." Thrown to the earth,
she remounts for the *third* time and finally hits her stride: "There is
nothing in the world but [Babe] and I think I can stay up forever." Actually Babe throws her again, but in the process the bronc is exhausted
and subdued. Thus Ray, like the black cowboy Marvel Rogers in Crawford's *Bronc Rider*, has ridden her bronc to a standstill and proved she

has true grit. And when the judges award her a special prize buckle, Ray reveals her true identity to the crowd and television cameras: "I knock off my hat, undo the rubber band, comb with my fingers, and shake out my braid. . . . At first there's silence. Everyone gapes at me and then at each other and then at me again. The quiet hangs like a Seattle fog, as we stand there, facing off in the long afternoon light. And finally from far away, clear and proud, Evelyn shouts: 'Rayona!' . . . And when I raise the silver buckle high above my head, the rest of the crowd joins in."⁵⁹

"The ride on Babe is a boundary I can't recross," Ray concludes. She is a *real cowgirl* now, by virtue of her horsemanship, her western duds, and her new Cowboy Code demeanor. Christine's boyfriend Dayton brags, "She's got guts," adding, "she gets it from Lee, Christine, a natural." Riding Babe, Ray reflects, "I was connected to a power I never knew existed." Viewing her image on the late-night news, she is awed by that power, a force which has, at last, brought her a certain degree of peace and acceptance of herself: "I fill the screen dark and brown. My hair is wild as a star on MTV. To see me, you'd think I could do anything I want." Ray now probably *can* do anything she wants. On the back of a bucking bronc, she has discovered her individuality. A female descendant of African American and Indian peoples, she has embraced horsemanship and a cowboy culture that Hispanic Americans, Anglo-Americans, and Celtic Americans introduced to her ancestors a century earlier. And in seeing, for the first time, the beauty and strength of the "dark and brown" wild-haired girl on the television screen, Ray has discovered more than her pride in descent from African and Indian peoples. She has discovered that she is proud to be a North American cowgirl.⁶⁰

CHAPTER SEVEN

"Hooked on an 8 Second Ride"
The Rodeo Cowboy as Contemporary
Ancestor and Popular-Culture Hero

I've got two words to say to you: *Cowboy Up.*
—Tuff to Lane in *8 Seconds* (1993)

In the 1990s the western and its rodeo subgenre returned triumphantly to American literature, poetry, art, music, and movies. Prominent among the rodeo offerings of the early 1990s was a solid movie directed by John G. Avildsen, written by Monte Merrick, and called simply *8 Seconds* (1993). It is the most recent in a long line of rodeo popular arts, replicating and embellishing upon themes of *The Lusty Men* (1952), *The Bronc Rider* (1965), *Moving On* (1970), *Junior Bonner* (1972), *For All Our Cowboy Friends* (1981), and many other rodeo movies, books, poems, paintings, and songs. Although not the most ambitious or significant work of the rodeo arts, *8 Seconds* accomplishes its business with strength and effect.

The movie traces (and embellishes upon) the life of Oklahoman Lane Frost, a world-champion bull rider who tragically lost his life in the 1989 Cheyenne Frontier Days Rodeo. Luke Perry and Stephen Baldwin post solid performances as Frost and his traveling buddy and best friend, roughstock champ Tuff Hedeman. With their cowboy-poet pal Cody Lambert (Red Mitchell), the bull riders travel the now-familiar southwestern rodeo road in Tuff's Cadillac from Del Rio to Cheyenne, sleeping in cramped motel rooms, drinking beer and brawling in western barrooms, and chasing their dreams of a world-championship belt buckle. Unlike Baldwin's hard-drinking, outspoken Tuff, Perry's Lane is humble about his bull-riding prowess, speaking in a soft, authentic Oklahoma twang and showing the gentler side of the cowboy way. Lane falls head over heels for rodeo barrel racer Kellie Kyle (*Northern Exposure*'s Cynthia Geary) in a romance plot that is, at times, just a bit too sweet. Although Lane wins his buckle at the 1987 National Finals Rodeo, he is haunted by a desire to please his uncommunicative father, former champion Clyde Frost (James Rebhorn), and this problem temporarily threatens his marriage to Kellie. The two go through infidelity and hard times before they reconcile and plan a new home and a life in the Oklahoma countryside. Their dreams are gored by a Brahma bull in Cheyenne. At movie's end, Kellie and Tuff resign themselves to Lane's death and move ahead with their lives, resolving to respect and continue to give life to Lane Frost's courage and gentlemanly Cowboy Code legacy.

8 Seconds sits firmly upon a base of live arena bull-riding scenes filmed on location in San Antonio, Texas. These colorful, exciting, and violent vignettes serve as the introduction to, transitions for, and dramatic conclusion of the much less compelling romance and family-strife components of the story line. Like rodeo-movie cowboys Jeff McCloud and Junior Bonner before him, Lane is drawn irresistibly to the treacherous side of rodeo; he craves the danger of riding Brahma bulls. Junior Bonner's obsession with and ultimate mastery over Sunshine is echoed in Frost's yearning and ultimate success in riding the "unrideable" Brahma Red Rock. Yet like his predecessors, Lane Frost is no bull-hater. When he first meets Kellie, she is suspicious of bull riders (whom she characterizes as crazed "little men with big egos" and "skinny butts"). He tries to win her over, joking that "bulls ain't got nothin' against ya. They just wanta buck ya off and git on with their business." Kellie remains unconvinced until Lane delivers a roughstock soliloquy reminiscent of Jeff McCloud's speech to Louise Merritt in *The Lusty Men.* "I got a lot of respect for them bulls," Lane informs her. "Ya know when one of them comes bustin' out of the gate it's like you're tied onto a tornado . . . it's not like you're tryin' to break his spirit, you're just tryin' to stay with him jump for jump. It's like every wild or free thing in the world is right there in the palm of your hand."

Some critics have derided Avildsen's movie, poking fun at Lane's "aw-shucks" demeanor, his sappy courtship of Kellie, and the "personality transplant" one critic deems necessary for Perry's Frost to spurn his wife and father at midmovie and then somehow come back to them again. Yet in the end the overdrawn romance and family-discord themes of *8 Seconds* prove inconsequential. For this sturdy, well-acted movie is not at all about marriage and family—it is about cowboys and rodeo. And in this sense, its most important theme is the evolving friendship of Lane Frost and Tuff Hedeman: *8 Seconds* is the story of how Lane and Tuff teach each other what it means to be a cowboy.

Stephen Baldwin's inspired portrayal of Tuff ranks with the greatest rodeo-cowboy hero portrayals. Baldwin's Tuff has the look, gait, voice, and attitude of a *real cowboy*. But Tuff also has a "mean and hateful" side. Initially he is disdainful of Lane, labeling him a "puss" for his gentle ways and chivalrous behavior. "You can't be a cowboy and a nice guy, Lane," he chides. "It just don't work like that. We've got an image to uphold. Drinkin', lovin', fightin', cowboyin'. . . . You ain't got what it takes." But Tuff is also jealous of Lane's riding prowess and cannot understand how Lane has combined humility with skill to become "one of the best goddamned bullriders in the circuit." On the other hand, Tuff possesses a courage and steadfastness that Lane admires and seeks to emulate. Thus in a character juxtaposition closely resembling that of Pepper Martin and Sonny Gilstrap of *The Cowboy Way* (which appeared the same year), Lane and Tuff represent *both* sides of the same Cowboy

Code. To make themselves whole, they must learn from each other, shedding their failings and cultivating each other's strengths. Tuff eventually learns some manners from Lane, and by movie's end he shows the Code humility, hospitality, and honesty so essential to a true cowboy. What Lane learns from Tuff is grit and determination, for they don't call him "Tuff" for nothing. "When I was four years old," Tuff informs Kellie, "I got my hand slammed in a car door. Never did cry or nothin'. So they started callin' me 'tough nut.' It got shortened."

This all comes to a head after a bull stomps Lane's groin in Del Rio, Texas. Lying in a first-aid tent in excruciating pain, Lane seeks but gets no consoling from Tuff. Nonchalantly reading a copy of *Rodeo Sports News,* Tuff drolly assures Lane that his "dick [is] still there" but "hangin' by a thread . . . you don't wanna see it." In self-pity, Lane states that he might go home and forget about rodeo. Tuff becomes furious: "Well, maybe you just oughta quit, Lane. Go home, work your daddy's ranch, live to be a hundred. Sit in your rockin' chair. Watch the sun go down. That'd be nice, wouldn't it? Real special. And then, before you croak, one last little thought's gonna keep goin' through that pretty little head of yours over and over and over again. 'I'm a puss. I was the best god-damned bullrider in the circuit and I chickened out.' I've got two words to say to you: *Cowboy Up.*" Sobered by this tongue-lashing, Lane learns his lesson. The next time we see him he is, in obviously great pain, mounting the bull Double Trouble in the next go-round in Del Rio. "You got the guts now," Tuff assures him. Lane rides Double Trouble and at last becomes a *real cowboy.*

"The American West was settled in a spirit of courage, determination, and friendship," reads the introductory epigraph to *8 Seconds.* "The Old West may be gone, but the spirit survives." From the movie's perspective, the spirit survives in rodeo cowboys like Lane and Tuff, who adhere to the Cowboy Code, bringing nineteenth-century values to twentieth-century society. Like his predecessors, Lane Frost represents the values of "country people . . . down-to-earth, [and] sincere." Like *Urban Cowboy*'s Bud Davis and many other rodeo-cowboy heroes, Lane "sure would like to have some [land] . . . someday" and somehow re-create the nineteenth century in the twentieth. Like Bud, but unlike Jeff McCloud, J. W. Coop, and Junior Bonner, Lane seeks a woman partner, a cowgirl who shares his respect for "country people" and their ways. But as with Dawson Legate of Red Steagall's haunting ballad, this cannot be. The mythical rodeo man can follow only one of two paths. He can either keep "movin' on down that road" or he can die. Jeff McCloud and J. W. Coop die in the arena. So does Dawson Legate, after trying unsuccessfully to leave rodeo and settle down to a family and ranch on the Canadian prairie. Lane Frost shows Kellie the land he has purchased for their ranch, but the rodeo calls him back. Even though he has not ridden in months, Lane feels the urge to move on because "everybody's spectin' me up to Cheyenne." Of course they are expecting him. He is a world-champion cowboy. He lives by cowboy rules. "The Old West may be gone, but the spirit survives."[1]

That the "spirit" of the western genre lives on vibrantly in North American popular culture is a fact apparent to all but a handful of literary critics and "new" western historians. These scholars' isolation from mainstream American popular culture is evident in a March 1993 *New York Times Book Review* critique of Richard Slotkin's *Gunfighter Nation* (1992), a book that darkly examines the importance of western movies and literature in varied facets of modern American civilization. Although the critic finds the western themes of Slotkin's work of some importance in assessing American history and culture, she ultimately judges even this 1960s-flavored treatment as too old-fashioned for sophisticated postmodern critics. "This book," she writes definitively, "appears at a time when popular enthusiasm for the western has all but evaporated." Eight days later, Clint Eastwood's western blockbuster *The Unforgiven* (1992) swept the Academy Awards, winning four Oscars, including those for best picture and best director.[2]

In the late 1980s and early 1990s, beginning well before publication of the review just cited, the western genre was proving once again its classic stature in the American popular arts. The number and quality of movie and television westerns echoed trends apparent in literature, poetry, art, and music. The classic 1989 television miniseries *Lonesome Dove* (based on Larry McMurtry's Pulitzer Prize–winning 1985 novel) spawned eight western movies from 1990 to 1992, most notably *Dances with Wolves* (1990) and *City Slickers* (1991). Two Geronimo movies — *Geronimo* and *Geronimo: An American Legend* — appeared in 1993, as did *Tombstone*. In 1994 movie audiences lined up to see *8 Seconds*, *Bad Girls*, *City Slickers II*, *The Cowboy Way*, *Wyatt Earp*, and *eleven* other feature-length western movies. The 1992–1993 television season offered only four prime-time western series (including *Young Guns*), but the 1993–1994 season had *thirteen*, among them *Harts of the West*, Chuck Norris' *Walker, Texas Ranger*, and *Dr. Quinn, Medicine Woman*. Meanwhile, three western documentary miniseries appeared on cable and public television, followed by a television *Lonesome Dove* sequel and a *Bonanza* remake, with a *Gunsmoke* revival in the offing. This strong western lineup is rivaled only by that of the 1950s and early 1960s, when the western quite literally ruled American movie houses and television stations.[3]

Contemporary fascination with the West and things western is reflected in Michael Johnson's *New Westers: The West in Contemporary American Culture* (1996). Johnson writes about many facets of today's western-culture movement, with specific chapters on western clothing and fashion, literature, the cowboy poetry movement, historians, movies, country music, and dancing. He concludes that the participants in the movement "in their increasing numbers, passions, and activities constitute an event of the first magnitude."[4]

Johnson's work corroborates the Wrangler Western Index (1994), an extensive quantified marketing report and analysis of western influences on American consumer culture. Journalists and media reporters were most drawn to the Wrangler Index's report that 60 percent of men and 50 percent of women surveyed said that they wanted to be cowboys or cowgirls for at least a day, and 25 percent of those aged thirty-five to forty-nine said they would like to try cowboying for at least a year. Yet other facets of the index reflect more accurately the deep significance of the West and western lifestyle for North Americans. Western tour companies, for instance, reported a 22 percent increase in business from 1993 to 1994, and dude ranch bookings increased by 30 percent. The Country Western Line Dancing Association reported a 400 percent increase in membership from 1992 to 1993. Shopping malls throughout urban North America house popular western-wear outlets, and western art, ranging from Navajo jewelry to Remington sculptures, proliferates. Revenues from country-music sales more than doubled in the first half of the decade. Country-music radio stations ranked number one in fifty-seven of America's top 100 markets, including Detroit, Cleveland, Baltimore, Buffalo, Seattle, and San Diego (41.6 percent of all North American adults tune in at least once a week to country-music stations). In the summer of 1997, country musician Garth Brooks drew a quarter of a million people to a seemingly unlikely "rural venue"— New York City's Central Park. Moreover, this fascination with the West is manifesting itself demographically. The population growth in the Rocky Mountain region (Arizona, Colorado, Idaho, Montana, Nevada, New Mexico, and Utah) is now twice the national average, and the annual change in housing permits issued in the region jumped from plus 15 percent in 1991 to nearly plus 50 percent in 1992. Clearly, many Americans are moving west, and many more are buying western products and engaging in varied facets of western lifestyle.[5]

The Wrangler Index also addresses the rising popularity and importance of North American rodeo and rodeo cowboys. While rodeo is booming in the West, states east of the Mississippi River have also seen record-breaking increases in annual rodeo-ticket revenue during the

1990s. In 1993, for example, Illinois, Michigan, Ohio, and New York reported annual rodeo-ticket revenue increases of 66 percent, 99 percent, 135 percent, and 67 percent, respectively. Meanwhile, millions of Americans watch rodeo on television. TNN, ESPN, and other cablevision outlets regularly show live and prerecorded rodeo events. ESPN's *Wrangler World of Rodeo* series features eight annual rodeos, each viewed by up to 472,000 households. The National Finals Rodeo has been featured in same-day ESPN broadcasts since the mid-1980s. This annual ESPN offering of ten two-hour National Finals shows now attracts, on the average, 520,000 households per show. Although in no way rivaling the World Series or Super Bowl, the National Finals Rodeo is nevertheless one of the fastest-growing sports television venues in the industry.[6]

Advertisers have long used the rodeo mystique to market their products. As early as 1936, Camel cigarette ads featured brief vignettes about steer wrestler Dick Shelton, "World Champion All-Round Cowboy and Camel Smoker." In the late 1940s, Wrangler took the lead in marketing its jeans via a rodeo image, employing Rodeo Ben and RCA cowboy consultants to design a special brand of "rodeo jeans"—the 13MWZ." In 1962, as part of its ongoing rodeo-based promotions, Wrangler published a forty-nine-issue series of *Great Moments in Rodeo* comic books, featuring the stories of all-around champions Dean Oliver, Benny Reynolds, Harley May, and others who wore and endorsed Wrangler jeans. Today, Wrangler remains at the forefront of rodeo advertising. A recent magazine ad features 1950s and 1960s champion bull riders Freckles Brown and Jim Shoulders in 13MWZS: "Since 1947 cowboys have been putting on our jeans. Since 1947, bulls have been trying to get them off. . . . If you want real cowboy jeans, make sure you get the only ones designed by real cowboys. Wrangler 13MWZ Cowboy Cut Jeans."[7]

In the 1980s and 1990s, scores of advertisers jumped on the rodeo bandwagon,[8] promoting products ranging from soda pop to four-wheel-drive vehicles. Resistol now advertises its hats with a "Triple Threat"—roughstock champs Jim Sharp, Ty Murray, and Tuff Hedeman—who all "ride with Resistol." Coca-Cola magazine ads feature a bull rider ready to "turn out" above the Coke logo and slogan Can't Beat the Real Thing. Levi Strauss, not to be outdone by its Wrangler competitors, uses a rodeo-cowboy arena scene as background for an ad urging readers to buy Levi's "for rough going" and adding, "Go to rodeo—America's most exciting sport." Isuzu Motors Limited informs us that its sports-utility Rodeo is a "darn good getaway vehicle" whose four-wheel-drive capabilities can "follow your lead" down "deserted back roads. . . . Not since you were a scout have you been so ready to handle what lies ahead—be it mud, snow, ice, rain, or loose gravel. . . . How's that for freedom of choice?"[9]

All of this rodeo-specific advertising coalesces each year on ESPN's coverage of the Las Vegas National Finals Rodeo. Sponsors include Dodge (trucks), Coca-Cola, Coors, Copenhagen/Skoal, Justin (boots), Resistol, Seagram, Purina, and of course Wrangler. Nearly all of the advertising is cowboy- or rodeo-specific, tapping the mythical dimension of rodeo to appeal to the audience. The rodeo man who emerges from these advertisements is an archetypal Turnerian adherent to the Code of the West. Like the rodeo cowboys of movies, television, literature, poetry, art, and music, he is individualistic, courageous, skilled, resourceful, plain-spoken, humble, loyal, and democratic. His relationship with women is, of course, elusive, as rodeo advertisers tap individualistic themes like those popularized thirty years ago by Ian and Sylvia in "Someday Soon." Thus one attractive, smitten woman admiringly describes her cowboy lover in a Wrangler advertisement: "He's crazy about the rodeo. He *says* he's crazy about me. I don't know, maybe he's just plain crazy." Someday soon, goin' with him, someday soon (in Wrangler jeans, of course).[10]

One should proceed with caution in ascribing significance to popular culture. Having said that, I am nevertheless struck by the continuous presence of rodeo cowboys in modern North American popular culture. Throughout the twentieth century, the rodeo-cowboy hero has played an important minor role in the western genre of movies, literature, poetry, art, and music. This pattern continues today, with prime-time rodeo sports broadcasts, rodeo images in advertising, movies like *8 Seconds* and *The Cowboy Way*, and other artistic rodeo works ranging from Ken Kesey's *Last Go Round* to Paul Zarzyski's *Roughstock Sonnets* to Walter Piehl's impressionistic *Sweethearts of the Rodeo* paintings to Garth Brooks' hit songs "Rodeo" and "The Beaches of Cheyenne" to, as we have seen throughout this book, much more.

To be sure, the rodeo cowboy is not the only contemporary popular-culture hero. Nor should we overintellectualize or attach *too* much significance to his role. One could certainly argue that it is modern urban themes, not rural ones, that dominate contemporary popular arts, from rap music to television series featuring inner-city police, doctor, and lawyer heroes. All I am saying here is that the rodeo-cowboy hero has appeared for so long and in so many popular art forms that we must pay attention to him. His persistent presence in modern North American movies, literature, poetry, art, and music demands an answer to a final difficult question: *Why* is the rodeo cowboy a contemporary North American popular-culture hero?[11]

Not so long ago, the first generation of American Studies scholars believed that they had laid the groundwork for interpreting and understanding the Myth of the West in American history and popular culture. In the 1950s and 1960s, Henry Nash Smith, John William Ward, Leo Marx, and others analyzed and interpreted the western genre in, respectively, *Virgin Land: The American West as Symbol and Myth* (1950), *Andrew Jackson: Symbol for an Age* (1953), "The Meaning of Charles Lindbergh's Flight," *The Machine in the Garden: Technology and the Pastoral Ideal in America* (1964), and other important works. This myth/symbol school, as it came to be called, of American Studies offered a straightforward interpretation of the western and its significance to Americans. From the *Leatherstocking Tales* to cowboy movies, they argued, westerns have been a major genre in the American arts because they strike a responsive chord, tapping deep emotions in the American people. One obvious reason for this is that the western tells the epic story of an American people crossing a continental frontier and taming its wild forces, planting and nurturing the seeds of North American civilization. Yet, the myth/symbolists argued further, the real power of the western stems from an inherent irony or tragedy within this story. For in civilizing the wild frontier, American pioneers simultaneously destroyed a natural world, a frontier lifestyle, and a code of behavior that they truly valued and loved. The power of the western, then, writes John William Ward, is found in "the field of energy defined by the poles of Nature and Civilization," the wild and the tame. And this polarity accounts for what Ward and other myth/symbol scholars describe as the "persistent nostalgia of our advanced industrial and technological society in the twentieth century"—a nostalgia that manifests itself in the persistence of the western genre.[12]

In the late 1960s and early 1970s, poststructuralist literary critics and "new" western historians proved true the physical law that for every action there is an equal and opposite reaction. This second generation of American Studies scholars—raised and trained in the fires of 1960s ferment and political activism—found much wanting in the upbeat works of Smith, Ward, and Marx. Their opening volley was Bruce Kucklick's seminal 1972 essay "Myth and Symbol in American Studies," which labeled Smith's classic *Virgin Land* atheoretical and a prime example of "a scholarly genre" that "has not adequately defined what it is about." Kucklick quoted Alan Trachtenberg's critique of *Virgin Land* as a book that "prefers to exemplify rather than theorize."[13]

Although most of the new critics agreed that the western provided a key to understanding American civilization, they proceeded to paint a much less positive portrait of that civilization, the western myth it fostered, and those today who celebrate that myth. Most of their critique was aimed at the code of values portrayed in the western myth. Whereas Smith and his colleagues emphasized Turnerian traits of individualism, democracy, equality, ingenuity, and courage, poststructuralist literary scholars and "new" western historians argued otherwise. Richard Slotkin, Jane Tompkins, Blake Allmendinger, Patricia Nelson Limerick, Richard White, and others pointed to negative frontier traits such as violence, coarse behavior, wastefulness, and anti-intellectualism (these scholars seemed unaware that Turner had also delineated these traits as typically western). Moreover, the new scholars' dark portrait of the West and the western genre adopted a neo-Marxist analysis of class conflict, racism, and sexism—issues of prime concern to their own 1960s generation. The result was an interpretation of the western that turned the myth/symbol school's analysis on its head.[14]

Today, after twenty-five years of revisionism, it is time to search for a synthesis. It is time to think seriously about American Studies, to salvage the best of the old and new methodologies, discard the rest, and move on in our search for the meaning of the West and the western in North American history and culture.

A good place to begin is with "The Quest for the National Character," David Potter's essay first published nearly forty years ago. Potter was an American Studies scholar whose concept of "character" corresponds quite closely to a more contemporary folkloric use of the term "myth." In this usage a myth is not a falsehood—rather, it is a strongly held idea or set of ideas that has great meaning to a people. Potter searches in his essay for the true American character, and he arrives at an impasse, or rather, a paradox. Potter sees two prime, equally powerful, and contradictory interpretations (myths) of American character, those of Frederick Jackson Turner and Alexis de Tocqueville. In Turner's view, the American character is democratic, individualistic, courageous, ingenious, anti-intellectual, and idealistic (traits that, as we have seen, closely correspond to frontier Cowboy Code values). Tocqueville, the brilliant French observer, saw the American character in a much less favorable light. He thought that American' love of freedom would ultimately be overwhelmed by majoritarian democracy and egalitarianism. Tocqueville's American was, at heart, a conformist and a materialist. Given a choice between liberty and equality—freedom or security— Tocqueville foresaw the American opting for equality and security every time.[15]

Potter was never quite able to unravel his paradox, but it has great relevance to this study of rodeo and rodeo cowboys. Turner's and Tocqueville's interpretations, of course, fit perfectly into the frontier/civilization dialectic—John William Ward's "poles of Nature and Civilization" and Elizabeth Atwood Lawrence's juxtaposition of "wild and tame"—that have provided the "field of energy" for my study. Turner's American represents an older, preindustrial American culture; Tocqueville's American is more modern and urbane. Turner's American represents the frontier, Tocqueville's represents civilization; one is wild, one is tame. Yet the paradox remains. Which is the true American character (myth)? Is the American an urban conformist or a frontier individualist? Is there more than one myth, or is there a possible synthesis? If there is a synthesis, what does Turner's American share with Tocqueville's?

Contemporary "cognitive dissonance theory" can be of some help here. Cognitive dissonance, psychologists tell us, is a form of "psychological discomfort" found in individuals who entertain "inconsistent . . . opinions and values." For example, a person who regularly takes his or her spouse and family to church on Sunday but spends the rest of the weekend in an adulterous relationship probably suffers from cognitive dissonance. So does a person who smokes cigarettes before and after visiting the doctor's office for lung-cancer treatments. When individuals suffer from cognitive dissonance, they naturally try to reduce it; indeed, they must reduce it in order to maintain mental health. Although

changes of behavior can certainly remedy cognitive dissonance, ratio-
nalization and other avoidance behaviors are common antidotes. Thus
the adulterer may try to convince himself that there are "two kinds of
love," and the smoker may embrace pseudoscientific studies discount-
ing a relationship between cigarettes and cancer. There are other ways
to cope with cognitive dissonance. I would argue here that *mythologization* is also an effective way to reduce cognitive dissonance.[16]

The industrial revolution, one could argue, has caused cognitive dissonance of epic proportions. Formerly agricultural people find themselves in a world of cities and high technology. They know well the incredible advantages this transition has brought them: a record high
standard of living and gross national product, longer lives and lower
infant mortality, democratic political institutions and accessible public education, and countless consumer amenities, from hot tubs to mi-
crowave entrées to laptop computers. Yet these modern folk cannot help
but look around them and ponder the cost of the changes their society
has so rapidly undergone. They see that they have paid a high price for
modernity. The family unit has frayed. Cities and suburbs fail to nur-
ture the tight communities and neighborhoods of old. Low-cost, high-
quality handmade merchandise has disappeared. People have lost direct
contact with the natural world—the mountains, prairies, bodies of water, and fresh air—as they spend more and more time in crowded and
unhealthy urban environments. This clash between the embrace of modernity and a yearning for the past creates a classic case of cognitive dissonance.

This dissonance began more than 160 years ago, amid the Jacksonian
advent of the American industrial revolution. As the dissonance began,
so did attempts to deal with it through mythologization. Historians and
literary scholars have argued that Jacksonian Americans embraced folk
heroes like Davy Crockett, Daniel Boone, and Mike Fink, the *Leatherstocking Tales* of James Fenimore Cooper, and the down-home politics
of "Old Hickory," "Old Tip," and "Honest Abe" as a salve for the psycho-

logical aches and pains of modernity. Later, as Henry Nash Smith has shown, the Kit Carson dime novels and an emerging western genre captured the attention of a nation of Gilded Age shopkeepers and factory workers who also revered President Teddy Roosevelt, the Dakota cowboy and "Rough Rider." In the 1920s and 1930s the movie western came of age, and while the common folk flocked to see Gene Autry and Roy Rogers, the intellectuals pursued what historian T. Jackson Lears has described as a revolt against "modernity."[17]

Following World War II, and extending to the present day, North Americans continue to answer the contradictory calls of our cognitive dissonance. The late 1940s and 1950s gave us Missouri's Harry Truman and Kansas' Ike Eisenhower, the first (but not last) presidents from west of the Mississippi. The 1950s fostered television and movie westerns by the thousands. In 1960 John F. Kennedy offered Americans the vision of a "New Frontier," and his successor held court from the LBJ Ranch. Even the hippies jumped on board in their own unique way, donning leatherstockings and Indian beads and calling for a "return to the land" in a voice that sounded remarkably Jeffersonian. In 1968, a year that gave us the Tet offensive, LBJ's political demise, the King and Kennedy assassinations, and the Chicago riots, what was the most watched television program in North America? It was *The Andy Griffith Show* (1960–1968), the compelling and humorous saga of life in a small, contemporary Appalachian community. (Less artistically ambitious rural shows proliferated: *The Real McCoys, The Beverly Hillbillies, Green Acres, Petticoat Junction,* etc.). While 1970s Americans turned their attention to Watergate, *The Waltons,* and *Little House on the Prairie,* they elected to the presidency Jimmy Carter, a sometime peanut farmer and devout Christian (and nuclear engineer). Of course, the denouement of mythologization as an antidote for cognitive dissonance came with President Ronald Reagan. Although Reagan had not grown up on a farm or served in combat, he had played cowboys and frontier soldiers galore in movies and on television. His stint on television's *Death Valley Days* served as training for presidential holidays spent, LBJ-style, on his California "ranch."[18]

Meanwhile, as an integral part of mythologization, contemporary North Americans have continually coped with and alleviated cognitive dissonance in the everyday details of their personal lives. Their strategies are far too numerous and complicated to discuss here, and a few examples will have to suffice. For instance, gardening and yard work readily assuage the tensions of urban and suburban living for some North Americans—thus the grandchildren of farmers continue to till their fields, as it were, creating their own backyard Gardens of Eden. Or they seek recreation in the natural world on weekends, trekking to the mountains to ski or backpack, leaving the pressures of their city lives behind. They do not necessarily leave the amenities behind, however. Their trek might take place in a high-cost recreational vehicle, bound for a comfortable cabin or vacation home in the "wild" (where they can watch *Gunsmoke* and *Bonanza* reruns via satellite dish). That recreational vehicle probably sports a name like Bronco, Winnebago, Explorer, Cherokee, or Rodeo to reconfirm the frontier quality of their vacation. On the road they might tune in a country-music radio station or play a new-age cassette of "Native American flute music." Their diet might also verge on the "wild," emphasizing health via a salad and fruit juices, "natural" granola desserts, or boxed cereals that taste "just like wild hickory nuts." Skiing and hiking keep the body fit, and sports and "working out" do for the urban North American what a hard day in the fields did for his grandparents. Attire for treks or for weekends at home might be casual and "western," with Eddie Bauer answering the needs of the urban rustic.

I believe that these examples, and many, many more like them, lead ultimately to a synthesis that might fulfill David Potter's "Quest for the National Character." Note the concurrence of old and new—frontier and civilization, wild and tame, Turnerian and Tocquevillian—elements in each example. Nature calls the North American, but he arrives in a Winnebago and decked out in Eddie Bauer duds. The American listens to country music, but it is performed with electric guitars and arrives via highly commercialized metropolitan radio stations (or at heavily amplified stadium-concert venues). John F. Kennedy advocates not just a frontier, but a *New* Frontier. Andy Griffith's Mayberry clings lovingly to its old ways in the midst of an impersonal modern civilization. The hippies espouse an all-American agrarian philosophy while simultaneously claiming to be a modern and radical *counter*culture. *The Waltons* rely on nineteenth-century values and common sense to meet the challenges of the Great Depression and World War II. Jimmy Carter is a peanut farmer who also happens to be a Naval Academy graduate in nuclear engineering. Ronald Reagan, whose "aw-shucks" demeanor makes him our surrogate grandfather on the ol' homestead, is also the grim and savvy leader of a cold war fight-to-the death against a Communist "evil empire."

David Potter sought a synthesis of Turner's and Tocqueville's contradictory and paradoxical assessments of American character—a synthesis of Turner's individualistic frontier American and Tocqueville's conformist contemporary American. I would argue that Potter's paradox is a direct result of cognitive dissonance—the conflicting values of formerly Turnerian agricultural people who have become Tocquevillian urbanites and lost their ties to the land. To reduce this dissonance, Americans have turned to myth—not myth as falsehood, but rather myth as a strongly held set of beliefs. This myth has produced many phenomena like those just discussed. In the process, it has also produced a new popular-culture hero—a *contemporary ancestor*—who fuses the historic American with the modern American.

This contemporary-ancestor hero is the end result of a long evolution in American folk and literary traditions. Beginning in the Jacksonian era and stretching into the Gilded Age, American folk and literary heroes were staunchly antiprogress. Daniel Boone kept "movin' on" every time he saw a neighbor's smoke or heard the sound of axes, and so did Davy Crockett, Mike Fink, and Cooper's Leatherstocking. In Mark Twain's classic *Adventures of Huckleberry Finn,* Huck and Jim float serenely down their beloved Mississippi, only to lose their idyll in the jaws of a smoke-belching steamboat. And John Henry, the last of the antimodern folk heroes, dies "with his hammer in his hand, Lord Lord." He defeats the steam-driven hammer, but only at the cost of his own death and martyrdom to a vanished way of life. Interestingly, at the same time that John Henry battled the steam hammer, another folk hero, Casey Jones, put his hand on the throttle and let a steam locomotive engine roar him to a much different kind of martyrdom. During the Gilded Age, a new kind of folklore and popular-culture hero emerged — a contemporary ancestor who combined his frontier individualism with *machinery* to achieve preindustrial ends via industrial means.[19]

In the twentieth century, this new contemporary-ancestor hero proliferated in folklore and popular culture. Sergeant Alvin York brought a homespun Appalachian accent to America's entry into the total global warfare of World War I. A little earlier, in the North American Southwest, Pancho Villa outfoxed General "Black Jack" Pershing with folkloric trickster antics and his Model T Ford, celebrated in folk song as "La Cucaracha." Charles Lindbergh, the "Lone Eagle," rose meteorically to 1920s fame, one could argue, because he epitomized Turnerian frontier strengths while simultaneously seated in the cockpit of a modern transoceanic aircraft (Amelia Earhart feminized that same mystique a decade later). Audie Murphy, the son of Texas sharecroppers, hunted game on his native grasslands before earning more combat medals than any other World War II soldier; he subsequently pursued a Hollywood career that included scores of grade-B cowboy movies. More recently, astronaut John Glenn epitomizes the small-town values and courageous Code behavior that Tom Wolfe has dubbed *the right stuff.*[20]

The rodeo-cowboy hero, of course, rides alongside his fellow contemporary ancestors, from Sergeant York to Charles Lindbergh to Harry

Truman to the Apollo astronauts. As with his cohorts, the rodeo man's mystique is based on actual historical circumstances. Gone are nearly all of the old rancher critics who once claimed he was not a *real cowboy*. In the second half of the twentieth century, the rodeo man has come to represent the most vibrant remaining form of traditional cowboy culture. Painstakingly preserving and honoring cowboy traditions, he is one of the staunchest adherents to the legendary Code of the West. And modern-day North Americans can see the rodeo hero any time of the year, from their television-room couch or in the comfort of grandstand seats while drinking big plastic cups full of draft beer. In the arena, the rodeo man acts out the taming of the West, roping calves, bulldogging steers, and riding the wild broncs. When his job is done—when he has symbolically tamed the wild frontier to make way for civilization—the rodeo-cowboy hero has to "move on down the road." He hits that rodeo road, not astride his horse but in a pickup truck or aboard a jet airplane, en route to the next Holiday Inn and the next rodeo show. He is a nineteenth-century man in a twentieth-century world—an *urban cowboy*, an *electric horseman*, helping the Apollo astronauts and John Wayne and Ronald Reagan and Lane Frost keep guard over the New Frontier.

And when the rodeo is over, modern-day North Americans continue to admire the rodeo man in movies and on television, in novels and poetry, in art, and in country music. It may be a late-night rerun of Mitchum's Jeff McCloud in the classic *Lusty Men;* or Larry McMurtry's novel *Moving On;* or Ian and Sylvia's "Someday Soon"; or Copland and de Mille's *Rodeo;* or Michael Dorris' *A Yellow Raft in Blue Water;* or John Avildsen's *8 Seconds;* or one of thousands of other popular-culture representations of rodeo and rodeo cowboys. Whatever the form, the rodeo-cowboy hero will always be there. He may not be the most important contemporary popular culture hero, but he is most certainly persistent. And his longevity and popularity stem ultimately from his character traits. The rodeo hero is ubiquitous because he is consummately American, embodying Turnerian traits and complete loyalty to this Cowboy

Code and to his fellow cowboys. It could be that he is only a fantasy or, as D. H. Lawrence once called Leatherstocking, a "wish-fulfillment." Then again, he may not be a fantasy at all. Or perhaps he is located somewhere between the "real" and the "ideal," between life and art. However one chooses to define myth, the rodeo man clearly embodies a vibrant myth. In choosing to pay homage to him, North Americans demonstrate their excellent taste. They can learn much from this rodeo-cowboy hero.

The interconnection of life and popular arts forms the core of the music and showmanship of Chris LeDoux, the retired world saddle-bronc champ and country-music singing star. *Chris LeDoux Live*, a video of his 1992 Bally's Casino performance (filmed during the Las Vegas National Finals Rodeo), takes the rodeo mystique one step beyond country music into the world of rock-and-roll videos. Although LeDoux is known as a country traditionalist, he sings in one song that there is in fact a "little long-haired outlaw inside my soul." This outlaw streak is immediately evident in the rock components of the *Live* video. LeDoux takes the stage amid smoke bombs, high-tech lighting effects, and the kind of guitar theatrics that might well drape a performance by a heavy-metal star. But it is rodeo hero Chris LeDoux here, dressed in jeans, boots, a royal-blue western shirt, and a bead-banded Stetson. His band, Western Underground, similarly attired, belts out a set based solidly on LeDoux's country and rodeo roots while simultaneously aspiring to the world of hard-core rock. Garth Brooks experimented successfully with the concept of a rock-and-roll rodeo song in "Rodeo," but it is the outlaw LeDoux who brings rodeo rock-and-roll home to roost. He does so in "Hooked on an 8 Second Ride."

"Hooked on an 8 Second Ride"[21] begins as a transition from "Seventeen," a lyrical ballad about a young man who answers the call of the rodeo road. "The sweet voice of freedom echoes down the Ages," LeDoux sings in conclusion to "Seventeen," "and calls another cowboy on his way." Playing a gentle acoustic guitar solo to leave the ballad, LeDoux suddenly strikes a strong and heavily amplified chord. A fog of smoke begins to rise from the drummer's platform, and the Western Underground's three guitarists move together center-stage. The crowd, made up largely of rodeo contestants and fans, immediately begins to dance and clap wildly. The electric guitars and drums move into a hard-rocking song, driven by hard-hitting rhythm-guitar chops and low-note guitar runs, exploding into 1970s-style high-note guitar solos.

As the vocal begins, LeDoux introduces the rodeo-cowboy hero, "Rollin' down a long highway / Down through New Mexico." He is "driftin' down that road" to "ride a bull in a rodeo," and

> He's hooked on a feelin'
> The tension of a natural high
> Don't know why it's appealin'
> All he knows is he's got to ride.

The hero, of course, is the same one LeDoux has been singing about for twenty years—the same hero LeDoux himself aspired to become and, having won "The World," proceeded to enshrine as a popular-music cultural icon. And now LeDoux has brought this rodeo hero up to date. The rodeo-cowboy hero is a *contemporary ancestor,* fused now from the Code of the West and rock-and-roll music.

> Climbin' over that chute gate
> He settles down inside
> The tension's risin' but he can't wait
> Until they turn that bull outside.

There is no logical explanation for the rodeo-cowboy hero's behavior, nor is there an explanation for the respect and adulation he commands in a modern, high-tech North American society. Whether he is real, or imaginary, or both, or neither, is beside the point. The only thing that matters now is that he is "Hooked on an 8 Second Ride." And so are we.

He's addicted to danger.
Ruled by passion and pride.
To pain and fear he's no stranger.
But his lust needs to be satisfied.
Hooked on an 8 second ride.
Hooked on an 8 second ride.
Hooked on an 8 second ride.

Introduction: Frontier, Civilization, and the Meaning of Rodeo

1. The standard works are Ernest Staples Osgood, *The Day of the Cattleman* (1929; reprint, Chicago, 1970); Edward Everett Dale, *The Range Cattle Industry* (Norman, Okla., 1930); Walter Prescott Webb, *The Great Plains* (Boston, 1931); Louis Pelzer, *The Cattleman's Frontier* (Glendale, Calif., 1936); Joe B. Frantz and Julian Ernest Choate Jr., *The American Cowboy: The Myth and the Reality* (Norman, Okla., 1955); Gene M. Gressley, *Bankers and Cattlemen* (New York, 1966); Terry G. Jordan, *Trails to Texas: Southern Roots of Western Cattle Ranching* (Lincoln, Nebr., 1981); David Dary, *Cowboy Culture: A Saga of Five Centuries* (New York, 1981); Richard W. Slatta, *Cowboys of the Americas* (New Haven, 1990).

2. The standard works are Henry Nash Smith, *Virgin Land: The American West As Symbol and Myth* (New York, 1950); Frantz and Choate, *American Cowboy*; Don D. Walker, *Clio's Cowboys: Studies in the Historiography of the Cattle Trade* (Lincoln, Nebr., 1981); Robert Murray Davis, *Playing Cowboys: Low Culture and High Art in the Western* (Norman, Okla., 1992); and William W. Savage Jr., *The Cowboy Hero: His Image in American History and Culture* (Norman, Okla., 1981).

3. Clifford P. Westermeier, *Man, Beast, Dust: The Story of Rodeo* (1947; reprint, Lincoln, Nebr., 1987).

4. Kristine Fredriksson, *American Rodeo: From Buffalo Bill to Big Business* (College Station, Tex., 1985); Mary Lou LeCompte, *Cowgirls of the Rodeo: Pioneer Professional Athletes* (Urbana, 1993). See also Kathleen Mullen Sands, *Charreria Mexicana: An Equestrian Folk Tradition* (Tucson, 1993), and Wayne S. Wooden and Gavin Ehringer, *Rodeo in America: Wranglers, Roughstock, and Paydirt* (Lawrence, Kans., 1996).

5. Beverly June Stoeltje, "Rodeo As Symbolic Performance" (Ph.D. diss., University of Texas, Austin, 1979); Elizabeth Atwood Lawrence, *Rodeo: An Anthropologist Looks at the Wild and the Tame* (Chicago, 1984); Smith, *Virgin Land*; John William Ward, *Andrew Jackson: Symbol for an Age* (New York, 1953); Roy Harvey Pearce, *Savagism and Civilization: A Study of the Indian and the American Mind* (1953; reprint, Berkeley, 1988); Leo Marx, *The Machine in the Garden: Technology and the Pastoral Ideal in America* (New York, 1964). See also Sands, *Charreria Mexicana*.

6. Lawrence, *Rodeo... the Wild and the Tame*, 7, 129–30. Turner's 1893 essay is available today in Frederick Jackson Turner, *The Significance of the Frontier in American History*, ed. Harold P. Simonson (New York, 1966). For more on the "Cowboy Code," see chaps. 1 and 3 herein.

7. Lawrence, *Rodeo... the Wild and the Tame*, 116, 129–30.

8. Ibid., 16–18, 85, 97–104, 108, 110, 117, 212–20. See also Savage, *Cowboy Hero*, 43–45, 107, 129–31.

9. David D. Lee, *Sergeant York: An American Hero* (Lexington, Ky., 1985); John William Ward, "The Meaning of Charles Lindbergh's Flight," *American Quarterly* 10 (Spring 1958): 3–16.

10. I build here on the work of Smith, Ward, Marx, and the American-Studies school cited in notes 5 and 9 above, while incorporating some of the analyses of Savage, *Cowboy Hero*; Kent L. Steckmesser, *The Western Hero in History and Legend* (Norman, Okla., 1965); and John G. Cawelti, *The Six-Gun Mystique* (Bowling Green, Ohio, 1982). See also chap. 7 herein.

11. Richard M. Dorson, *America in Legend: American Folklore from the Colonial Period to the Present* (New York, 1973), xiv; Lawrence Levine, "The Folklore of Industrial Society: Popular Culture and Its Audiences," *American Historical Review* 97 (December 1992): 1372, 1399.

12. See Harold P. Simonson's review of Jane Tompkins, *West of Everything: The Inner Life of Westerns* (New York, 1992), in *Pacific Northwest Quarterly* 84 (January 1993): 30; and Alvin Davis' review of Blake Allmendinger's *The Cowboy: Representations of Labor in an American Work Culture* (New York, 1992), in *Montana, Magazine of Western History* 44 (Summer 1994): 74–75.

13. Many thanks to Mike Magie for his thoughts on this subject.

Chapter 1. "Real Cowboys": A Brief History of Rodeo

1. Theodore Roosevelt, *Ranch Life in the Far West* (1888; reprint, Flagstaff, Ariz., 1985), 42–43.

2. Ibid., 33, 38; E. C. ("Teddy Blue") Abbott and Helena Huntington Smith, *We Pointed Them North: Recollections of a Cowpuncher* (1939; reprint, Norman, Okla., 1986), 87, 143.

3. The standard works are Clifford P. Westermeier, *Man, Beast, Dust: The Story of Rodeo* (1947; reprint, Lincoln, Nebr., 1987); Kristine Fredriksson, *American Rodeo: From Buffalo Bill to Big Business* (College Station, Tex., 1985); Elizabeth Atwood Lawrence, *Rodeo: An Anthropologist Looks at the Wild and the Tame* (Chicago, 1984); Beverly June Stoeltje, "Rodeo As Symbolic Performance" (Ph.D. diss., University of Texas, Austin, 1979). My folkloric analysis is derived from the methodology of Richard M. Dorson, *American Folklore and the Historian* (Chicago, 1971), 1–14, 25, 186–99.

4. Westermeier, *Man, Beast, Dust*, 32–37.

5. Mary Lou LeCompte, "The Hispanic Influence on the History of Rodeo, 1823–1922," *Journal of Sport History* 12 (Spring 1985): 21–30, 38; Mody Boatright, "The

American Rodeo," *American Quarterly* 16 (Summer 1964): 195–97; Lawrence, *Rodeo . . . the Wild and the Tame*, 80–81. See also Kathleen Mullen Sands, *Charreria Mexicana: An Equestrian Folk Tradition* (Tucson, 1993), and Wayne S. Wooden and Gavin Ehringer, *Rodeo in America: Wranglers, Roughstock, and Paydirt* (Lawrence, Kans., 1996).

6. Ben Ferguson interview (typed transcript), Ellensburg, Wash., Public Library, KIT-76-61sa, 5–6.

7. Howard Thomas interview (typed transcript), ibid., KIT-75-85sa, 16.

8. *Ellensburg (Wash.) Evening Record*, July 11–15, 1923.

9. Ibid., September 13–17, 1923; Howard Thomas interview, 13; Lillian Pope interview, Ellensburg, Wash., Public Library, KIT-75-21sa, 1; Chalmer Cobain interview, Ellensburg, Wash., Public Library, KIT-75-22sa, 13.

10. *Ellensburg Evening Record*, September 14, 17, 1923.

11. Michael Allen, "'Let 'er Buck!' How the Ellensburg Rodeo Was Born," *Columbia* 4 (Summer 1990): 12; "Ellensburg's Rodeo Grounds: Frontier Cooperation Started Washington's World-Famous Rodeo," *Ketch Pen* (Rodeo Historical Society), n.s., 6 (July 1993): 18–19.

12. Don Russell, *The Wild West: A History of the Wild West Shows* (Fort Worth, 1970), 1–2, 121–27; Barbara Williams Roth, "The 101 Ranch Wild West Show, 1904–1932," *Chronicles of Oklahoma* 43 (Fall 1966): 416–31.

13. Quotes from *Buffalo Bill's Wild West*, facsimile reproduction program (orig., Hartford, Conn., 1885), Buffalo Bill Historical Center, Cody, Wyo., n.p. See also Joseph Schwartz, "The Wild West Show: 'Everything is Genuine,'" *Journal of Popular Culture* 3 (Spring 1970): 656–66.

14. Russell, *Wild West*, 114, 117–19.

15. Fredriksson, *American Rodeo*, 21–26, 37–40, 56.

16. Ibid., 40–51, 65.

17. Mary Lou LeCompte, *Cowgirls of the Rodeo: Pioneer Professional Athletes* (Urbana, 1993), 100–43; Teresa Jordan, *Cowgirls: Women of the American West* (Garden City, N.Y., 1984), 187–96; Michael Allen, "Rise and Decline of the Early Rodeo Cowgirl: The Career of Mabel Strickland, 1916–1941," *Pacific Northwest Quarterly* 83 (October 1992): 126–27.

18. Roy Bird and Luann Bird, "'Punkin' Roller Rodeos: A Little Touch of the Old West," *Journal of the West* 17 (1978): 34–43. My differentiation, here and throughout, between authentic folk festival rodeos and more commercial folk-based rodeos is based on Richard M. Dorson's methodology in *American Folklore and the Historian* (Chicago, 1971), 1–14, 25, 186–99. Note that today's International Professional Rodeo Association (IPRA; see Glossary) rodeos are sometimes called

"punkin' rollers"; although professionally sanctioned, they are not sanctioned by the Professional Rodeo Cowboys Association (PRCA).

19. Bird and Bird, "Punkin' Roller Rodeos," 34–43; Stoeltje, "Rodeo As Symbolic Performance," 374–451; *Official Program, 1994 Ellensburg Rodeo* (Ellensburg, Wash., 1994); *Pendleton Roundup, 1995 Official Program* (Pendleton, 1995). For precise definitions and explanations of the events of the classic rodeo program, see the glossary.

20. Fredriksson, *American Rodeo*, 88–89.

21. Thanks to J. C. Mutchler, a New Mexico cowboy temporarily exiled in Yale University's American Studies Ph.D. program, for his advice here (even though he does not agree with all that I say). Many of us in the field eagerly await J.C.'s doctoral dissertation on contemporary southwestern cattle ranch culture.

22. Chalmer Cobain interview, KIT-75-22sa, 13; A. C. Greene, "Empty Saddles: Were the Old Rodeo Cowboys Better?" *American West* 24 (January–February 1987): 28–35.

23. For cowboy authenticity, see Fredriksson, *American Rodeo*, 13–15, 57–59, 92 (quotation on 59). See also Westermeier, *Man, Beast, Dust*, 50–58. J. C. Mutchler notes that some contemporary ranch hands continue the old cowboy tradition of questioning the rodeo men's authenticity.

24. In *Rodeo . . . the Wild and the Tame*, 129–30, Lawrence argues there are "striking parallels" between rodeo cowboys and working cowboys.

25. Ibid.; Richard M. Dorson, *America in Legend: American Folklore from Colonial Times to the Present* (New York, 1973), 150–53; Frederick Jackson Turner, *The Significance of the Frontier in American History*, ed. Harold P. Simonson (New York, 1966). Thanks to an anonymous reviewer for citing the quick-witted retort (versus slow drawl) mode of cowboy vernacular in Carl Peters Benedict, *A Tenderfoot Kid on Gyp Water* (Dallas, 1943), 16–17.

26. Lawrence, *Rodeo . . . the Wild and the Tame*, 129–30. Although I take several exceptions, Lawrence makes a strong argument that rodeo cowboys are direct descendants of working cowboys.

27. Biographical information in Willard Porter, *Who's Who in Rodeo* (Oklahoma City, 1982), 116–17, 170–73.

28. Lawrence, *Rodeo . . . the Wild and the Tame*, 93–94; Fredriksson, *American Rodeo*, 103–12, 119–20, 183–200.

29. Fredriksson, *American Rodeo*, 103–12, 119–20, 183–200; Jane Stern and Michael Stern, "Raging Bulls," *New Yorker*, September 14, 1992, 94–96.

30. Porter, *Who's Who in Rodeo*, 182–83.

31. Fredriksson, *American Rodeo*, 183–200, outlines this commercialization but

does not employ folkloric analysis. See also the Sterns' "Raging Bulls."

32. "36th National Finals Rodeo," *USA Today*, December 2–11, 1994, (special section) 2.

33. Bird and Bird, "Punkin' Roller Rodeos," 40. Chris Huck and Debbie Huck, *Montana Rodeos* (Helena, Mont., 1984), surveys all of the Montana PRCA and punkin' roller shows.

Chapter 2. "Goin' Down That Road": The Rodeo Cowboy in Movies and Television

1. *The Misfits* (1961).

2. Henry Nash Smith, *Virgin Land: The American West As Symbol and Myth* (New York, 1950). The *Leatherstocking Tales* are *The Deerslayer* (1841), *The Last of the Mohicans* (1826), *The Pathfinder* (1840), *The Pioneers* (1823), and *The Prairie* (1827).

3. John G. Cawelti, *The Six-Gun Mystique* (Bowling Green, Ohio, 1984), 61–94; Smith, *Virgin Land*, 59–70; Thomas Schatz, *Hollywood Genres* (Philadelphia, 1981), 45–80; *Stagecoach* (1939); *Shane* (1953).

4. For contemporary westerns, see William W. Savage Jr., *The Cowboy Hero: His Image in American History and Culture* (Norman, Okla., 1979), 41–46.

5. Ibid.; Phil Hardy, *The Western* (New York, 1983), 281, 312. For *contemporary ancestor*, see David D. Lee, *Sergeant York: An American Hero* (Lexington, Ky., 1985); John William Ward, "The Meaning of Charles Lindbergh's Flight," *American Quarterly* 10 (Spring 1958): 3–18; and chaps. 3 and 8 herein.

6. The only previously published scholarship focusing exclusively on rodeo movies is James Hoy's "Rodeo in American Film," *Heritage of the Great Plains* 23 (Spring 1990): 26–32. Clifford P. Westermeier discusses some rodeo movies in "Sagebrush Galahads: The Cinema Cowboys," *Red River Valley Historical Review* 5 (Fall 1980): 27–54, as do William Savage in *Cowboy Hero*, 44–45, 130–31, and Wayne S. Wooden and Gavin Ehringer in *Rodeo in America: Wranglers, Roughstock, and Paydirt* (Lawrence, Kans., 1996), 221–31.

7. Kalton C. Lahue, *Winners of the West: The Sagebrush Heroes of the Silver Screen* (New York, 1970), 36; Dwayne Erickson, "Stampede Fever," *American Cowboy* 1 (August 1994): 29.

8. Westermeier, "Sagebrush Galahads," 38–39.

9. *The Lusty Men* (1952); Hoy, "Rodeo in American Film," 26; Westermeier, "Sagebrush Galahads," 37–38.

10. All quotations in the preceding paragraphs are from *The Lusty Men*.

11. Gerald Pratley, *The Cinema of John Huston* (Cranbury, N.J., 1977), 126–30; Scott Hammen, *John Huston* (Boston, 1985), 91–99; Lawrence Grobel, *The Hustons*

(New York, 1989), 486–88; Hoy, "Rodeo in American Film," 26–27.

12. All quotations from *The Misfits* (1961).

13. Hammen, *John Huston*, 98–99; *The Misfits*.

14. *The Misfits*.

15. *Here Come the Nelsons* (1952).

16. Westermeier, "Sagebrush Galahads," 45; Savage, *Cowboy Hero*, 131; Neil Summers, "Stoney Burke," *The Official TV Western Book* (Vienna, W.Va., 1989), 94–95; "The Care and Handling of Tigers," *The Wide Country* (April 25, 1963), 16 mm, Motion Picture, Broadcasting, and Sound Division, Library of Congress, Washington, D.C. Thanks to Mary Hanneman for sharing her research.

17. *Stoney Burke* (April 22, 1963), 16 mm, Motion Picture, Broadcasting, and Sound Division, Library of Congress, Washington, D.C.

18. *The Honkers* (1972); *Goldenrod* (1977); Westermeier, "Sagebrush Galahads," 45–46; Hoy, "Rodeo in American Film," 28–29.

19. *J. W. Coop* (1972); Hoy, "Rodeo in American Film," 28–30; Westermeier, "Sagebrush Galahads," 45–47. See chap. 6.

20. *Junior Bonner* (1972); Terrence Butler, *Crucified Heroes: The Films of Sam Peckinpah* (London, 1979), 75–79; Savage, *Cowboy Hero*, 44–45.

21. *Electric Horseman* (1979); Hoy, "Rodeo in American Film," 30–31. For *Lonely Are the Brave* (1962), see Savage, *Cowboy Hero*, 44.

22. *Urban Cowboy* (1980); Hoy, "Rodeo in American Film," 30; Don Graham, "Texas Videos: The Best Texas Movies on Tape," *Texas Monthly* 19 (July 1991): 99.

23. *My Heroes Have Always Been Cowboys* (1990); Soren Anderson, "Like a Thrown Bull Rider, 'Cowboys' Falls Flat on Its Tummy," *Tacoma (Wash.) Morning News Tribune*, n.d., in possession of Michael Allen.

24. For examples of the "country boy in the city" taletype, see Yankee Jonathan in Richard M. Dorson, *America in Legend: American Folklore from Colonial Times to the Present* (New York, 1973); *Tarzan's New York Adventure* (1942); *Coogan's Bluff* (1968); and *Crocodile Dundee* (1986).

25. *The Cowboy Way* (1994).

26. Smith, *Virgin Land*; Leo Marx, *The Machine in the Garden: Technology and the Pastoral Ideal in America* (New York, 1964); John William Ward, *Andrew Jackson: Symbol for an Age* (New York, 1953); Michael Allen, *Western Rivermen, 1763–1861: Ohio and Mississippi Boatmen and the Myth of the Alligator Horse* (Baton Rouge, 1990); Harold P. Simonson, "Frontier History As Art," *Antioch Review* 24 (Summer 1964): 201–11.

27. Smith, *Virgin Land*; Marx, *Machine in the Garden*; Ward, *Andrew Jackson*; Allen, *Western Rivermen*; Simonson, "Frontier History As Art."

28. Here and in chaps. 3 and 7, I expand on the rodeo cowboy's status as a *contemporary ancestor,* drawing from Lee's *Sergeant York* and Ward's "Meaning of Charles Lindbergh's Flight."

Chapter 3. "Wild Side of Life": The Rodeo Cowboy in Folklore and Literature

1. Larry McMurtry, *Horseman, Pass By* (1961; reprint, New York, 1989), 137–38.

2. Ibid., 90, 113, 130–31, 181–82, 206.

3. Ibid., 131, 201–2.

4. Ibid.

5. Ramon F. Adams, *The Cowboy Dictionary* (orig. *Western Words*, 1968; reprint, New York, 1993), iii–viii; John O. West, *Cowboy Folk Humor* (Little Rock, 1990), 9–32; Elizabeth Atwood Lawrence, *Rodeo: An Anthropologist Looks at the Wild and the Tame* (Chicago, 1984), 72–73.

6. Adams, *Cowboy Dictionary,* v–vi; West, *Cowboy Folk Humor,* 27, 30; Lawrence, *Rodeo . . . the Wild and the Tame,* 72.

7. James H. Penrod, "Folk Beliefs about Work, Trades, and Professions from New Mexico," *Western Folklore* 27 (No. 3, 1968): 183; Lawrence, *Rodeo . . . the Wild and the Tame,* 90; Clifford P. Westermeier, *Man, Beast, Dust: The Story of Rodeo* (1947; reprint, Lincoln, Nebr., 1987), 64–65.

8. Howard Thomas interview, March 25, 1975, typed transcript, Ellensburg, Wash., Public Library, KIT-75-8sa, 19–22.

9. Kristine Fredriksson, *American Rodeo: From Buffalo Bill to Big Business* (College Station, Tex., 1985), 112; David G. Brown, *Gold Buckle Dreams: The Rodeo Life of Chris LeDoux* (Greybull, Wyo., 1989), 165–68.

10. Lawrence, *Rodeo . . . the Wild and the Tame,* 210, 87; Clovis Chartrand interview, October 6, 1975, typed transcript, Ellensburg, Wash., Public Library, KIT-75-41sa, 12–13.

11. Fredriksson, *American Rodeo,* 123; Lawrence, *Rodeo . . . the Wild and the Tame,* 160, 183; Jan H. Brunvand, "Rodeo Clown Jokes," *Northwest Folklore* 1 (No. 2, 1966): 31.

12. Fredriksson, *American Rodeo,* 123.

13. Ollie Osborn interview, September 1981, typed transcript, Ollie Osborn File, National Cowgirl Hall of Fame, Hereford, Tex., 9; Westermeier, *Man, Beast, Dust,* 23–25.

14. Red Steagall, *Ride for the Brand: The Poetry and Songs of Red Steagall* (Fort Worth, 1993), 87–91, and chap. 5 herein; Fredriksson, *American Rodeo,* 126; Lawrence, *Rodeo . . . the Wild and the Tame,* 209.

15. Howard Thomas interview, 17, 22–23.

16. Vera McGinnis, *Rodeo Road: My Life As a Pioneer Cowgirl* (New York, 1974); Foghorn Clancy, *My Fifty Years in Rodeo* (San Antonio, 1952); Gene Lamb, *Rodeo Back of the Chutes: The Hilarious and Factual Story of Professional Rodeo* (Denver, 1956); Thelma Crosby and Eve Ball, *Bob Crosby: World Champion Cowboy* (Clarendon, Tex., 1966). See also Jim Davis, *We Remember Pete Knight* (n.p., n.d.), ProRodeo Hall of Fame, Colorado Springs; Sam Brownell, *Rodeos and "Tipperary"* (Denver, 1961); Rankin Crow, *Rankin Crow and the Oregon Country* (Ironside, Ore., 1970); David G. Brown, *Gold Buckle Dreams;* Tom Hadley with J. Dallas White, *Tom Hadley's World of Rodeo: 45 Years of Cowboy Fun* (Kerrville, Tex., 1989); Robert N. Gray (ed.), *Mr. Rodeo Himself: Cecil Cornish, His Life and Treasures* (Waukomis, Okla., 1990); and Ken Adams, *Rodeos, Pig Races, and Other Cowboy Stories* (Phoenix, 1994).

17. Lamb, *Rodeo Back of the Chutes,* 1. For southwestern folk humor and the "Alligator Horse" motif, see Michael Allen, *Western Rivermen, 1763–1861: Ohio and Mississippi Boatmen and the Myth of the Alligator Horse* (Baton Rouge, 1990), 6–26.

18. Lamb, *Rodeo Back of the Chutes,* 245, 248–53.

19. Adams, *Rodeos, Pig Races, and Other Cowboy Stories,* 45–46. For McCarrol, Knight, and Brown variants, see Teresa Jordan, *Cowgirls: Women of the American West* (Garden City, N.Y., 1984), 191; Davis, *We Remember Pete Knight;* Gray (ed.), *Cecil Cornish,* 70.

20. Lamb, *Rodeo Back of the Chutes,* 25–34.

21. Gray (ed.), *Cecil Cornish,* 30–31; Clancy, *Fifty Years in Rodeo,* 221–22; Lamb, *Rodeo Back of the Chutes,* 35–45.

22. Westermeier, *Man, Beast, Dust,* 94–95, 100–106. The Turtles' 1936 Boston declaration is in the archives of the National Cowboy Hall of Fame and Western Heritage Center, Oklahoma City.

23. Lamb, *Rodeo Back of the Chutes,* 42–43; Fredriksson, *American Rodeo,* 40, 42.

24. Lamb, *Rodeo Back of the Chutes,* 37, 40–44.

25. Ibid., 37.

26. LeDoux in Brown, *Gold Buckle Dreams,* v.

27. David D. Lee, *Sergeant York: An American Hero* (Lexington, Ky., 1985), x.

28. B. M. Bower, *Rodeo* (New York, 1928); Gene Lamb, *Rodeo Cowboy* (San Antonio, 1959); Stanley Noyes, *Rodeo Clown* (New York, 1961). William Crawford donated each of these rare works to the ProRodeo Hall of Fame.

29. McMurtry, *Horseman, Pass By,* 241.

30. *Hud* (1963).

31. Ibid.

32. Larry McMurtry, *Moving On* (New York, 1970), x.

33. Ibid., 29.

34. Ibid., 31, 40–41, 77, 158.

35. Ibid., 100, 102, 168.

36. Ibid., 237, 322, 363.

37. While this analysis is my own, a helpful discussion is in Mark Busby, *Larry McMurtry and the West: An Ambivalent Relationship* (Denton, Tex., 1995).

38. McMurtry, *Moving On*, 178, 660.

39. William Crawford, *The Bronc Rider* (Oxnard, Calif., 1965).

40. For the status of *The Bronc Rider* among rodeo aficionados, see Lawrence, *Rodeo . . . the Wild and the Tame*, 117. For examples of technical detail and realism, see Crawford, *Bronc Rider*, 75–78, 115–17.

41. Crawford, *Bronc Rider*, 62, 79, 87, 147, 153.

42. Ibid., 26–28, 31, 58, 88, 91, 101, 146–47, 179, 234, 252.

43. Ibid., 64, 72, 74, 90, 96–97. For a feminist critique of *The Bronc Rider*, see Lawrence, *Rodeo . . . the Wild and the Tame*, 117.

44. Crawford, *Bronc Rider*, 37–38, 43, 44, 49, 141.

45. Ibid., 208, 213–14, 222.

46. Ibid., 147. Lawrence, *Rodeo . . . the Wild and the Tame*, 117, mounts the major liberal critique of Crawford because, to her credit, Lawrence is one of the few serious scholars who have actually read Crawford. For the multiethnic theme in Crawford's work, see Crawford, *Bronc Rider*, 34–35, 102, and chap. 6 herein.

47. Herbert Harker, *Goldenrod* (New York, 1972); Billy Wilcoxson, *10 Karat Hole in a Donut* (Albuquerque, 1973); Aaron Fletcher, *Cowboy* (New York, 1977); Janice Kaplan, *First Ride* (New York, 1982). Various Wrangler and Dell rodeo comic books are in the ProRodeo Hall of Fame, Colorado Springs.

48. Cyra McFadden, *Rain or Shine* (New York, 1987), 3–12.

49. Ibid. Quotations on 9–10, 12.

50. Ibid., 20.

51. Ibid., 145–48.

52. Ibid., 236.

53. Ibid., 4, 10, 200–201.

54. Ibid., 3–4, 7, 10.

55. Ibid., 3.

56. Ibid., 11–12, 227–37, 249.

57. James Hoy, *Cowboys and Kansas: Out of the Tall Grass Prairie* (Norman, Okla., 1995), 167–69. See also Howard [Jack] Thorp, *Songs of the Cowboys* (Boston, 1908); John Lomax, *Adventures of a Ballad Hunter* (New York, 1947); Glenn Ohrlin, *The Hell-Bound Train: A Cowboy Songbook* (Urbana, 1973); John White, *Git Along Little Dogies:*

Songs and Songmakers of the American West (Urbana, 1975); Hal Cannon, *Cowboy Poetry: A Gathering* (Salt Lake City, 1985); and Guy Logsdon (ed.), *"The Whorehouse Bells Were Ringing" and Other Songs Cowboys Sing* (Urbana, 1989).

58. Cannon, *Cowboy Poetry*, x; Hoy, *Cowboys and Kansas*, 171; Logsdon (ed.), *"The Whorehouse Bells Were Ringing,"* xiv–xv.

59. Cannon, *Cowboy Poetry*, 8–10; Logsdon (ed.), *"The Whorehouse Bells Were Ringing,"* 77–85.

60. Curley Fletcher, *Songs of the Sage: The Poetry of Curley Fletcher* (Salt Lake City, 1986), v–xiii, 11–14.

61. Ibid. "The Castration of the Strawberry Roan" is in Logsdon (ed.), *"The Whorehouse Bells Were Ringing,"* 86–96; I quoted the Baxter Black variant, 92–94.

62. Ohrlin, *Hell-Bound Train*, passim; Hal Cannon, *New Cowboy Poetry* (Salt Lake City, 1990), viii.

63. Wilbur Shepperson and Judith Winzeler, "Cowboy Poetry: The New Folk Art," *Nevada Historical Society Quarterly* 29 (No. 4, 1986): 254–65; Hoy, *Cowboys and Kansas*, 169–73.

64. Richard M. Dorson, *American Folklore and the Historian* (Chicago, 1971), 25, 189–99; Shepperson and Winzeler, "Cowboy Poetry," 264–65; Hoy, *Cowboys and Kansas*, 169–73.

65. Cannon, *Cowboy Poetry*, 49–51, 81–83, 101–3, 134–36, 153–55.

66. Red Steagall, *Ride for the Brand* (Fort Worth, 1993), 13–15, 87–93. Steagall's audiocassette is *Ride for the Brand: A Collection of Cowboy Poetry by Red Steagall* (RS Records, n.d., RS 1175).

67. Paul Zarzyski, *Roughstock Sonnets* (Kansas City, Mo., 1989), x–xiii.

68. Ibid., x, 60–61.

69. Ibid., 2.

70. Ibid., 26–27. See also Paul Zarzyski (poems) and Barbara Van Cleve (photographs), *All This Way for the Short Ride: Roughstock Sonnets, 1971–1996* (Santa Fe, 1996).

71. Paul Zarzyski and Justin Bishop, *Ain't No Life after Rodeo* (Sacramento, 1992). See also Zarzyski's foreword to Bob Wade, *Wreckin' and Ridin'* (Salt Lake City, 1996).

Chapter 4. "Getting It Right": The Rodeo Cowboy in Art

1. I first heard this story told by a former Westermeier graduate student at a Western History Association meeting in Wichita, Kansas, in 1988. Since then I have heard several variants.

2. Clifford P. Westermeier, *Man, Beast, Dust: The Story of Rodeo* (1947; reprint, Lincoln, Nebr., 1987), 13–15; "Clifford P. and Therese S. Westermeier," biographi-

cal essay, Clifford P. and Therese S. Westermeier Collection, Special Collections, University of Colorado Libraries.

3. Westermeier, *Man, Beast, Dust,* 13–15; "Clifford P. and Therese S. Wester-meier."

4. Westermeier, *Man, Beast, Dust,* 13–15; "Clifford P. and Therese S. Wester-meier."

5. Clifford P. Westermeier, "Art and Artists of the Cowboy," unpublished essay, Westermeier Collection, quotation on p. 35. For an introduction to cowboy art, see Ed Ainsworth, *The Cowboy in Art* (New York, 1968), and Joe Beeler, *Cowboys and Indians: Characters in Oil and Bronze* (Norman, Okla., 1967).

6. Westermeier, "Art and Artists of the Cowboy," 30–33.

7. Paul Frenzeny and Jules Tavernier, "Rodeo, or Rounding Up Cattle," *Harper's Weekly,* May 2, 1874, 387 (thanks to Ron Tyler); "101 Ranch Wild West" (posters), "Colonel Tim McCoy's Real Wild West" (posters), and "Pawnee Bill's Historic Wild West" (posters), all in Western History Collection, University of Oklahoma, Norman.

8. Valona Varnum Crowell, *The Artist and the Bucking Horse* (Taos, N.M., n.d.); "In Search of Sunsets: Images of the American West, 1850 to Present," Tacoma Art Museum, September 12–November 22, 1992, catalog, in possession of Michael Allen.

9. Artist unknown, "Ellensburg Rodeo" (poster, ca. 1920s), courtesy of Joel Smith, Ellensburg, Wash.; Wallace Smith, "Pendleton Roundup, Let 'er Buck" (poster, 1925), *American Cowboy* 1 (July–August 1994): 19.

10. Mary Carolyn Hollers George, *Mary Bonner: Impressions of a Printmaker* (San Antonio, 1982), 3–38, 74–81; Charles Simpson, *El Rodeo: One Hundred Sketches Made in the Arena During the Great International Contest (1924). Reproduced in Colour and Black and White* (London, 1925), Archives, ProRodeo Hall of Fame, Colorado Springs. The original artwork for *El Rodeo* resides in the National Cowboy Hall of Fame and Western Heritage Center, Oklahoma City.

11. Jo Mora, *Trail Dust and Saddle Leather* (Lincoln, Nebr., 1987), v; Stephen Mitchell, *Jo Mora: Renaissance Man of the West* (Ketchum, Idaho, 1994), 23. Mora's *Sweetheart* illustration is on the cover of the Byrds' *Sweetheart of the Rodeo* (1968, cs 9670).

12. Laurel E. Wilson, "'I Was a Pretty Proud Kid': An Interpretation of Differ-ences in Posed and Unposed Photographs of Montana Cowboys," *Clothing and Tex-tiles Research Journal* 9 (Spring 1991): 49–58; Wilson, "The American Cowboy: De-velopment of the Mythic Image," in P. Cunningham and S. Lab (eds.), *Dress in American Culture* (Bowling Green, Ohio, 1993), 80–94; Michael Allen, "Rise and

Decline of the Early Rodeo Cowgirl: The Career of Mabel Strickland, 1916–1941," *Pacific Northwest Quarterly* 83 (October 1992): 122–27. The most extensive collection of cowgirl clothing on display is at the National Cowgirl Hall of Fame, Hereford, Tex.

13. Tyler Beard, *100 Years of Western Wear* (Salt Lake City, 1993), 36–38, 47, 59; Main Gallery, ProRodeo Hall of Fame, Colorado Springs.

14. Westermeier Collection, Oversize #4.

15. Ibid.

16. *The Great American Rodeo* [catalog to the show] (Fort Worth, 1976), 15–16.

17. Ibid., 22–25, 46–53, 62–65. Thanks to Ron Tyler for a firsthand reminiscence of the impact of the Fort Worth show.

18. Ibid., 26–33, 34–45, 54–69.

19. Garry Winogrand, *Stock Photographs: The Fort Worth Fat Stock Show and Rodeo* (Austin, 1980), quotation from foreword.

20. "From Broncs to Easels: Rodeo Participants Turned Professional Artists Comprise Uncommon Art Organization," *Equine Images* 10 (October–November 1996): 20; "11th Annual PRCAA 'Showcase' 1996" and "History Update" (1994), press releases, PRCAA, 1830 Markwell Avenue, Oklahoma City, OK 73127.

21. Hays in *Southwest Art* 20 (July 1990): 30; Papas, ibid., 19 (September 1989): 129; Murray Tinkelman, *Rodeo Art of Murray Tinkelman* (New York, 1982); "The Art of Delmas Howe, 'Pantheon Series,' at Umbrello Gallery, October 18, 1990, Los Angeles, CA," program photocopy in possession of Michael Allen (thanks to Walter Piehl); Blake in Angela Howell, "Purebred Cowboy Art," *American Cowboy* 1 (August 1994): 52–55.

22. Karen Dahood, "Sweetheart of the Rodeo," *Southwest Profile* 12 (January 1989): 31–34; Theresa Johnson, "Brushing Up on Rodeo," *Missoulian* (Missoula, Mont.), January 6, 1989; Amy Kuebelbeck, "Sweetheart of the Rodeo," *Grand Forks (N.D.) Herald*, November 20, 1987.

23. Walter Piehl to Michael Allen, October 30, 1995, in possession of Michael Allen.

24. *Sweethearts of the Rodeo: Contemporary Rodeo Art*, catalog (Colorado Springs, 1990), ProRodeo Hall of Fame, Colorado Springs; Walter Piehl to Michael Allen, August 27, 1994, in possession of Michael Allen. All other quotations from Dahood, "Sweetheart of the Rodeo," and Johnson, "Brushing Up on Rodeo." Piehl is currently painting two collections of works employing the themes of cowgirls and roping.

25. David Mattison, "A. D. Kean: Canada's Cowboy Movie-Maker," *Beaver* 69 (March 1989): 29; "R. A. Bird, Photographer," *Alberta History* 31 (Autumn 1983):

20–27. See also Cunningham-Dillon Photo Collection, Western History Collection, University of Oklahoma, Norman.

26. Joe Koller, "Salute to R. R. Doubleday," *Hoof and Horns* 22 (September 1952): 3; Kay Stansbury, "Ride 'em Cowboy—for Doubleday," *Postcard Collector* 3 (May 1985): 18–19.

27. Ron Tyler, *The Rodeo of John Addison Stryker* (Austin, 1977), vi–xxxiv, quotation on xii. See also Erwin E. Smith, *Life on the Texas Range* (Austin, 1952), 78–81.

28. Louise L. Serpa, *Rodeo* (New York, 1994), Notes by Larry McMurtry; B. Byron Price, "Louise Serpa's *Rodeo*," *Ketch Pen* 8 (Summer 1995): 12–13; Winogrand, *Stock Photographs*; Geoff Winningham, *Going Texan: The Days of the Houston Livestock Show and Rodeo* (Houston, 1972), 5.

29. Douglas Kent Hall, *Rodeo* (New York, 1976); "Broncs, Bulls, and Buckaroos: The Ellensburg Rodeo Photographs of Rob Fraser," Clymer Gallery, Ellensburg, Wash., August 30, 1996, program notes in possession of Michael Allen. See also Sue Rosoff, "Rodeo Odyssey," work in progress, prospectus in possession of Michael Allen.

30. Rosamund Norbury, *Behind the Chutes: The Mystique of the Rodeo Cowboy* (Missoula, Mont., 1993), quotation from dust jacket.

31. Ibid., passim, quotations on 70 and dust jacket.

32. Westermeier, "Art and Artists of the Cowboy," 36.

Chapter 5. "I Ain't Rich but Lord I'm Free": The Rodeo Cowboy in Song

1. "Ian and Sylvia," in Jon Pareles and Patricia Romanowski (eds.), *The Rolling Stone Encyclopedia of Rock and Roll* (New York, 1983), 268–69.

2. Ian Tyson, "Someday Soon," Ian and Sylvia, *Northern Journey* (Vanguard, 1964, cv 79154). Thanks to Bill Malone for noting the similarity of this "rambling" theme to that of the folk song "The Wagoner Lad."

3. Frederick Jackson Turner, *The Significance of the Frontier in American History*, ed. Harold P. Simonson (New York, 1966); Richard M. Dorson, *America in Legend: American Folklore from Colonial Times to the Present* (New York, 1973), 150–53; Elizabeth Atwood Lawrence, *Rodeo: An Anthropologist Looks at the Wild and the Tame* (Chicago, 1984), 97, 129–30.

4. Guy Logsdon (ed.), *"The Whorehouse Bells Were Ringing" and Other Songs Cowboys Sing* (Urbana, 1989), xiii–xv. Classic collections of cowboy songs are Howard [Jack] Thorp, *Songs of the Cowboys* (Boston, 1908), and John A. Lomax, *Cowboy Songs and Other Frontier Ballads* (New York, 1910). I have relied heavily on Logsdon and on Glenn Ohrlin, *The Hell-Bound Train: A Cowboy Songbook* (Urbana, 1973).

5. Dorson, *America in Legend*, 134, 136.

6. Ohrlin, *Hell-Bound Train*, xii, xvii, 73–75; Curley Fletcher, *Songs of the Sage: The Poetry of Curley Fletcher* (Salt Lake City, 1986), 11–14.

7. Ohrlin, *Hell-Bound Train*, 80–83, 88–90, 93–94.

8. For folk-based and commercial rodeo-music traditions, see ibid., 73, 76–79, 84–85, 220–22; Lawrence, *Rodeo . . . the Wild and the Tame*, 97–104. Many thanks to Guy Logsdon for his letter of September 21, 1993, in my possession.

9. Guy Logsdon to Michael Allen, September 21, 1993. Baker recorded all of his albums at FF&S Sound Recordings, 2400 West Broadway, Columbia, MO 65201.

10. Chris LeDoux is quoted in Michael Corcoran, "A Cowboy Earns His Spurs," *Spokesman Review* (Spokane, Wash.), February 5, 1992. For noncommercial rodeo music, see also Ohrlin, *Hell-Bound Train*, and Charles Wellington Furlong, *Let 'Er Buck!* (New York, 1921).

11. Bill Malone, *Southern Music, American Music* (Lexington, Ky., 1979), 134–40; Paul Nelson, "Folk Rock," in Kim Miller (ed.), *The Rolling Stone Illustrated History of Rock and Roll* (New York, 1976), 216–21. The interrelated musical subgenres of folk, folk rock, and country rock and their relationship to country-western music form a complex subject far beyond the reach of this chapter. Perhaps a few generalizations will suffice: (1) Folk rock emerged when "folksingers," most notably Bob Dylan and the Byrds, added electric guitars and drums to their musical arsenal; (2) folk rock naturally evolved into country rock because country-and-western music is also closely related to Anglo and Celtic American (and to a lesser degree African American) folk traditions; (3) the main difference, to my mind, between 1960s and 1970s country rockers and their straight Nashville counterparts was the length of their hair. Indeed, one could argue that with some very important exceptions, it was the country rockers who were the purists at that particular moment in the history of country-western music. It took "outlaws" like Willie Nelson and Hank Williams Jr.—who possessed certifiable redneck credentials to balance their counterculture loyalties—to fuse the two groups. For a discussion of the counterculture and rodeo arts, see chap. 6 herein.

12. Judy Collins, *Who Knows Where the Time Goes* (Elektra, 1968, EKS 74033); Byrds, *Sweetheart of the Rodeo* (Columbia, 1968, CS9670); "Byrds: Sweetheart of the Rodeo," *Rolling Stone* (August 27, 1987), 151; Roger McGuinn and Jacques Levy, "Chestnut Mare," on Byrds, *The Best of the Byrds: Greatest Hits Volume II* (Columbia, 1972, KC 31795).

13. Great Speckled Bird, *Great Speckled Bird* (Ampex, 1969, A10103); Buffy Sainte-Marie, "He's an Indian Cowboy in the Rodeo," *Moonshot* (Vanguard 1972, VSD 79312); Mick Jagger and Keith Richards, "Wild Horses," on Flying Burrito Brothers, *Close Up the Honky Tonks: The Best of the Flying Burrito Brothers, 1968–1972*

(A&M Records, 1972, A&M sp-3631); Mason Proffit, *Bareback Rider* (Warner Brothers, 1973, bs 2704); Michael Martin Murphey, "Cosmic Cowboy," on Nitty Gritty Dirt Band, *Dirt, Silver, and Gold* (United Artists, 1976, ua-la670-l3).

14. Chris LeDoux, "The Cowboy and the Hippie," *Gold Buckle Dreams* (American Cowboy Songs 1987 acs 22).

15. Lawrence, *Rodeo . . . the Wild and the Tame*, x, 97; David G. Brown, *Gold Buckle Dreams: The Rodeo Life of Chris LeDoux* (Greybull, Wyo., 1986). Quotation in Corcoran, "A Cowboy Earns His Spurs."

16. "Chris LeDoux, Western Entertainer, Songs of Rodeo, Cowboy, and Ranch Life," Wolverine Gallery, PO Box 572, Greybull, WY 82426.

17. Quotations from Chris LeDoux, "A Cowboy's Got to Ride," *Gold Buckle Dreams*, and LeDoux, "I've Got to Be a Rodeo Man" (quoted in Lawrence, *Rodeo . . . the Wild and the Tame*, 101).

18. Chris LeDoux, "A Cowboy's Got to Ride"; Ledoux, "I've Got to Be a Rodeo Man" (quoted in Lawrence, *Rodeo . . . the Wild and the Tame*, 101); Ledoux, "Goin' and a' Blowin'," *Gold Buckle Dreams*.

19. Chris LeDoux, "National Finals Rodeo" and "He Rides the Wild Horses," *Gold Buckle Dreams*.

20. Chris LeDoux, "Our First Year," ibid., and "The Greatest Prize," quoted in Brown, *Gold Buckle Dreams*, 225.

21. Chris LeDoux, "So You Want to Be a Cowboy," *Gold Buckle Dreams*.

22. Malone, *Southern Music, American Music*, 148–49; Red Steagall and the Coleman County Cowboys, *For All Our Cowboy Friends* (mca, 1977, mcac-680).

23. Red Steagall, "Rodeo," and "For All Our Cowboy Friends," *For All Our Cowboy Friends*.

24. Red Steagall, "The Night the Copenhagen Saved the Day," ibid.

25. Red Steagall, "Bandito Gold," ibid.

26. Red Steagall and Glen Sutton, "Tight Levis and Yellow Ribbons," quoted in Brown, *Gold Buckle Dreams*, 161–62; Steagall, "Two Pairs of Levis and a Pair of Justin Boots," *For All Our Cowboy Friends*.

27. Red Steagall, "Dawson Legate," *For All Our Cowboy Friends*.

28. Red Steagall, "Freckles Brown," ibid.

29. For contemporary rodeo influence on country music, see: Lawrence, *Rodeo . . . the Wild and the Tame*, 97–104; Brown, *Gold Buckle Dreams*, 1, 93, 105, 195; Alanna Nash, "New Country: Sweethearts of the Rodeo," *Stereo Review* 51 (December 1986): 109; "Showdown at Cheyenne," *48 Hours*, August 25, 1988, 2–4 (typed transcript); Gerry Wood, "After Bucking the Rodeo Circuit, Singer Reba McEntire Finds Country Music a Cinch," *People's Weekly* 21 (April 1984): 85–86; and Alanna Nash, *Be-*

hind Closed Doors: Talking with the Legends of Country Music (New York, 1988), 310–13, 315, 323.

30. Larry Bastian, "Rodeo," *Garth Brooks Ropin' the Wind* (Capitol, 1991, CDP 7 96330 2).

31. George Strait, "Amarillo by Morning," *George Strait, Greatest Hits* (MCA, 1985, MCAC-5567).

Chapter 6. "If You're a Cowboy, You're a Cowboy": Rainbow Rodeo Riders and the Archetypal Anti-Archetype

1. "Showdown at Cheyenne," *48 Hours,* August 25, 1988 (typed transcript).

2. Ibid., 11–12.

3. Ibid., 4–5, 12–13.

4. The literature of "multiculturalism" and the "culture wars" is immense. An interpretive introduction is Arthur Schlesinger Jr., *The Disuniting of America: Reflections on a Multicultural Society* (New York, 1992). Bernard Goldberg is noted for his critique of the leftist bias of television journalism, and so it is possible that he wanted to focus his *48 Hours* interview with Brian Riley on Riley's Cowboy Code ways.

5. Ibid., 10, 16.

6. Hal Cannon, Preface to Curley Fletcher, *Songs of the Sage: The Poetry of Curley Fletcher* (1931; reprint, Salt Lake City, 1986), vi–vii.

7. Richard W. Slatta, *Cowboys of the Americas* (New Haven, 1990); Philip Durham and Everett L. Jones, *The Negro Cowboys* (New York, 1965); Terry G. Jordan, *North American Cattle-Ranching Frontiers: Origins, Diffusion, and Differentiation* (Albuquerque, 1993); Alan Lomax, *Cajun Country: Don't Drop the Potato,* videotape (North Carolina Public Television, 1990); Grady McWhiney, *Cracker Culture: Celtic Ways in the Old South* (Tuscaloosa, 1988); Peter Iverson, *When Indians Became Cowboys: Native Peoples and Ranching in the American West* (Norman, Okla., 1994); Virginia Cowan-Smith and Bonnie Domrose Stone, *Aloha Cowboy* (Honolulu, 1988). Teresa Jordan, *Cowgirls: Women of the American West* (New York, 1984).

8. My thesis is based on an analysis of the sources cited in the following note.

9. Mary Lou LeCompte, "The Hispanic Influence on the History of Rodeo," *Journal of Sport History* 12 (Spring 1985): 21–38; Kathleen Mullen Sands, *Charreria Mexicana: An Equestrian Folk Tradition* (Tucson, 1993); Clifford P. Westermeier, "Black Rodeo Cowboys," *Red River Valley Historical Review* 3 (Summer 1978): 4–26; Colonel Bailey C. Hanes, *Bill Pickett, Bulldogger: The Biography of a Black Cowboy* (Norman, Okla., 1977); Mary Lou LeCompte, *Cowgirls of the Rodeo: Pioneer Professional Athletes* (Urbana, 1993); Glen Mikkelsen, "Indians and Rodeo," *Alberta His-*

tory 35 (Summer 1987): 13–19; Iverson, *When Indians Became Cowboys;* Texas Department of Corrections, *Texas Prison Rodeo* (program, 1984); "A Day at the Gay Rodeo," *Seattle Weekly,* September 21, 1994, 24–25.

10. Michael Allen, "Spit in the Ocean; or, 'Greasewood City: You Can't Get There from Here,'" *Ellensburg Anthology '83* (Ellensburg, Wash., 1983), 30–34, Local History Collection, Ellensburg, Wash., Public Library. Theodore Roszak, *The Making of a Counter Culture: Reflections on the Technocratic Society and Its Youthful Opposition* (Garden City, N.Y., 1969) delineates hippie antimodernism, as does Timothy Miller, *The Hippies and American Values* (Knoxville, 1991), 91–93. The expression "greening of America" is drawn from Charles Reich's mediocre book *The Greening of America* (New York, 1970). My favorite example of the difference between hippies and neo-Marxists is the theme of the Beatles' song "Revolution," in which John Lennon sings, "If you go carryin' pictures of Chairman Mao / You ain't gonna make it with anyone anyhow."

11. Ken Kesey with Ken Babbs, *Last Go Round: A Real Western* (New York, 1994). It is not clear how the two divided the workload, but it appears Kesey did much of the writing while Babbs did the research and illustrations.

12. Ibid., vi, 221.

13. Ibid., 11, 19, 20–22, 85–88, 142, 170, 210, 234.

14. Ibid., 25, 77, 153–54, 161–62, 167, 187–88.

15. For the nature theme, see ibid., 67–68, 138–39.

16. For Code behavior, see, for example, ibid., 102–4, 137–39, 187–88, 221.

17. Ibid., 84.

18. *J. W. Coop* (1972). See chap. 2 herein.

19. Richard Meyer, "The Outlaw: A Distinctive American Folk Type," *Journal of the Folklore Institute* 17 (1980): 93–124; Stephen Tatum, *Inventing Billy the Kid: Visions of the Outlaw in America, 1881–1981* (Albuquerque, 1982); *J. W. Coop;* William Crawford, *The Bronc Rider* (Oxnard, Calif., 1965), 33; *Convict Cowboy* (1995); *Urban Cowboy* (1980).

20. Perhaps inadvertently, *Stir Crazy*'s screenwriters borrow the multiethnic name of professional baseball player César Geronimo of the Cincinnati Reds.

21. Blake Allmendinger, *The Cowboy: Representations of Labor in an American Work Culture* (New York, 1992), 106: "*Stir Crazy* traces the convict's submission to prison authority and his return to domestic society through participation in the cowboy's work process. It also demonstrates the prison's attempt to define the rehabilitation process as theatrical art."

22. *Stir Crazy* (1980).

23. For the possibility of gay working cowboys, see Allmendinger, *Cowboy,* 50–

55. For gay rodeo, see "A Day at the Gay Rodeo," *Seattle Weekly*, September 21, 1994, 24–25; "Like It or Not, Enumclaw Hopes Trouble Won't Mar Gay Rodeo," *Tacoma News Tribune*, September 10, 1993; and "State High Court Upholds Ban on Gay Rodeo," *Reno Gazette-Journal*, October 22, 1988.

24. David Link, "Babylon Sister," *Reason* 26 (February 1995): 63; "No Rodeos, Gay or Not," *Reno Gazette-Journal*, November 12, 1988; Allmendinger, *Cowboy*, 80–81.

25. Darrell Yates Rist, *Heartlands: A Gay Man's Odyssey across America* (New York, 1992), 97–98, 100, 112. An unexplored aspect of gay fascination with rural culture is the burgeoning gay square-dance scene.

26. Ibid., 116, 103, 109, 114, 111, 115.

27. Ibid., 112–13, 105, 103–4.

28. Ibid., 119.

29. Tom Robbins, *Even Cowgirls Get the Blues* (Boston, 1976), 128–33.

30. See Teresa Jordan and Mary Lou LeCompte, cited in notes 7 and 9 of this chapter, and Michael Allen, "Rise and Decline of the Early Rodeo Cowgirl: The Career of Mabel Strickland, 1916–1941," *Pacific Northwest Quarterly* 83 (October 1992): 122–27.

31. William W. Savage Jr., *The Cowboy Hero: His Image in American History and Culture* (Norman, Okla., 1979), 106–7. See also chap. 2 herein.

32. Roberta Beed Sollid, *Calamity Jane: A Study in Historical Criticism* (1958; reprint, Helena, Mont., 1995). Larry McMurtry introduced the possibility of a bisexual Calamity Jane in *Buffalo Girls* (New York, 1990).

33. Hilda E. Wenner and Elizabeth Freilicher, comps., *Here's to the Women: 100 Songs for and about American Women* (Syracuse, N.Y., 1987), 261–63; Kesey, *Last Go Round*; *Urban Cowboy*; Gail Gilchrist, *The Cowgirl Companion: Big Skies, Buckaroos, Honky Tonks, Lonesome Blues, and Other Glories of the True West* (New York, 1993), 107.

34. Aaron Copland, *"Billy the Kid" and "Rodeo," Complete Ballets: Leonard Slatkin and the St. Louis Symphony Orchestra* (EMI 4DS-37357); Agnes de Mille, *American Dances* (New York, 1980), 132–35; Neil Butterworth, *The Music of Aaron Copland* (Gloucester, U.K., 1985), 91–93.

35. Paul Zarzyski and Justin Bishop, "Fannie Sperry Steele (Buckin' Horse Suffragettes)," recording and copyrighted typescript in possession of Michael Allen, with thanks to Paul Zarzyski.

36. Crawford, *Bronc Rider*, 34–35; *The Cowboy Way* (1994). For the Hispanic influence in cowboy and rodeo culture, see notes 7 and 9, this chapter.

37. Sands, *Charreria Mexicana* (Tucson, 1993), 254–55, 245, 255–57.

38. Brackette F. Williams, "Introduction: Nat Love Rides into the Sunset of Slavery and Racism," in Nat Love, *The Life and Adventures of Nat Love, Better Known in the Cattle Country As 'Deadwood Dick,' by Himself: A True History of Slavery Days, Life on the Great Cattle Ranges and on the Plains of the 'Wild and Wooly' West, Based on Facts, and Personal Experiences of the Author* (1907; reprint, Lincoln, Nebr., 1995), vii–x.

39. Ibid.

40. For historic black rodeo men, see note 9 of this chapter and Paul W. Stewart and Wallace Yvonne Ponce, *Black Cowboys* (Broomfield, Colo., 1986), and Steven Byers, "Charles Sampson," *People's Weekly* 20 (October 24, 1983): 51–52; *The Bulldogger* (poster), National Cowboy Hall of Fame, Oklahoma City (I have not located a copy of the movie); Eric Easter et al. (eds.), *Songs of My People: African-Americans, a Self-Portrait* (Boston, 1992), 42–45; Mark Ross, Zack Miller, and Justin Bishop, "Bill Pickett," in Paul Zarzyski and Justin Bishop, *Ain't No Life after Rodeo* (Sacramento, 1992). *Black Rodeo* (1972) is discussed in Westermeier, "Black Rodeo Cowboys," 22–23.

41. Crawford, *Bronc Rider*.

42. Ibid., 99–106.

43. Ibid., 102, 105, 106, 250–51.

44. See chap. 2 herein.

45. For historic Indian working and rodeo cowboys, see notes 7 and 9 of this chapter; Rowena Alcorn, "Jackson Sundown," *Montana, Magazine of Western History* 33 (Autumn 1983): 46–51; and Mikkelsen, "Indians and Rodeo," 13–19. Quotations from Peter Iverson, "When Indians Became Cowboys," *Montana, Magazine of Western History* 45 (Winter 1995): 30.

46. James Welch, *Winter in the Blood* (New York, 1974), 24, 26, 30; Crawford, *Bronc Rider*, 172–73; John L. Doyle, "Rodeo Roper," *Southwest Art* 19 (June 1989): 124; Buffy Sainte-Marie, "He's an Indian Cowboy in the Rodeo," *Moonshot* (Vanguard, 1972, VSD-79312).

47. Hal Borland, *When the Legends Die* (1963; reprint, New York, 1989), 17, 88, 100, 116, 124, 148, 161, 215.

48. Craig Lesley, *Winterkill* (New York, 1984).

49. Ibid., 29–33, 85, 89, 193, 284, 314–15.

50. Ibid., 29–30, 54–57, 60, 217–18, 221–22.

51. Ibid., 35–36, 52, 60, 223–24, 319–20, 328. Craig Lesley, like Hal Borland, uses the powerful male hunter/great beast/ritual hunt taletype that can be traced, in American literary tradition, from James Fenimore Cooper's *Deerslayer* and Thomas Bangs Thorpe's "The Big Bear of Arkansaw" to William Faulkner's "The Bear" and Robert De Niro's movie role as *The Deer Hunter* (1978).

52. Arthur Schlesinger Jr., *The Disuniting of America: Reflections on a Multicultural Society* (New York, 1992), 10, 16.

53. Ibid., 27, 30, 134.

54. Ibid., 18–19.

55. Michael Dorris, *A Yellow Raft in Blue Water* (New York, 1987).

56. Ibid., 7, 39, 44, 47, 51.

57. Ibid., 13, 29, 35, 36–37, 159, 170–71.

58. Ibid., 110, 112–13, 153.

59. Ibid., 117–19, 121–22. Dorris' account of Ray's ride on Babe succeeds amid factual errors numerous enough to keep rodeo fans blushing. Ray has only been on a horse once in her life, so her success in disguising herself as Foxy and riding in a men-only event is unrealistic, to say the least. The fact that Babe belongs to Christine's boyfriend (and Lee's former best friend) Dayton is important to Dorris' story line but defies the reality of standard rodeo roughstock contracting procedures. Moreover, Babe's on-again, off-again wild/tame behavior in the arena is incongruous for a bucking horse. Ray's success in riding Babe for *twenty-four* (count 'em!) seconds and then remounting and riding her *twice* again, all three rides within one minute (plus an additional fourth ride the next morning), is as unbelievable a feat as it is illegal. Indeed, it is a great testament to Dorris' literary talents that one actually *wants* to ignore all of these glitches and go on reading his story.

60. Ibid., 120, 132.

Chapter 7. "Hooked on an 8 Second Ride": The Rodeo Cowboy as Contemporary Ancestor and Popular-Culture Hero

1. *8 Seconds* (1993); Soren Anderson, "Eight Seconds Is Simple, Sentimental, and Entertaining," *Tacoma News Tribune*, February 25, 1994.

2. Peggy Pascoe's review of Richard Slotkin's *Gunfighter Nation: The Myth of the Frontier in Twentieth-Century America* (New York, 1992) is discussed in Gerald Thompson, "The New Western History: A Critical Analysis," *Continuity* 17 (Fall 1993): 11 n. 13.

3. News Release, "Wrangler Western Index," Wrangler, Inc., c/o Martin Public Relations, 707 E. Main Street, Richmond, VA 23219. See also M. J. Van Deventer, "Make Me a Cowgirl for at Least a Day," *Persimmon Hill* 22 (Summer 1994): 80. Many thanks to Wrangler, Inc., and Dr. Laurel Wilson, University of Missouri, Columbia.

4. Michael Johnson, *New Westers: The West in Contemporary American Culture* (Lawrence, Kans., 1996), 1–12, 13, 324–28.

5. News Release, "Wrangler Western Index," passim.

6. Ibid.; Telephone interview, Phil Fredrickson, Professional Rodeo Cowboys Association, September, 29, 1995.

7. A good introduction to the use of cowboy mystique in advertising is in William W. Savage Jr., *The Cowboy Hero: His Image in American History and Culture* (Norman, Okla., 1979), 109–22. Ads mentioned are in *Portland Sunday Oregonian,* February 16, 1936, 12; *Great Moments in Rodeo,* Nos. 1–49, Archives, ProRodeo Hall of Fame, Colorado Springs; and *American Cowboy* 1 (February 1995): n.p.

8. Kristine Fredriksson surveys the contemporary rodeo-advertising business in *American Rodeo: From Buffalo Bill to Big Business* (College Station, Tex., 1985), 186–200. See also James P. Forkan, "Rodeo Circuit Plans to Rope Advertisers," *Advertising Age,* September 24, 1984, 68, and Janice Steinberg, "Roundup in the City," *Advertising Age,* August 29, 1988, 58.

9. Resistol ad in *Bull Riders Only* (program, 1993), back cover page, in possession of the author; Coca-Cola ad courtesy of The Coca-Cola Company, P.O. Drawer 1734, Atlanta, GA 30301; Duane Valentry, "Levi Strauss: The Father of Western Garb," *Persimmon Hill* 19 (Autumn 1991): 37; "The Isuzu Rodeo," sales brochure, in possession of the author.

10. "PRCA Sponsorships: Sponsor Contacts and Program Summaries" (1994), report for Professional Rodeo Cowboys Association. Many thanks to Mark Furrier of the PRCA for the data. And thanks to Ruth Airlie of the ProRodeo Hall of Fame for sharing her 1992 and 1993 National Finals Rodeo videos.

11. In "The Folklore of Industrial Society: Popular Culture and Its Audiences," *American Historical Review* 97 (December 1992): 1369–99, Lawrence Levine argues for the significance of twentieth-century popular culture and offers a methodology for the collection, analysis, and interpretation of pop-culture material.

12. Henry Nash Smith, *Virgin Land: The American West As Symbol and Myth* (New York, 1950); John William Ward, *Andrew Jackson: Symbol for an Age* (New York, 1953); Roy Harvey Pearce, *Savagism and Civilization: A Study of the Indian and the American Mind* (1953; reprint, Berkeley, 1988); John William Ward, "The Meaning of Charles Lindbergh's Flight," *American Quarterly* 10 (Spring 1958): 3–16; Leo Marx, *The Machine in the Garden: Technology and the Pastoral Ideal in America* (New York, 1964). Quotation from John William Ward's afterword to James Fenimore Cooper, *The Prairie* (New York, 1964), 407.

13. Bruce Kucklick, "Myth and Symbol in American Studies," *American Quarterly* 24 (October 1972): 435–49.

14. See Thompson, "New Western History: A Critical Analysis." I summarize the work of these authors in "The 'New' Western History Stillborn," *Historian* 57 (Au-

tumn 1994): 201–8, and "Cowboyphobia: A Diagnosis and Cure; or, The Emperors Wear No Duds," *Journal of the West* 36 (October 1997): 3–6.

15. David Potter, "The Quest for the National Character," in John Higham (ed.), *The Reconstruction of American History* (New York, 1962), 197–220.

16. Leon Festinger, *A Theory of Cognitive Dissonance* (Evanston, Ill., 1957), 1–31. A good summary is in Elliot Aronson, *The Social Animal* (San Francisco, 1980), 146–52.

17. For rural nostalgia in the Jacksonian epoch, see Marvin Meyer, *The Jacksonian Persuasion: Politics and Belief* (Stanford, 1957); Ward, *Andrew Jackson;* and Michael Allen, *Western Rivermen, 1763–1861: Ohio and Mississippi Boatmen and the Myth of the Alligator Horse* (Baton Rouge, 1990), 24–26, 214–24. For the Gilded Age and progressive era, respectively, see Smith, *Virgin Land,* and T. Jackson Lears, *No Place of Grace: Anti-Modernism and America, 1880–1920* (New York, 1981).

18. Richard Kelly, *The Andy Griffith Show* (Winston-Salem, 1985), ix–14. While not subscribing to my overarching rural-nostalgia interpretation, Timothy Miller, *The Hippies and American Values* (Knoxville, 1991), 91–93, does document the hippie rural commune movement. Most of this interpretation of post–World War II America is my own, although I continually marvel at the insights of the University of Montana's redoubtable Harry W. Fritz, who first got me thinking about the extent to which Marvin Meyer's Jacksonian "restoration theme" applies to the Carter-Reagan era.

19. Allen, *Western Rivermen,* 24–26, 217. For Casey Jones, see Richard M. Dorson, *America in Legend: American Folklore from the Colonial Period to the Present* (New York, 1973), 235–41; in the same work, see also "Mose the Bowery Boy," 99–108, and "Gib Morgan," 216–27. The classic overview is Marx, *Machine in the Garden.*

20. David D. Lee, *Sergeant York: An American Hero* (Lexington, Ky., 1985), 54–57, 121–24; Ward, "The Meaning of Charles Lindbergh's Flight"; Tom Wolfe, *The Right Stuff* (New York, 1979), 16–64.

21. The conclusion is based on Chris LeDoux, "Hooked on an 8 Second Ride," *Chris LeDoux Live,* videocassette (Liberty Records, 1993, c3-0777-7-40351-3-2).

The following is a much-abridged listing of a rich and complex occupational folk vernacular. I include here only terms that will assist uninformed readers in understanding the main text of this book. The terms and definitions of this lingo are drawn from numerous sources, but I am particularly indebted to Walter Piehl (who meticulously copy-edited the first draft), Jim Hoy, the late Willard Porter, Chris and Debbie Huck, and of course, Ramon F. Adams for his *Cowboy Dictionary* (originally published in 1968 as *Western Words*; reprint, New York, 1993).

All-around/all-round champion. At the end of each rodeo season, the overall Professional Rodeo Cowboys Association (PRCA) money-winner who competed in at least two different events is proclaimed the "all-around champion." See *National Finals Rodeo; Points system.*

Arena director. The arena director runs the rodeo arena before, during, and after the show, making sure that the events move smoothly and according to the rules. Sometimes the duties of the arena director are combined with those of the *Producer* and/or *Stock contractor.*

Arena-trained. A rodeo cowboy who has not learned his skills on a ranch is said to be "arena-trained." This means that he was actually trained in the rodeo arena—through calf-roping clubs, 4-H, high-school and college rodeo competitions, or rodeo schools. See *Ranch-trained.*

Bareback bronc riding. Bareback bronc riding is not "ranch-related" (working cowboys used saddles when busting broncs). Bareback bronc riding requires the cowboy to exhibit style in staying atop an unsaddled bucking bronc while holding on to a leather handle (called "bareback riggin'") cinched around the bronc's withers; one free hand must remain always in the air. Those who ride the required eight seconds are scored subjectively by two judges on a scale of 100—50 points for riding style and 50 points for the difficulty of the bronc. Criteria for style include the technique and sweep of the cowboy's spurring and his degree of control; broncs score high for continuous, high-kicking, powerful, and irregular bucking. A score in the 70s is usually competitive; there is very little grade inflation in rodeo. Cowboy shorthand for this bareback event is "the bares"; compare *Saddle bronc riding,* which is called simply "bronc riding."

Barrel racing. First introduced in Texas rodeos in the 1930s, barrel racing is not ranch-related (working cowboys did not race barrels at the roundup) and is today the only women's event in PRCA-sanctioned rodeos. In this timed event, cowgirls guide their horses in a cloverleaf pattern around three barrels. They ride fast and cut the barrels close to score a winning time, often around seventeen to eighteen. Knocking over a barrel costs the cowgirl a five-second penalty. The introduction of barrel racing led to the phasing out of women's participation in roughstock and timed-event competitions and exhibitions by the 1940s. PRCA-sanctioned rodeo became, for all practical purposes, a gender-segregated sport.

Barrier. A spring-loaded rope that is stretched across the opening of a calf-roping or bulldogging chute and released to give the calves or steers a head start. If the roper or 'dogger and his horse move too soon to pursue the cattle, the cowboy is penalized ten seconds for "breaking the barrier."

Biting the dust. Being thrown from a bronc or bull.

Brahma. A breed of cattle imported by western ranchers from India. Cross-bred Brahmas proved especially suited for rodeo bull-riding events. See *Bull riding*.

Bronc/bronco. From the Spanish. A wild (unbroken) horse. A cowboy who rides broncs is called a "bronco buster," "bronc fighter," "bronc breaker," or most often, "bronc rider." See *Bareback bronc riding* and *Saddle bronc riding*.

Buck. When a bronc tries to throw a cowboy off his back, he is said to "buck." There are dozens of verbs denoting the various ways broncs buck, including *blow, blow up, boil, break in two, crawfish, crow hop, explode, jackknife, pitch, sunfish, swallow his head, throw,* and *windmill.* See *Sunfish*.

Buck off. A thrown cowboy is "bucked off"; also "dusted," "drilled," or "turfed." A cowboy bucked off over the head of a bronc or bull is "dashboarded."

Buckle bunny. The rodeo equivalent of a rock-and-roll "groupie" is a buckle bunny. She is a rodeo aficionada, but her motives may also be amorous.

Bulldogging. See *Steer wrestling*.

Bull riding. The finale of most rodeos, bull riding is the most dangerous and, arguably, the most exciting rodeo event. Bull riders circle a plaited length of rope around a 1,500–1,800-pound Brahma (or Brahma-cross) bull, mount the beast, place one hand in a braided-in handhold, tighten the rope, and explode out of the chute in hopes of an eight-second ride. As in bareback bronc riding, two judges score the cowboy on a scale of 100—50 points for style and 50 points for the difficulty of the bull. Bull riders need not spur or "mark out" the bull to be scored. Rodeo shorthand for the bull-riding event is "the bulls."

Bust. Rodeo cowboys use the verb *bust* to denote their temporarily subduing horses by riding them or cattle by jerking them over with a rope. The term's origins lie in the "bronco busters" of the working-cowboy era.

Calf roping. This timed event is a ranch-related classic on the rodeo program. The mounted cowboy's job is to catch, rope, and tie a running calf as quickly as possible. The calf gets a head start by way of a "barrier" rope and runs full speed as the cowboy pursues, throws a loop around the calf's head, and jerks him to a standstill. Then the cowboy quickly dismounts, throws the calf to the ground, and ties three of his legs together with a "piggin' string." A time under ten seconds is usually necessary to win.

Chaps. Leather leggings that cowboys and rodeo men wear over their jeans. Originally, working cowboys wore chaps to protect their legs from the animals and other elements of nature, but today's rodeo cowboys wear them largely for show (the flopping of the chaps and fringe can enhance the appearance of—and score for—a bronc rider's spurring action).

Chutes. Enclosures that hold and/or release livestock into the rodeo arena.

Circuit. A series of rodeos is called a "circuit." Professional rodeo cowboys travel or "ride the circuit." The PRCA has divided North America into circuits, each with its own finals competition. See *Road.*

Clown. After a bull rider has completed his ride or been thrown, rodeo clowns (usually two) distract the bull while the cowboy retreats to safety. During this process the "bullfighter" clown often gets dangerously close to the bull, while the "barrel man" keeps a safer distance, sometimes taunting the bull from inside a reinforced barrel.

Corporate sponsor. Modern rodeo is characterized by corporate sponsors who subsidize prize purses, roughstock, scoreboards, and other items in return for acknowledgment during the course of the rodeo performance.

Corriente. Roping stock, native to Mexico, that are the preferred breed for *Timed events.*

Cowboy Christmas. The period of time on or around the Fourth of July, when a great number of rodeos occur.

Cowboy Turtles Association. The "Cowboy Turtles Association" was the first name used by the group that was to become the Rodeo Cowboys Association and, ultimately, the Professional Rodeo Cowboys Association. Formed in 1936, the Cowboy Turtles aimed to improve the lot of the rodeo cowboy by bargaining collectively for higher prize purses, mandatory entry-fee/prize-purse combination (to prevent skimming by unscrupulous promoters), and professional, standardized judging. According to oral tradition, rodeo men chose the name Turtles because they had been "slow as turtles" in getting organized. See *Professional Rodeo Cowboys Association.*

Cowboy's Prayer. A traditional rodeo-specific prayer recited after the *Grand entry* at many rodeos.

Cream puff. An easy-to-ride bronc or bull; also called a "pup."

Crow hopping. Mild bucking. By not kicking its back legs high, and thus bucking stiff-legged, a "crow-hopping" bronc hinders his rider's attempt to earn a high score.

Dally. A cowboy term from the Spanish *dar la vuelta* (to take a turn). After roping a steer, rodeo cowboys "dally" their ropes by taking several fast turns around the saddle horn. Calf ropers tie "hard and fast" to the horn.

Day money. The prize money paid to the winners of each performance or "go-round" is "day money," which is distinguished from the much larger championship purse of the "last go-round" or "short-go" or "average."

Dink. A horse or bull that bucks poorly, ensuring a low score.

Draw. The animal picked for a rodeo cowboy to ride, bulldog, or rope is his "draw." Cowboys used to draw the numbers of these animals from a hat; today drawing is done by computer. In roughstock events, a "good draw" is an animal that bucks for a spirited and consistent eight seconds, thus earning a high score. A "bad draw" is an animal that does not buck with spirit or consistency for the eight seconds or one that is impossible to ride. In timed events, a good draw runs straight and without hesitation.

Dude. A noncowboy; an easterner. A term of utmost derision.

Duds. Cowboys and rodeo cowboys call dress-up clothes their "duds"; these include hats, neckerchiefs, snap-button shirts and vests, prize-buckled belts, Levi's, and boots.

Entry fee. In rodeo, unlike many other sports, contestants pay an entry fee to compete in each event.

Exhibition event. Any rodeo event, such as a *Specialty act,* that is not scored for competition is an exhibition event. Before the RCA banned women's competition in ranch-related events during and after World War II, many women's roughstock and timed events were labeled "exhibitions."

Flank strap. A sheepskin-covered strap around a bull's or bucking bronc's flanks. Snugged in this position, it enhances the animal's natural instinct to throw off the rider. The *Pickup man* releases the flank strap immediately after eight seconds have passed.

Gear. Any equipment the rodeo man may use in his work. See *Riggin'*.

Girls' Rodeo Association. See *Women's Professional Rodeo Association*.

Goose egg. A disqualified roughstock rider scores a "goose egg," or zero; in timed events, a "no time."

Go-round. When all contestants have competed once in an event, they have completed the first "go-round," or "long-go." Those who have placed highest then compete in a "short-go" or "last go-round" or "average," which is the championship round. These "go-rounds" usually stretch over a weekend or several days.

Grand entry. This ritual, probably a variant of the circus or Wild West show "grand entry," marks the beginning of all authentic rodeo folk festivals. Scores of colorfully costumed, flag-bearing horsemen and horsewomen gallop single file into the rodeo arena. There they may ride in a continuous figure-eight or cloverleaf drill pattern for up to five minutes while being joined by still more riders, who may or may not include the mounted rodeo contestants (ropers and barrel racers). The grand-entry riders may be local rodeo-board members, the rodeo queen and princesses, sponsor representatives, and rodeo posse members. After all riders have entered, they halt and salute the American and/or Canadian national flags and anthems, and then conclude by galloping single file from the arena. Immediately following the grand entry, the bareback bronc-riding event begins the formal competition of the rodeo.

Hand. One who is proficient in cowboying or rodeo skills is a "hand" and, of course, aspires to be a "top hand."

Hazer. A hazer assists a steer wrestler (bulldogger). On a second horse, he rides out from a box on the right side of the chute (the steer wrestler rides from the left box). He rides alongside the steer's right hip to prevent the animal from turning away from the steer wrestler. See *Steer wrestling.*

Hobbled stirrups. Stirrups connected by a leather thong or rope beneath a bronc's belly are said to be "hobbled." Rodeo contestants no longer hobble stirrups. Before World War II, hobbling was done to help women (and some men) bronc riders stay aboard. But it could also cause injury to the rider if the bronc fell.

Hooked. Getting horned by a bull; a bull known for hooking is called a "hooky."

Hung-up/hang-up. When a roughstock rider gets his hand caught in his riggin' or rope and cannot dismount his bronc or bull, he is said to be "hung-up." A saddle bronc rider who catches his spurs in the saddle is also hung-up. A hung-up cowboy is said to "hang and rattle." Hang-ups are extremely dangerous and can prove deadly.

International Professional Rodeo Association. In 1929 the business side of rodeo—the rodeo producers, stock contractors, and local governing boards—formed the Rodeo Association of America (RAA). This group aimed to professionalize rodeo by standardizing prizes, rules, and judging, and facilitating better communication within the rodeo community. Because rodeo cowboys viewed the RAA as representing only the business end of rodeo, they formed their own professional organization—the Cowboy Turtles Association—which often challenged the RAA. In 1946 the RAA combined with the southwestern National Rodeo Association (NRA) to form the International Rodeo Association (IRA), known today as the International Professional Rodeo Association (IPRA). In the interim, however, the Turtles' heirs, the Professional Rodeo Cowboys Association (PRCA), became the supreme arbiter of rodeo rules and judging standards, temporarily reducing the IPRA to lesser administrative functions, beauty contests, and animal-safety coordination. In today's burgeoning rodeo scene, the IPRA has resurfaced as the "other" professional rodeo organization, sanctioning a number of non-PRCA rodeo shows east of the Mississippi River. On a professional level, today's IPRA shows fall somewhere between PRCA and "punkin' roller" rodeo. See *Professional Rodeo Cowboys Association; Punkin' roller.*

International Rodeo Association. See *International Professional Rodeo Association.*

Juicy. A "showy" bronc or bull that might help earn a cowboy a high score is "juicy."

Kiss. Getting hit in the face by the top of a rodeo bull's head is a bull rider's "kiss."

"Let 'er buck!" A folk expression of early roughstock riders, perhaps with working-cowboy origins. "Let 'er buck" signaled the rider's readiness to leave the chute and ride his bronc. Today's roughstock riders call "Outside!" or simply nod their heads.

Lingo. Vernacular speech. Rodeo cowboys speak their own lingo.

Long-go. See *Go-round.*

Madison Square Garden Rodeo. Founded in 1920, New York City's annual Madison Square Garden show was one of the most prestigious of all North American rodeos through World War II. It was supplanted by the PRCA -sanctioned National Finals Rodeo in 1959.

Marking out. The first requirement of a bronc rider's skills. The rider "marks out" when he leaves the chute with his spurs in the bronc's neck and forward of the bronc's shoulders, with his cowboy boot toes turned out. This position is the legal beginning of any qualified ride; proficient marking out also enhances bucking and raises a cowboy's score. Failure to mark out results in a *Goose egg* and disqualification.

Mugger. A "mugger" is a member of a wild-cow-milking or wild-horse-race team. On foot, he subdues a roped cow or horse.

Muley. A hornless steer.

National Finals Rodeo. Founded in 1959 by the Rodeo Cowboys Association, the National Finals Rodeo is the finale of each year's rodeo season. The week-long competition features each event's top fifteen cowboys and cowgirls. Hosted by Oklahoma City for many years, the NFR is now held each December in Las Vegas.

National Rodeo Association. See *International Professional Rodeo Association.*

Pickup man. Two mounted "pickup men" assist bronc riders in dismounting, remove the flank strap from broncs (or bulls), and drive the animals from the arena so that the rodeo can continue safely and without interruption. The work requires supreme skill and horsemanship.

Piggin' string. After a calf roper has roped his calf, he secures it by tying three of its feet together with a "piggin' string," a six-foot braided rope.

Points system. In the Professional Rodeo Cowboys Association, cowboys are ranked by the amount of prize money they earn annually. $1 = one point. National Finals Rodeo competitors are thus the top fifteen money-winners in their events. Ultimately, the NFR world champions and all-around champion are ranked by dollars earned.

Producer. The individual or committee in charge of a rodeo. Producers orchestrate and ensure the execution of each component of the event. The producer may be amateur, professional, or semiprofessional, contracted by the local rodeo board. See *Arena director; Stock contractor.*

Professional Rodeo Cowboys Association. Organized rodeo cowboys evolved through three related professional incarnations—the Cowboy Turtles Association (CTA, 1936–1945), Rodeo Cowboys Association (RCA, 1945–1975), and Professional Rodeo Cowboys Association (PRCA, 1975–present). The CTA was founded in 1936 to promote cowboys' interests in their dealings with rodeo management (Rodeo Association of America). After staging successful strikes to ensure professionalization through better judging, higher prize purses (with entry fees added), and a standardized rules system, the Cowboy Turtles changed their name to the Rodeo Cowboys Association and finally the Professional Rodeo Cowboys Association. Today the PRCA is the single most important professional organization in rodeo, and the most famous North American rodeos are "PRCA-sanctioned" and regulated (the International Professional Rodeo Association is a regional body that sanctions smaller rodeos, primarily east of the Mississippi River). See *Cowboy Turtles Association; International Professional Rodeo Association.*

Pulling leather. A bronc or bull rider must ride with one hand, keeping his free hand in the air. If the cowboy intentionally touches the saddle, horse, or bull with his free hand, he is disqualified for "pulling leather"; if his touch is unintentional, he is also disqualified, but cited for "touching" or "slapping."

Punkin' roller. A small non-PRCA rodeo is called a "punkin' roller," a term originally used to deride "green" cowboys. Today many punkin' roller rodeos are
much-respected bastions of noncommercial and authentic small-town rodeo
folk traditions. Although IPRA rodeos are officially sanctioned shows, they are
sometimes called "punkin' rollers."

Ranch-related events. Some rodeo events are rooted in actual cowboy ranch
workways. Calf roping, team roping, and saddle bronc riding, for example, are
all ranch-related events. By contrast, very few working cowboys ever engaged
in bareback bronc riding, steer wrestling, or bull riding, so these are "nonranch"
events—they are not "ranch-related."

Ranch-trained. A rodeo cowboy who learned his trade as a working cowboy on a
cattle ranch is said to be "ranch-trained." See *Arena-trained.*

Reride. If judges deem a bronc or bull rider's first ride as unfair to the rider, for
any number of reasons, he is granted a "reride." For example, if the bronc or
bull bucks weakly or does not buck at all, thus irreparably hurting the cowboy's
score, the judges would grant a reride.

Riggin'. Working cowboys referred to horse-riding gear—saddles and their various parts—as "rigging" or "riggin'." More specifically, the word denoted the various saddle cinches (straps extended under the horse's belly and "cinched up"
to make the saddle secure). Rodeo roughstock riders continue to use the term,
with exceptions. Bareback bronc riders refer to their handhold cinch as their
"rig" or "riggin'," and saddle bronc riders usually refer to their saddle as their
"rig," "pack," or just plain "saddle." Bull riders generally call their rigging their
"rope."

Road. A powerful metaphor for the itinerant rodeo lifestyle. Rodeo cowboys talk
often about "movin' down that road," "hittin' the road," or their lives on the
"rodeo road." This itinerant, rambling motif is ascribed to other important
occupational folk heroes, such as riverboatmen, loggers, roughnecks, truck
drivers, and even beatniks and hippies. It is a very important motif in popular
depictions of the rodeo cowboy as folk hero.

Rodeo. From the Spanish verb *rodear* ("to encircle"). The noun *rodeo* means
"roundup"—the semiannual cattle-country work event during which cowboys
counted, sorted, branded, and medicated their cattle and, when the work was
done, engaged in work-related contests. The roundup ultimately evolved into
the North American rodeo contest, a kind of folk festival. Competitors and aficionados accent the first syllable of *rodeo*, not the second as in the Spanish pro-
nunciation. A "rodeoer" is someone who competes in rodeo—someone who
goes "rodeoing" or likes "to rodeo."

Rodeo Association of America. See *International Professional Rodeo Association.*

Rodeo Cowboys Association. See *Professional Rodeo Cowboys Association.*

Rosin. To secure their grip on a bull rope or riggin', roughstock riders apply a powdered, crystallized sap substance known as "rosin" and "work it in" (heat it by friction).

Roughstock. Bucking broncs and bulls.

Roughstock events. Rodeo roughstock events are saddle bronc riding, bareback bronc riding, and bull riding. These events are scored both quantitatively and qualitatively—the cowboy must ride eight seconds to qualify, at which time the judges give him a numerical score based on his style. In contrast, timed events such as calf roping and bulldogging are scored only by the clock. See *Bareback bronc riding; Bull riding; Saddle bronc riding; Timed events.*

Saddle bronc riding. Considered the classic rodeo event by many rodeo fans, saddle bronc riding is ranch-related—a direct descendant of the bronc busting of historic working cowboys. Saddle bronc riding requires the cowboy to exhibit riding style while staying mounted atop a saddled bucking bronc for eight seconds. Astride a regulation (PRCA-approved, or "association") saddle, the cowboy maintains his balance with a "buck rein" (halter rope) in one hand; the free hand must remain always in the air. Those who "mark out" and ride the eight seconds are scored subjectively by two judges on a scale of 100–50 points for the style and 50 points for the difficulty of the bronc. Criteria for riding style include the sweep of the cowboy's spurring (from neck to cantle) and his degree of control; broncs score high for powerful, high-kicking ("snappy" and "showy") jumps. See *Marking out.*

Show. Most rodeo folk call the rodeo a "show" (or "perf," for "performance"), although this usage in no way implies that they think of themselves as entertainers, as opposed to cowboys.

Slack. When there are too many paid entrants to fit into a rodeo program, some of the contestants compete in "slack" competitions before or after the regular show. Of course, there can also be "slack" in a calf roper's rope.

Specialty act. Noncompetition portions of the rodeo program are filled by contracted "specialty acts" such as trick riders, clowns, trained horses, trick ropers, etc.

Steer wrestling. A nonranch event, "steer wrestling" was first introduced in 1903 as an exhibition event called "bulldogging" by Bill Pickett, the famed African American cowboy. A mounted steer wrestler and his mounted "hazer" quickly pursue a running steer out of the chutes. Riding up alongside the racing steer, the hazer keeps him in line while the wrestler slides off his saddle and grabs the steer's horns. Digging his boot heels into the ground, the wrestler pulls the steer down, twisting and throwing him until all four feet are pointed in the same direction. This event requires great horsemanship, agility, and strength; competitive times run five seconds or less. The modern event differs from Pickett's pioneering bulldogging in that Pickett and others sometimes bit the steer's lip to subdue the beast and then raised both hands in the air to signal the end of the run.

Stetson. A famed brand of cowboy hat. Rodeo cowboys often refer to their "Stetson," not their hat. Another popular brand of hat is Resistol. Because of the significance attached to headwear in North American cowboy culture, these names evoke powerful images.

Stock contractor. The person, persons, company, or companies that provide the stock used in a rodeo—roping calves, steers, broncs, and bulls. Stock contractors may be professionals or amateurs, and in small-to-medium-sized rodeos they may also serve as *Producer* and/or *Arena director*.

Sunfish. A bucking bronc that, at the top of his jump, rolls his body to one side and turns his belly toward the sky is "sunfishing." See *Buck*.

Team roping. This is a timed, ranch-related event in which a pair of mounted cowboys pursue, rope, and stop a running steer as quickly as possible. The steer gets a head start out of the gate and runs at full speed as the two cowboys pursue. First, one cowboy (the "header") throws a loop around the steer's horns, slowing him considerably, "setting," and turning him. The second roper ("heeler") quickly lassos the moving steer's hind legs. Finally, the riders stretch the steer between them, and the run is complete.

Timed events. Rodeo's timed events include barrel racing, calf roping, team roping, steer roping, and steer wrestling and are scored only by the clock. They contrast with *Roughstock events* (saddle and bareback bronc riding, and bull riding), which are scored both quantitatively and qualitatively. Cowboys call a rodeo man who specializes in one or more timed events a "timey." See *Calf roping; Steer wrestling; Team roping*.

Timekeepers. The officials who watch and record the clock on all timed and roughstock events.

Top. A highly complimentary adjective in rodeo lingo. A "top hand" is a mighty good cowboy.

Turtles. See *Cowboy Turtles Association*.

Vaquero. In the Southwest, a cowboy—especially a cowboy of Mexican ancestry—is called a "vaquero."

Wannabe. A rodeo hanger-on, a man who wishes he were a cowboy but seldom, if ever, enters an event, is a "wannabe." One step up from a *Dude*.

War bag. A rodeo cowboy's carrying case or duffel bag. It may contain not only all of his personal effects (clothing, chew, toiletries, dress boots, etc.) but also his riggin' and other equipment. See *Riggin'*.

Well. The "well" is the inside of a bull's spin; for a rodeo man, "falling into the well" is dangerous business indeed.

Women's Professional Rodeo Association. The Girls' Rodeo Association (GRA), organized in 1948, changed its name to Women's Professional Rodeo Association (WPRA) in 1981. This group first organized in reaction to the diminishing status of women in professional rodeo. Before World War II, women had played a small but important role in rodeo, performing as relay racers and trick riders as well as competing against one another in nearly all of the other rodeo events. Yet a combination of factors—wartime gas shortages, fear of arena injuries and deaths, the practices of influential rodeo producer Gene Autry, and prejudice— had reduced cowgirls solely to barrel racing by 1947. The GRA aimed to resuscitate women's rodeo by professionalizing barrel racing in PRCA shows and, more important, sanctioning segregated all-cowgirl rodeos with a complete program of timed and roughstock events. The WPRA continues this tradition today; some cowgirls push to return to PRCA shows the all-women timed and roughstock exhibitions and competitions last seen in the 1920s and 1930s.

A beginning researcher investigating the history of rodeo cowboys in popular cul-ture is like a dude attending his first rodeo—he needs a good program to help sort the roughstock from the timed events. What follows is a brief, abridged program introducing the standard works on each of the major facets of this study. Each bib-liographical category is named after an event in the classic rodeo program, and we start with the "Grand Entry" . . .

"Grand Entry": The Essential Books

Making the grand entry in this Roundup is a small but sturdy posse of rodeo histo-rians and anthropologists whose work has built the field. They are Clifford P. Westermeier, *Man, Beast, Dust: The Story of Rodeo* (1947, reprint, Lincoln, Nebr., 1987); Elizabeth Atwood Lawrence, *Rodeo: An Anthropologist Looks at the Wild and the Tame* (Chicago, 1984); Kristine Fredriksson, *American Rodeo: From Buffalo Bill to Big Business* (College Station, Tex., 1985; Mary Lou LeCompte, *Cowgirls of the Ro-deo: Pioneer Professional Athletes* (Champaign-Urbana, 1993); and Beverly June Stoeltje, "Rodeo As Symbolic Performance" (Ph.D. diss., University of Texas, Aus-tin, 1979).

"Saddle Broncs": Primary Sources

Just as the saddle bronc event is the signature component of any good rodeo, pri-mary sources form the backbone of the study of rodeo history. However, rodeo folk are grounded so firmly in oral, as opposed to written, tradition that ferreting out primary sources becomes problematic. I took the case-study approach and zeroed in on the oral history collection of the Local History Room of the Ellensburg, Wash., Public Library. There I found an abundant supply of taped narratives (and printed transcripts) by Kittitas County cowboys, rodeo hands, and other old-timers. The only two places to find plentiful published primary accounts by rodeo men are the National Cowboy Hall of Fame in Oklahoma City and the ProRodeo Hall of Fame in Colorado Springs. There researchers will find scores of firsthand rodeo reminis-cences, most of them published privately in obscure and limited editions. For start-ers, see Vera McGinnis, *Rodeo Road: My Life As a Pioneer Cowgirl* (New York, 1974); Foghorn Clancy, *My Fifty Years in Rodeo* (San Antonio, 1952); Gene Lamb, *Rodeo Back of the Chutes: The Hilarious and Factual Story of Professional Rodeo* (Denver, 1956); Robert N. Gray (ed.), *Mr. Rodeo Himself: Cecil Cornish, His Life and Treasures* (Waukomis, Okla., 1990); Sam Brownell, *Rodeos and "Tipperary"* (Denver, 1961);

and David G. Brown, *Gold Buckle Dreams: The Rodeo Life of Chris LeDoux* (Greybull, Wyo., 1989).

"Calf Roping": The Movies

Roping and tying a fast-moving calf requires years of practice, and the student of rodeo movies should also prepare thoroughly before galloping into the arena. The place to start is the theory of the western genre in literature. Henry Nash Smith, *Virgin Land: The American West As Symbol and Myth* (Cambridge, Mass., 1950), and John G. Cawelti, *The Six-Gun Mystique* (Bowling Green, Ohio, 1984), provide the best of, respectively, the old and new schools of thought, and so do the books cited in "Brahma Bull Riding" below.

Next comes the western movie, with Thomas Schatz, *Hollywood Genres* (Philadelphia, 1981), and Phil Hardy, *The Western* (New York, 1983), laying the groundwork for an analysis of the genre, while Jim Hoy's "Rodeo in American Film," *Heritage of the Great Plains* 23 (Spring, 1990): 26–32; Clifford P. Westermeier's "Sagebrush Galahads: The Cinema Cowboys," *Red River Valley Historical Review* 5 (Fall 1980): 27–54, and William W. Savage Jr., *The Cowboy Hero: His Image in American History and Culture* (Norman, Okla., 1979), zero in on the cowboy and rodeo-cowboy subgenre in movies. The list of significant rodeo movies (and television shows) is, of course, short and sweet: *The Lusty Men* (1952); *The Misfits* (1961); *Stoney Burke* (1962–1963); *Hud* (1963); *J. W. Coop* (1972); *Junior Bonner* (1972); *Electric Horseman* (1979); *Urban Cowboy* (1980); *The Cowboy Way* (1994); and *8 Seconds* (1994).

"Bulldogging": Literature

Bill Pickett used to bulldog a steer by biting its lower lip until the pain forced the critter to capitulate. An exploration of rodeo literature, I can assure you, is a much more pleasant chore. Begin with the theoretical works just cited for the western genre and in the "Brahma Bull Riding" section. Then move to oral traditions with Ramon F. Adams, *The Cowboy Dictionary* (orig. *Western Words*, 1968; reprint, New York, 1993); John O. West, *Cowboy Folk Humor* (Little Rock, 1990); and the primary-source reminiscences cited in the "Saddle Broncs" section. Rodeo literature with strong themes of ethnicity or sexuality is cited under "Team Roping." Cowboy poetry and its rodeo subgenre are discussed in the folk song literature of the "Barrel Racing" segment and in Wilbur Shepperson and Judith Winzeler, "Cowboy Poetry: The New Folk Art," *Nevada Historical Society Quarterly* 29 (No. 4, 1986): 254–65; and James Hoy, *Cowboys and Kansas: Out of the Tall Grass Prairie* (Norman, Okla., 1995), 167–73. Finally, the list of rodeo novels and poetry collections is, like a bulldogging steer, lean and mean: Larry McMurtry, *Horseman, Pass By* (1961; reprint, New York, 1989) and *Moving On* (New York, 1970); William Crawford, *The Bronc Rider* (Oxnard, Calif., 1965); Cyra McFadden, *Rain or Shine* (New York, 1987); Hal Cannon, *Cowboy Poetry: A Gathering* (Salt Lake City, 1985); Curley Fletcher, *Songs of the Sage: The Poetry of Curley Fletcher* (Salt Lake City, 1986); Red Steagall, *Ride for the Brand* (Fort Worth, 1993); and Paul Zarzyski, *Roughstock Sonnets* (Kansas City, Mo., 1989).

"Bareback Broncs": Art

The bucking bronc is the classic motif of the rodeo subgenre of western art. To learn about this important subject, you will find that art galleries and libraries prove as valuable as a good seat behind the bucking chutes. Cowboy art in general is a huge field, so start with Ed Ainsworth, *The Cowboy in Art* (New York, 1968), and Clifford P. Westermeier's unpublished essay "Art and Artists of the Cowboy," Archives, University of Colorado Libraries. Westermeier takes his subject into the rodeo-cowboy subgenre, which then branches out into different media—painting and printmaking, sculpture, posters, clothing art, and photography. Good introductions to each of these are Joe Beeler, *Cowboys and Indians: Characters in Oil and Bronze* (Norman, Okla., 1967); Valona Varnum Crowell, *The Artist and the Bucking Horse* (Taos, N.M., n.d.); Laurel E. Wilson, "'I Was a Pretty Proud Kid': An Interpretation of Differences in Posed and Unposed Photographs of Montana Cowboys," *Clothing and Textile Research Journal* 9 (Spring 1991): 49–58; Tyler Beard, *100 Years of Western Wear* (Salt Lake City, 1993); Ron Tyler, *The Rodeo of John Addison Stryker* (Austin, 1977); and Garry Winogrand, *Stock Photographs: The Fort Worth Fat Stock Show and Rodeo* (Austin, 1980). Wild West show and rodeo poster art is featured in the Western History Collection of the University of Oklahoma and at the National Cowboy Hall of Fame, Pendleton Roundup Hall of Fame, and ProRodeo Hall of Fame.

"Barrel Racing": Country Music

To aficionados, the sight of a cowgirl on a fast horse rounding her last barrel and "heading for home" at breakneck speed is beautiful music. To pursue the subject of the rodeo subgenre of country music, one should start with cowboy and rodeo folk song traditions. Glenn Ohrlin and Guy Logsdon have carried the mantle of early cowboy-song collectors N. Howard "Jack" Thorp and John and Alan Lomax. Ohrlin's *The Hell-Bound Train: A Cowboy Songbook* (Urbana, 1973) and Logsdon's *"The Whorehouse Bells Were Ringing" and Other Songs Cowboys Sing* (Urbana, 1989) contain all of the important tunes. Next comes some background on the more commercialized forms of country music and country rock, which Bill Malone serves up ably in his seminal work *Southern Music, American Music* (Lexington, Ky., 1979).

Finally, there is the rodeo-music subgenre itself. Because no one has before now collected or analyzed this music, it is best to start by just listening to the songs. As my notes to chapter 5 indicate, the music is scattered far and wide, usually as isolated rodeo cuts on more eclectic long-play recordings. To focus, I recommend three classic albums devoted solely to rodeo music: Johnny Baker, *Songs of the Rodeo* (FF&S Sound Recordings, Columbia, Mo., 1964); Chris LeDoux, *Gold Buckle Dreams* (American Cowboy Songs, ACS 22, 1987); and Red Steagall and the Coleman County Cowboys, *For All Our Cowboy Friends* (MCA, 1977, MCAC-680).

"Team Roping": Ethnicity and Sexuality

Roping teams consist of a "header" and a "heeler." Students of "multiculturalism" in rodeo popular culture would be well advised to "head" the secondary theoretical and historical material first, before completing the job by "heeling" the primary sources. In the theoretical literature, Arthur Schlesinger Jr. succinctly defines "multiculturalism" and discusses today's "culture wars" in *The Disuniting of America: Reflections on a Multicultural Society* (New York, 1992). The role of the 1960s hippie (as distinguished from "new left") counterculture in fostering the Myth of the West and promulgating artistic venues for that myth is first presented in my "Spit in the Ocean; or, 'Greasewood City: You Can't Get There from Here,'" *Ellensburg Anthology '83* (Ellensburg, Wash., 1983), 30–34, Local History Room, Ellensburg Public Library.

Since my book deals more with rodeo cowboys than working cowboys, I refer "headers" of the literature of historic female, gay, Hispanic, black, and Indian *working* cowboys to note 7 in chapter 6. Prison, female, gay, Hispanic, black, and Indian *rodeo* cowboys and cowgirls are discussed in, respectively, Texas Department of Corrections, *Texas Prison Rodeo* (program, 1984); Mary Lou LeCompte, *Cowgirls of the Rodeo: Pioneer Professional Athletes* (Champaign-Urbana, 1993); "A Day at the Gay Rodeo," *Seattle Weekly*, September 21, 1994, 24–25; Mary Lou LeCompte, "The Hispanic Influence on the History of Rodeo," *Journal of Sport History* 12 (Spring 1985): 21–38; Kathleen Mullen Sands, *Charreria Mexicana: An Equestrian Folk Tradition* (Tucson, 1993); Clifford P. Westermeier, "Black Rodeo Cowboys," *Red River Valley Historical Review* 3 (Summer 1978): 4–26; and Peter Iverson, *When Indians Became Cowboys: Native Peoples and Ranching in the American West* (Norman, Okla., 1994).

"Heelers" had best focus on looping a few choice critters. Here are my top picks: Ken Kesey with Ken Babbs, *Last Go Round: A Real Western* (New York, 1994); William Crawford, *The Bronc Rider* (Oxnard, Calif., 1965); Darrell Yates Rist, *Heartlands: A Gay Man's Odyssey Across America* (New York, 1992), 97–119, passim; Nat Love, *The Life and Adventures of Nat Love, Better Known in the Cattle Country As "Deadwood Dick," by Himself. . . .* (1907, reprint, Lincoln, Nebr., 1995); Craig Lesley, *Winterkill* (New York, 1984); and Michael Dorris, *A Yellow Raft in Blue Water* (New York, 1987).

"Brahma Bull Riding": The Myth of the West, Cowboy Code, and the Rodeo-Cowboy Hero

Every rodeo worth its salt ends with a wild session of Brahma bull riding, and now that our run through this Rodeo Sources Roundup Program is about over, it's time to take on the toughest critter of them all, the *significance* of the rodeo hero in North American popular culture. So ease on down into the chute and onto that Brahma, partner, and get ready to spin!

The classic delineation of the Myth of the West and its significance in popular culture is of course Henry Nash Smith, *Virgin Land: The American West As Symbol and Myth* (Cambridge, Mass., 1950), and I have noted the work of Smith and his colleagues John William Ward, Marvin Meyer, and Roy Harvey Pearce in the introduction and chapter 7. Leo Marx's *The Machine in the Garden: Technology and the Pastoral Ideal in America* (New York, 1964) and David Potter's "The Quest for the National Character" in John Higham's *The Reconstruction of American History* (New York, 1962), 197–220, are especially important here to build a base for the *contemporary ancestor* idea, which I draw and rework from John William Ward, "The Meaning of Charles Lindbergh's Flight," *American Quarterly* 10 (Spring 1958): 3–16, and David D. Lee, *Sergeant York: An American Hero* (Lexington, Ky., 1985).

Even with all this western myth theory under your belt, your Brahma has only just now busted loose. To transcribe western myth into rodeo-cowboy popular culture, you had better rosin up your riggin' and hang on tight. A recent article by Lawrence Levine—"The Folklore of Industrial Society: Popular Culture and Its Audiences," *American Historical Review* 97 (December 1992): 1369–99—lays down a method for analyzing the significance of popular culture, and I first read about cognitive dissonance theory in Elliot Aronson, *The Social Animal* (San Francisco, 1980), 146–52. To address cowboy studies directly, I recommend starting with William W. Savage Jr.'s classic *The Cowboy Hero: His Image in American History and Culture* (Norman, Okla., 1979) and of course Elizabeth Atwood Lawrence's *Rodeo . . . the Wild and the Tame* (Lawrence delineates the rodeo applications of the Cowboy Code throughout, especially on pp. 129–31). There is a succinct introductory discussion of the Cowboy Code in Richard M. Dorson, *America in Legend: American Folklore from the Colonial Period to the Present* (New York, 1973), and the Cowboy Code emanates from every page of E. C. ("Teddy Blue") Abbott and Helena Huntington Smith, *We Pointed Them North: Recollections of a Cowpuncher* (1939; reprint, Norman, Okla., 1954).

Finally, there is the debate over American Studies and the "new" western history—a debate that is obviously central to this book's conclusions. I realize that my methods and sources are unabashedly old-school; those who seek the more "cutting-edge" methods of the poststructuralists and "new" western historians should begin with Richard Slotkin's trilogy—*Regeneration Through Violence* (1973), *The Fatal Environment* (1985), and *Gunfighter Nation* (1992)—and then proceed into the literary criticism of Jane Tompkins, *West of Everything: The Inner Life of the Western* (New York, 1992), and Blake Allmendinger, *The Cowboy: Representations of Labor in an American Work Culture* (New York, 1992). The attitude of "new" western historians toward the cowboy hero and the Myth of the West is evinced in the last chapter of Richard White's *It's Your Misfortune and None of My Own: A New History of the American West* (Norman, Okla., 1991). I summarize criticism of the "new" western history in "The 'New' Western Stillborn," *Historian* 57 (Fall 1994): 201–8, and "Showdown at the P.C. Corral," *Columbia* 9 (Spring 1995): 3–5. Richard White and I debate the matter in "Reply from an Empty Grave" and "Michael Allen Responds," *Columbia* 9 (Fall 1994): 4–6.

Thus, in this Brahma bull riding event, I have tried to synthesize, placing the classic works of the old American Studies school into a rodeo context, with a touch of William Savage, Elizabeth Atwood Lawrence, David D. Lee, and cognitive dissonance theory thrown in for good measure. I hope it all adds up to an eight-second ride and a good score. And I hope it provides a good introductory bibliography for all you cowboys and cowgirls. But before sauntering out of the arena and movin' on down that rodeo road, I ask you to consider very carefully one more author, Frederick Jackson Turner. Only a dude would try to take on a Brahma bull without reading, and rereading, Turner's classic 1893 work, *The Significance of the Frontier in American History*, ed. Harold P. Simonson (New York, 1966).

'Nuf said, amigos. Adios.

WITHDRAWN